'This bold and timely book helps us redefine the way we think about business and serves as a compelling blueprint for the future.' *Arianna Huffington, Editor-in-Chief,* The Huffington Post

'More than ever before, the world, both developed and developing, is going to need its businesses to survive and prosper. As a start, the 2,000-year-old history of anti-business sentiment needs first to be understood and then acted upon. Gaps need to be closed; gaps not just of perception but of reality. And it will be businesses, not society, who will need to make the bigger moves. This intelligent, practical book suggests what those moves should be. Of immediate value, I believe that only three years from now it will be seen to have been a trail-blazer.' *Sir Martin Sorrell, CEO, WPP*

'The mission statements of corporations often include shareholders, customers and employees, but as Browne shows, a commitment to society at-large has been largely absent. Rather than transparency and engagement, businesses have become more closed and isolated. *Connect* shows why and how business must radically change to thrive in the 21st century.' *John Hennessy, President, Stanford University and Board Member, Google*

'This book redefines three discredited words: Corporate Social Responsibility. Far too often they exist as a bit of window dressing or conscience-salving. John Browne wants to put them at the centre of businesses – both because it's right and because success in business is inextricably linked with sustainability. It's all the more compelling because of Browne's own years at the top in business.' *Alan Rusbridger, Former Editor-in-Chief, the* Guardian

'*Connect* provides a clear understanding of the value of connected leadership. This is beyond CSR or philanthropy. Companies must play a stronger role as global corporate citizens and do so authentically and with a sense of urgency.' *Peter T. Grauer, Chairman, Bloomberg LP*

'*Connect* offers a radical and different way of thinking about business. Typically of John Browne, he has put together an inspiring call-to-arms to create the companies society deserves.' *Alastair Campbell, Writer, Communicator and Strategist*

'John Browne argues that the relationship between business and the society it seeks to serve is vital, but the idea of Corporate Social Responsibility is dead. His interviews with top business leaders show, however, that a new connected paradigm is possible and it can be highly profitable. This book delivers huge insight into a vital topic that affects everyone.' *Tony Hall, Director-General, BBC*

'Browne aims to rehabilitate Corporate Social Responsibility, and move it from the periphery of a Board's agenda to the centre. Through a mixture of careful analysis and compelling anecdote, he succeeds where others have failed.' *Sir Howard Davies, Chairman, Royal Bank of Scotland*

'Lord Browne delivers a beautifully written tour de force, spanning ancient China to Silicon Valley. Rich with personal examples and extensive global interviews, he makes the powerful and persuasive argument that CEOs must connect with government and society to build sustainable organisations. A must-read.' *David Yoffie, Professor, Harvard Business School*

'Every business leader can learn from *Connect*. John Browne skillfully draws on deep historical research, clear insight into the future and his unique business experience to provide a path to business success in our turbulent times.' *Senator George J. Mitchell (United States Special Envoy for Northern Ireland, 1995–2001)*

'Big business is vilified, lauded and feared in equal measure. This stimulating book shows that this predicament is far from new. John Browne and colleagues analyse the challenges and offer some timely counselling to leaders who seek to establish some bond of trust and authenticity between the Boardroom and the Street.' *John Van Reenen, Professor, London School of Economics*

'John Browne, in this fast-paced book, lays out the enormous challenges that companies and society face together. For many, business is the antagonist, but Browne shows that corporate enterprise is central to the well-being of society. He demonstrates from his rich experiences how commercial success depends on integrity and building trust.' *Jerry Brown, Governor of California*

Connect

HOW COMPANIES SUCCEED
BY ENGAGING RADICALLY
WITH SOCIETY

John Browne

with **Robin Nuttall**
and **Tommy Stadlen**

PUBLICAFFAIRS

New York

PublicAffairs books are available at special discounts for bulk purchases in
the United States by corporations, institutions, and other organizations. For
more information, please contact the Special Markets Department at the
Perseus Books Group, 2300 Chestnut Street, Suite 200, Philadelphia, PA
19103, call (800) 810-4145, ext. 5000, or e-mail
special.markets@perseusbooks.com.

Typeset in India by Thomson Digital Pvt Ltd, Noida, Delhi

A CIP catalog record for this book is available from the Library of
Congress.

LCCN: 2015954472

ISBN 978-1-61039-697-4 (hardcover)

ISBN 978-1-61039-698-1 (e-book)

First published in the United Kingdom by WH Allen in 2015.

UK ISBN 9780753556924

First Edition

10 9 8 7 6 5 4 3 2 1

'. . . so that more light may enter.'
To Nghi

Contents

Prologue

The opera was Jorge Martín's harrowing *Before Night Falls*. It was late May 2010 and I was in Fort Worth, Texas, to see the premiere of this work by a friend about oppression, AIDS and death. As I handed my credit card to the hotel reception, I glanced across the lobby to the bar. Four television screens were tuned to different networks, each showing the same image: a live feed from the subsea camera below BP's Deepwater Horizon rig, capturing the apparently endless flow of oil into the sea, now in its sixth week. I was watching the reputation of the company in which I had worked for forty-one years gushing out of the Macondo well into the Gulf of Mexico.

For a second I felt relieved no longer to be in charge. Quickly, though, these images and the scathing commentary made me angry. How had this happened? BP was going to be torn apart. The scenes reminded me of the day in 1989 I flew over Prince William Sound just as the *Exxon Valdez* was spilling its oil. This was going to be far bigger and BP appeared helpless in the middle of a crisis. Anger gave way to sadness as I reflected on the eleven lives that had been lost and on my own experiences of the horror of industrial accidents. And I began to realise that even after three years away from BP, the well-being of its people remained a big part of my emotional life.

My trip to Texas that week exposed me to the powerful, visceral outrage directed towards BP. I had seen something similar only twice before, once directed against Union Carbide for the Bhopal tragedy in 1984 and then against Exxon for the *Valdez* spill. People felt violated by the accident itself and affronted by BP's public statements which could never match the enormity of the event. The company's connection with the US population was too weak to support it in such a major crisis. The cracks were widening by the second and a new corporate villain was born. BP along with 'Big Oil' was back in the dock.

This book is not about the environment, oil spills or the energy industry. It is about the need for business to connect with society. My aim is to articulate and explore the recurring rift between big business and the rest of society, and to propose a way in which companies can prosper by connecting with the world around them. In an era of unremitting transparency, the world requires much more from the private sector. The consequences of repeating the mistakes of the past are greater today than they have ever been. There is an enormous prize for companies which choose to meet these new demands with respect, authenticity and openness, making society's needs part of their business model. This is about much more than philanthropy or 'Corporate Social Responsibility'. It is about how companies connect with society.

This increasingly determines their competitive advantage: research undertaken for this book by McKinsey & Company estimates the related value at stake to be approximately 30 per cent of corporate earnings.[1] The shares of companies which connect effectively outperform those of their competitors by more than 2 per cent every year.[2] That amounts to a performance boost of more than 20 per cent in a ten-year period. However, most companies fail to engage proactively, partly because they believe that their past behaviour has been right and partly because they do not know how to alter that behaviour.[3] Change is possible, but it requires CEOs to give enough time to this activity and recognise it as a core commercial imperative. Those who understand this will become tomorrow's leaders, helping their companies to become respected and successful, and to grow in harmony with society.

I hope that this book prompts readers to think again about business. People inside companies should no longer feel it inevitable that public opinion is against business. Those on the outside should look beyond stereotypes to see not only business's failings but also its inspiring contributions to humanity. This book is written from both points of view, with a Western perspective, but with an ambition to tell a global story which includes companies in emerging markets. Our research took us all over the world, visiting companies and interviewing more than eighty leaders from business, politics and civil society – from Hank Paulson and Sheryl Sandberg, to Eric Schmidt and Tim Berners-Lee. In conjunction with McKinsey, we also conducted a survey of over 2,000 executives in order to examine attitudes. The results provide a unique snapshot of how well business and society connect.

Despite its centrality to human progress and happiness, business has provoked anger and suspicion for more than two millennia. Chapter 1 sets the historical context. I begin in ancient China with research that suggests that the 'great divergence', which saw China fall behind the West, took place against the backdrop of a souring relationship between the state and enterprise. As we travel on, from *The Merchant of Venice* to Thomas Jefferson and then to Milton Friedman, we end up in the Manhattan office of Goldman Sachs CEO Lloyd Blankfein, a leading protagonist in the latest debate on corporate practices.

In the next few chapters I lay out the emergence of different actors as business 'stakeholders'. I explore how corporate behemoths crumbled because they failed to connect with them, and illustrate the success of leaders who forged 100-year dynasties through a more enlightened approach.

The chocolate barons, Hershey and Cadbury, achieved this feat of deep, enduring trust because they understood that employees not only reflect but also create brands. As we will see in Chapter 2, they were among the first industrialists to view workers as partners in the enterprise rather than simply factors of production. From the bloody Homestead Strike in Andrew Carnegie's steel mill to the recent Marikana Massacre in South Africa's mining belt, many have not grasped the fact that well-treated employees underpin reputation and performance.

Government and regulators, who wield the greatest power of all over business, are the focus of Chapter 3. Both fairly and unfairly, they have the potential to create or destroy huge amounts of value. Companies such as Uber, the car-booking service, understand that their multibillion-dollar valuations are built upon an ability to make their case to governments and society at large. Sometimes there is little that business can do, as we will discover from a pharmaceutical boss who was threatened during the 2009 swine flu crisis by officials. But often companies can prosper by actively connecting with government and demonstrating that both sides share the same goals. Decent operators understand that good regulation protects their reputation from the unscrupulous minority. However, danger lurks when companies wield undue influence; regulatory 'capture' has catastrophic consequences for everyone.

Developing countries pose particular challenges, which we examine in Chapter 4. Gone are the days when someone in the mould of Clive of India or Cecil Rhodes could treat large swathes of the British Empire as their personal bounty. Fierce backlashes against corporate colonialism, ranging from the Indian Mutiny to Colonel Gaddafi's nationalisation of Libyan oil reserves, reversed the balance of power. More recently, as I discovered in the dangerous past of Colombia, companies are held responsible for their host country's actions as well as their own.

If government is the most powerful stakeholder, the environment is perhaps the most complex. Much of my career has been spent balancing the fundamental human need for energy against the consequent risks to our environment. Mankind's unease at the commercial exploitation of nature was as evident in early Chinese texts as it was in Milton's *Paradise Lost*. As a voiceless victim, however, the environment never stood a chance against business until people such as Rachel Carson put concern for the environment on to the political agenda in the mid-twentieth century. She was helped in her campaign by the emergence of NGOs, an important but not universally responsible new watchdog of commerce. In Chapter 5 activists and executives who lived through a turning point in 'green' consciousness explain how the environmental responsibilities of companies are about to expand significantly.

In Chapter 6 I talk about the way technology shapes the connection between business and its various stakeholders. Digital technology is a tool of transparency which allows outsiders to scrutinise previously secret corporate behaviour. Technology, though, provides more than this; it is the means whereby business can meet the world's demands for health and prosperity. Nevertheless, society fears the harm that can be done by the irresponsible use of technology in the hands of companies driven by the expectations of profits from unconstrained activity.

In Chapter 7 I examine how reputations are made and lost based on companies' connections with society. Reputation is not something that can be 'managed': it is an outcome of authentic actions, not a construct of 'spin'. Companies build up a reservoir of goodwill which takes years to fill but only hours to empty. If the reservoir is insufficient, a crisis can be fatal. Often these crises are self-inflicted, but business also has the potential to induce fear and dread even when there is no evidence to suggest that a company has done anything wrong.

As we reflect on two millennia of anti-business sentiment, Chapter 8 addresses the failure of many corporate leaders to learn from the past and their inability to break the cycle of resentment. Corporate Social Responsibility, 'CSR', has failed in its role as the

system for handling external relationships because it is so disconnected from commercial activity and from the needs of real people.
I believe CSR is dead. The connection between business and the
world can only thrive if companies integrate societal and environmental issues deeply into their core business strategy and operations.
Critically, as traditional sources of competitive advantage are eroded,
connection with society represents a final frontier of competitiveness: an opportunity to build lasting distinctiveness.

Chapter 8 is the first chapter of the second part of the book,
which is set inside the boardrooms of companies at the leading
edge of change. We hear from leaders who are staking their careers
on the premise that this new way of connecting with society is
not only possible but also highly profitable. From my own experience and through extensive research on companies around the
world, I set out four tenets which articulate what companies can
do to achieve connected leadership.

First, they have to map their world. This means analysing their
stakeholders as precisely as their customers, understanding trends
and discontinuities, and quantifying the value at stake from external
relationships. Second, they need to define their contribution to
society clearly and powerfully. The contribution must be at the
heart of the company's purpose and at the nexus of its intercon-
nections with society. Third, companies should apply world-class
management to traditionally 'soft' societal topics. Fourth, they must
demonstrate a commitment to radical engagement, a completely
open, proactive and constructive approach to the outside world.

Over the course of three chapters, I illustrate how potent it
can be when companies deploy these four tenets of connected
leadership. Chapter 9, which focuses on the first two tenets, highlights the importance of context and the need to communicate
a contribution which goes beyond financial gain. The CEOs of
Unilever and IBM describe how a renewed sense of purpose
rescued two giants which had lost their direction. Later, an anthropologist explains how a Swedish banker, who demanded to see

sub-prime houses physically, kept connected to society's needs. That line of sight had been lost by so many bankers, a loss which contributed greatly to the global financial crisis of 2008.

Chapter 10 examines what happens when companies apply rigorous management techniques to societal connection. This chapter also observes how some company founders in Silicon Valley have significantly reset the role of CEO. In common with other writers on leadership, I strongly believe that CEOs should focus only on issues that define and enact the company's core purpose. In our case we believe that societal concerns, of course, need to be at the centre of that purpose.

A renewed connection with the external world is only possible if business people are willing to adopt an entirely new attitude. They need, as I argue in Chapter 11, to engage radically. This means being brave enough to embrace genuine openness, far-sighted enough to make friends before they need them and to communicate in a language that exudes authenticity rather than propaganda.

The four tenets may appear simple on paper. However, surprisingly few companies achieve them. For many executives the behaviour required is unnatural; cognitive biases, such as being over-optimistic and seeing all new decisions confirming your previous ones, are powerful barriers to reform in most boardrooms. Succeeding at the four tenets therefore requires a profoundly different point of view and the courage to question the status quo.

The nature of the relationship between business and society will change in the coming decades. The importance of specific issues will keep changing, the geographical theatres of action will shift and the cultural values of the main participants will continue to develop. But while the details will evolve, the fundamental importance to business and to society of a constructive alliance will only grow. In the Epilogue I anticipate the trends that will make it even more crucial for business to connect with society and to reduce its paradoxical unease with the force that keeps it alive.

Every year we witness new examples of companies whose bond of trust with society has been broken. As this book goes to press in the United States, the crisis over VW's emissions continues. When the news broke, VW's share price fell by a third. This single data point does not prove our research that the value at stake from a company's connection with society amounts to 30 per cent of earnings. But it is a reminder that these episodes will continue to be a significant cost unless there is a radical change in the way business views its relationship with society.

Since publishing *Connect* in Europe, readers and reviewers have tended to agree that CSR is not the answer. People recognize that taking a company's connection with society seriously means CEOs and line managers taking responsibility for it. Most CSR and sustainability departments are aware that they alone cannot fix this age-old problem.

This book is not designed to be encyclopaedic. Rather, it is guided by my own experience and by the research of my collaborators, Robin Nuttall and Tommy Stadlen. There is little new to be said about fundamentals of management or leadership. It is in their application in the real world that interest lies. I hope we will spark that interest.

Part One

The Business of Business

1

THE NOTHING NEW

Society

The Great Divergence

'Crooks and upstart industrialists exploit the common people with their dishonest practices. They appropriate the bounty of our natural resources as their own rich inheritance. But we will put down the wealthy traders and great merchants. We shall not give the advantage to the overbearing and aggressive.' These words might have been spoken anywhere in the world, at any time in history. In fact they belong to a Chinese government official of the first century BCE.

His name was Sang Hongyang, a shopkeeper's son whose mathematical ability and political nous propelled him to the position of Lord Grand Secretary in the Han Dynasty. He would later be executed for treason but for a time he was one of the biggest personalities of the day. His tirade against enterprise was delivered in 81 BCE at a set-piece debate, during a time of economic hardship. The country seethed with discontent. Many questioned the decision to place monopolies on salt and iron in the hands of a bloated and corrupt state. Salt prices were so high that some Chinese were forced to go without, and farmers made do with inferior and unsuitable tools produced by the iron monopoly.[1] Yet there remained a lingering distrust of the previous owners, the industrialists, who had amassed huge fortunes prior to government intervention.[2]

With a thirteen-year-old emperor on the throne, it fell to the de-facto leader and kingmaker, Huo Gang, to take action. A text known as the *Yan tie lun* (*Discourses on Salt and Iron*) tells how he summoned sixty of China's best thinkers to court for a debate on 'the grievances of the people'. Government representatives influenced by the pragmatic Legalist school take on the Confucian literati who demand an end to state monopolies. The government side dismiss the Confucians as 'poverty stricken frogs in a well', poorly dressed and therefore 'unqualified to hold forth on the affairs of state'. In return the Confucians excoriate their opponents' corruption.[3]

Sang is the government spokesman for much of the debate. He had earlier designed and implemented the state monopolies. Under a system called 'equable transportation', bureaucrats controlled commodity prices by buying staples where they were cheap and selling them where prices were higher. In his justifications for his policies, he returns repeatedly to an assault on private-sector power. Partly this represents bureaucratic envy and political expediency, but there is an unmistakable opposition to entrepreneurs. Vast private fortunes had been created in the early Han era as the strict controls of the previous dynasty gave way to liberalisation.

Confucian scholars sigh profoundly on the other side of the chamber as Sang defends state monopolies as a necessary intervention against dangerous tycoons.[4] Government, they believe, should not stifle entrepreneurial spirit. Their position is summed up by the Daxue of the Confucian School – in one of the earliest recorded paeans to economic competition[5] – by the phrase, 'Let the producers be many.' They believe that the monopolies are riddled with inefficiency and poor product quality.

At first sight the Confucians appear pro-business. In reality they share with their government adversaries a deep mistrust of profit and commercial activity. So-called secondary pursuits such as trade and artisanship are regarded with suspicion. The Confucians yearn for a time when the world valued things which could not be worn or eaten. If extended beyond basic necessities, trade promotes dishonesty: 'avaricious men become cheats and honest men avaricious'.[6]

The pre-eminent British sinologist Joseph Needham spent his life in search of an answer to one question: why was it that despite the towering achievements of early China, the scientific and

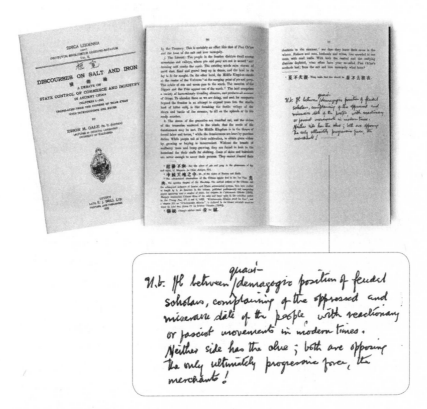

Joseph Needham's copy of the *Yan tie lun*, with a clue to the 'great divergence' between China and the West scrawled in the margin. Original text published 81 BCE.

industrial revolutions occurred in Europe and not in China? The distribution of fossil-fuel reserves, the quality of transport links and the development of overseas empires undoubtedly played a part.[7] Needham himself died without revealing a definitive answer to the 'great divergence' problem, but in the scrawled marginalia of his copy of the *Yan tie lun*, can be found a telling insight. 'Neither side has the clue,' he has written in blue ink. 'Both are opposing the only ultimately progressive force, the merchants!'

Disdain for commerce resulted in the consistent application of regulations which severely hampered industry's ability to contribute to the development of society. Enterprise was regarded by many early Chinese elites as dangerous and borderline immoral.[8] For example, when a list defining seven categories of criminals was published, in 97 BCE, to explain who would be conscripted for a military campaign, the last four categories were as follows: merchants; former merchants; sons of merchants; grandsons of merchants.

Necessary Evil

Despite the critical role it plays in mankind's development, business has never enjoyed a truly harmonious relationship with society. It is companies that feed, enrich, warm and delight us. Computers, cars and antibiotics would not have made it out of the laboratory without companies. There would be no movies, no mobile phones and no aeroplanes. Our homes would be cold and dark at night.

Antagonism towards business manifests itself in different guises. Edelman's annual 'Trust Barometer' identifies interesting differences in attitudes between developed and developing countries. Unlike their European and North American counterparts, citizens of emerging Asian economies tend to trust large companies far more than small businesses, which are often perceived as unreliable and dishonest.[9] British entrepreneurs, by contrast, have enjoyed a reputational renaissance, having been dismissed as spivs and second-hand car dealers in the mid-twentieth century. In the UK it is now big companies that are fighting for credibility.

On the other side of the Atlantic, the US is often considered the most business-friendly nation in the world. The archetypal American success story is one of an immigrant entrepreneur given the space to prosper by government and the respect of a population that celebrates rather than condemns successful private enterprise. But this is also a country that has witnessed periods of severe antagonism towards business sectors which have misbehaved. Some of the most memorable US presidents swept to power on a wave of public anger against corporate America. Thomas Jefferson took the White House on a ticket of shutting down the banks, which he dubbed 'more dangerous to our liberties than standing armies'. A few years later, Andrew Jackson took on and beat the most powerful financiers of his age. Jackson memorably invoked Jesus's removal of the moneylenders from the temple when he labelled the Second Bank of the United States a 'den of vipers and thieves'. And Theodore Roosevelt became known as the 'trust-buster' after he broke up the railroad, oil and banking monopolies of 'robber barons' such as J.P. Morgan and John Rockefeller.

Across the world, a feeling keeps returning that there is something grubby about business. One result of this has been the disproportionate entrepreneurial success of minorities who have been excluded from apparently more salubrious occupations. Some of the greatest British businessmen of the Industrial Revolution were Quakers. They were barred from the professions and the army because of their faith, but the establishment did not care if they chose to enter the lowly world of trade. It was considered a good match. The Quaker community maximised its limited opportunity and went on to build some of the most admired British firms.

Even more famously, Jews have thrived in finance throughout recorded history. This has been both a consequence and a cause of their persecution. Moneylending has been despised in the West for much of the last two millennia despite its function as the foundation of capitalism.[10] Successive societies have preferred not to sully their own with this task, preferring instead to outsource it to a group of expert outsiders who could be safely loathed for taking on the role. This warped attitude towards Jews and money-lending is a perfect microcosm of our perception of business down the ages as a necessary evil. It is one that Shakespeare explores in his play about capitalism, *The Merchant of Venice*. Shakespeare was drawn to the hypocritical approach to usury that marked Elizabethan England. Everyone agreed it was unpalatable but most conceded that the economy could not survive without it.[11] Even Shakespeare's own company, the Chamberlain's Men, could not have provided a home for the Bard without extensive loans.

With its comparison of honest merchants to dishonest money-lenders, *The Merchant of Venice* identifies another facet of our attitude towards business. Of all the industries, it is finance that

Wall Street bankers come face to face with activists demanding a 'Robin Hood Tax' on financial services companies. September 2013.

has consistently attracted the most opprobrium. A lingering sense in many cultures is that interest is unearned and therefore immoral. Francis Bacon cites the common argument that 'it is against nature for money to beget money'.[12] Of course, finance does not have a monopoly on unpopularity. Attitudes shift. One leading supermarket boss told us that the global financial crisis of 2008 was the best thing that could have happened to his organisation. It deflected a 'wall of noise' away from supermarkets and towards the banks. In 2013 the needle moved again; suddenly it was the tax affairs of consumer-goods firms such as Amazon and Starbucks that attracted public attention.

'The Nothing New'

'When my information changes, I alter my conclusions,' said the British economist John Maynard Keynes. Humans are notoriously slow to react to new information. In the case of business people, however, they also struggle to learn from the past. Today's scandals are merely tired reruns of ancient errors. The 2012 shooting of miners at Lonmin's platinum plant in South Africa was in some ways similar to the Homestead Strike in Pennsylvania in 1892, the darkest moment of Andrew Carnegie's life which resulted in the death of nine steelworkers. The same disregard for consumers and opposition to regulatory oversight that caused the European horse-meat fiasco of 2013 were present in 1906 when muckraking journalists exposed the squalor of Chicago's meatpacking district.

So with trust in business leaders at only 18 per cent, the current situation may be bad, but it is not particularly new.[13] In the scramble to respond to fast-moving events, many executives have not recognised that the problems they face are the problems of their predecessors. If they look carefully enough the solutions are visible in the runes of history. The opening line of *Murphy*, Samuel Beckett's deliberately unreadable novel, reads: 'The sun shone, having no alternative, on the nothing new.'

Lloyd Blankfein, the chief executive of Goldman Sachs, understands the cyclical nature of anti-business sentiment. In his view, 'there has been no real shift in human character that wasn't expressed in Greek tragedy'. We met in the forty-second-floor penthouse of Goldman's new headquarters in lower Manhattan. As he directed our gazes through floor-to-ceiling glass towards the gleaming ferries that shuttle his employees across the Hudson River to the New Jersey office at twice the speed of the public boats, he recalled that during many periods of American history, there was bitterness against corporations.

He began with President Jackson and his disassembly of big banks into small bodies, a policy that prefigured contemporary calls to break up institutions that are 'too big to fail'. Next was the Pecora Commission, the 1933 Senate hearings that cast bankers such as J.P. Morgan Jr. as the villains of the Great Depression. Blankfein then recalled the economic slump of the 1970s, when he emerged from university as the son of a postal clerk and a receptionist to a backdrop of high inflation and unemployment. The final stop on his tour took us to the present day and an era when banks in particular are subject to heavy criticism and scrutiny. He could not have taken over Goldman at a more challenging time, although as he put it, 'if you're already in the building when it catches fire, it's not courage, you simply have no choice'.

Blankfein believes that the most important characteristic for a CEO to possess is an instinct for what is cyclical and what is secular. He is convinced that broad public displeasure with business is the former rather than the latter, though he makes one important caveat. 'We've gone through these times before. I say with confidence that even though people say they will think this way for ever, they won't. When sentiment shifts, it takes memory with it. At the same time,' he adds, 'companies need to be seen to adapt and respond when it is necessary and important to do so. There are a lot of lessons from this most recent financial crisis and we needed to look at how we could improve and be a better institution. The public expects that type of self-reflection.'

The danger for those who recognise the cyclical nature of animosity against business is that they tend to emphasise its transience rather than the inevitability of its return. They are as unlikely to change course or to acknowledge the overall downward direction of the cycles as their colleagues who ignore the problem altogether.

My view is that the cycle can and must be moderated, if not broken. The fact that we are repeating mistakes made by merchants two hundred and two thousand years ago should be a source of embarrassment and a stimulus to reform. Many will suggest that such deep-rooted flaws are impossible to eradicate. But humans do in fact correct self-destructive patterns of behaviour. We tolerated racial and sexual discrimination from our beginnings and then, in a matter of decades, attitudes began to change dramatically in many countries. Western European nations spent the majority of their past locked in bloody and expensive wars. In the second half of the last century they finally realised they would be better off as allies and the fighting stopped. Change is possible.

Taking Care of Business

The current debate about business is characterised by polemic and tired paradigms rather than clear-eyed alternatives. People in business tend to adopt a patronising attitude to those who complain about corporate behaviour. Critics, they believe, do not understand how things work in the 'real world'. Society, on the other hand, has lost sight of the good that business does. Governments are caught somewhere between the two.

For the last forty years, two models have dominated the way people think about business. The first is shareholder value and the second is Corporate Social Responsibility. Shareholder value emerged as the prevailing Western business philosophy in the

1970s and 1980s. It was championed by the Chicago school of economics and in particular by Milton Friedman, who summarised his approach in an iconic article in 1970, entitled 'The Social Responsibility of Business is to Increase its Profits'. Friedman believed that the sole purpose of business is to make more money for its shareholders.

Shareholder value remains at the heart of business thinking today. But as logical as shareholder value may appear as an economic theory, it is fundamentally incomplete. It captures part of what should and does drive people, but not everything. In my experience most people do not go to work every day motivated only by the prospect of increasing the wealth of their investors; 89 per cent of the executives McKinsey surveyed for this book believe companies have a moral responsibility to address societal and environmental issues that go beyond legal requirements.[14] There are very few managers who could claim that they feel no responsibility to their staff, the environment or the well-being of their community, beyond what is legally required or strictly useful for their company. Excluding these intrinsic human impulses from considerations of shareholder value has contributed significantly to the perception that companies are indifferent to society's problems.

As McKinsey managing director Dominic Barton says, 'serving stakeholders is essential for maximising corporate value. Too often these aims are presented as being in tension: You're either a champion of shareholder value or you're a fan of the stakeholders. This is a false choice. Companies that bring a real stakeholder perspective into corporate strategy can generate tangible value even sooner. Creating direct business value, however,' he continues, 'is not the only or even the strongest argument for taking a societal perspective. Capitalism depends on public trust for its legitimacy and its very survival.'[15]

Corporate Social Responsibility (CSR) was an admirable attempt to improve companies' relationship with society and to broaden the scope of their duties. It told companies, as well as investors, to consider the well-being of employees, communities, governments and other groups. But CSR has failed both companies and society because the initiatives are almost always detached from the core commercial activities. At best they distract attention from the vast societal contribution made by the day-to-day business. At worst they represent a doomed endeavour to get away with irresponsible behaviour elsewhere. Business leaders have been voicing these concerns for some time, but while CSR has been declared dead intellectually, it remains the model by which most companies deal with society. Howard Davies, the chairman of RBS, who has served on numerous corporate boards, told us: 'In my experience, CSR is seen as largely rather separate from the business, handled by a separate team. That team is often very talented but their work is not usually seen as something that relates very closely to what the business actually does. It's sort of: "We carry out our business and then on Friday afternoon we think about CSR for half an hour." CSR is not the answer for companies who struggle to articulate the broader social value of their core business.'

It is the non-core nature of CSR that dissatisfies both sides of the debate. Executives view it as a distracting cost centre while NGOs criticise what they see as propaganda. Former McKinsey managing director Ian Davis argues that the CSR approach 'is too limited, too defensive and too disconnected from corporate strategy'.[16] Harvard Business School's Michael Porter summarises the result of these flaws as 'a hodgepodge of uncoordinated CSR and philanthropic activities disconnected from the company's strategy that neither make any meaningful social impact nor strengthen the firm's long-term competitiveness'.[17] Consistent with these perspectives, there is emerging evidence that CSR announcements tend to have a negative impact on share price, especially where there is limited 'hard' economic information content.[18]

This book sets out a new way for companies to connect with society that goes beyond a stale offering of CSR. I call it 'connected leadership'. It requires the integration of societal and environmental considerations into core business decision-making at every level of the company. Connected leadership can not only ensure long-term viability for business as a whole in an increasingly demanding and transparent environment, but also generate a source of competitive advantage for those who excel at a time when companies struggle to raise marketing or operations performance a few percentage points above their competitors. Crucially, connected leadership is predicated (most of the time) on mutual advantage; society would benefit considerably if it could enable a transition to this new paradigm, regardless of which firms gain the extra edge by engaging particularly well.

There are four tenets of connected leadership which, when mastered, can revolutionise a company's standing in society.

THE FOUR TENETS OF CONNECTED LEADERSHIP

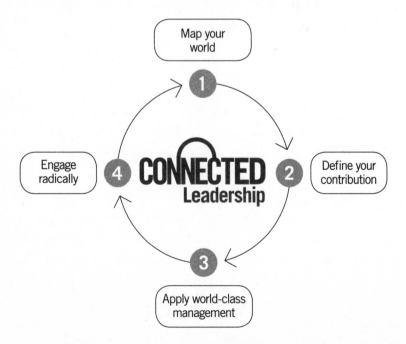

These four tenets are depicted in the diagram on the previous page and are explored fully in Part Two of the book.

The concept of connected leadership is based not on academic hypotheses but on the collective wisdom of those we have interviewed over the last two years, as well as my own experience in business and advising government. I am acutely aware that when I succeeded in businesses it was so often because I engaged effectively and sustainably with the external world. When I failed it was usually because I got this wrong. My ambition is to change the way people think about business. Business is the most powerful tool we possess in our quest for progress and prosperity. In my view we need to take more care of it, whether we are executives inside companies, citizens observing from the outside or government leaders tasked with oversight. In 1903 Teddy Roosevelt made the case for a rapprochement between the corporation and American society. 'We demand that big business give the people a square deal,' he said. 'In return we must insist that when anyone engaged in big business honestly endeavours to do right he shall himself be given a square deal.' What follows is our attempt to revive the campaign for that square deal.

Stories

On a shelf in my house sit three small pre-Columbian clay figures known as *canisteros*. I acquired them in Colombia in the early 1990s after BP had discovered a super-giant complex of oilfields in the guerrilla stronghold of Casanare. The development involved a contentious struggle to ensure both security and human rights, an episode that taught me that societal and environmental issues can never be considered peripheral to core business operations. The *canisteros* were itinerant merchants who went from town to town with baskets of goods. But they had another, more important function. As they criss-crossed the country they picked up news in one location and disseminated it in another. They became a walking depository of Colombia's collective experience. It was the stories they told that elevated them to the status of gods, worthy of reproduction in miniature form by reverent artists. Every time I walk past them I am reminded of two things. The first is that companies fail to connect with the external world at their peril. The second is that stories matter.

With stories we can make sense of the past and inspire change for the future; there is a reason that storytelling lies at the heart of all the great civilisations. The best leaders understand that stories of failure are just as important as tales of success. A.G. Lafley, twice CEO of Procter & Gamble, required failures in innovation or acquisitions to be analysed in detail. 'I think of my failures as a gift,' he said. 'My experience is that we learn much more from failure than we do from success.'[19]

A story-based approach is not without its pitfalls. Tom Peters's first book, *In Search of Excellence*, sold millions of copies and created the modern business-book genre. It was built around case studies of forty-three 'excellent' companies. Unfortunately for him, the inevitable happened. As soon as the book was published many of the vaunted firms started to falter and, in the case of the computer-game producer Atari, collapse. Peters's next book, *Thriving in Chaos*, begins with a simple sentence: 'There are no excellent companies.'

I have selected stories to illustrate broader arguments rather than to predict the future performance of specific companies. A company that happens to excel in certain areas may founder elsewhere and vice versa. My aim has been to provide snapshots in time of the very good and the very bad. Viewed together, I hope that they provide a new perspective on business and its relationship with society.

2

CHOCOLATE VILLAGES

Employees

Blood Money

In the early hours of 6 July 1892, two darkened barges carrying three hundred private security guards snaked down the Ohio River towards Carnegie Steel's flagship mill at Homestead, Pennsylvania. Each guard was armed with a revolver and a Winchester rifle. The plan, devised by plant boss Henry Frick and signed off by Andrew Carnegie himself, was simple. The guards from the Pinkerton Detective Agency were to secure the plant in the dead of night so that its unionised workforce could be replaced with cheaper strike-breakers.

Carnegie was determined to drive the union from Homestead and to squeeze more out of his workers. He instructed Frick to trigger a lockout by offering a new contract that he knew the union would never accept. Wages were to fall by up to a third; further pay cuts would follow if new technologies emerged; the plant was to be non-union. When, as expected, the workers rejected the deal, Frick locked the gates and set in motion one of the bloodiest labour conflicts of the era.

In the weeks leading up to the lockout, Homestead became
known as 'Fort Frick'. A three-mile-long, eleven-feet-high, barbed-
wire fence was erected around the perimeter. It was dotted with
giant searchlights and rifle holes and was rumoured to be electri-
fied. Frick was expecting a battle with his employees that would

The bloody battle between capital and labour at Homestead becomes
front-page news. July 1892.

be 'fought to the finish'. Carnegie's response was unequivocal: 'We'll approve of anything you do. We are with you to the end.'

Just after 2.30am, at the point where the Ohio River forks into the Monongahela, the flotilla was spotted by a union lookout. He telegraphed his comrades immediately: 'Watch the river. Steamer with barges left here.' The union was prepared. An emotional crowd of five thousand workers, townspeople and children was waiting for the Pinkerton guards as they pulled into sight of the plant's wharf. Leading the charge was Mother Finch, a silver-haired saloon owner who had witnessed forty strikes in her time. A brigade of Hungarians and Slavs joined forces with the skilled workers, relishing the chance to avenge countrymen who had been slain by Pinkerton guards in recent labour struggles across the country.

With day breaking, a hush descended as Captain Heinde, the tall, thickset commander of the private army, emerged on deck. 'If you men don't withdraw, we will mow every one of you down and enter in spite of you. You had better disperse, for land we will.' As chairman of the union's leadership committee, Hugh O'Donnell made one last attempt to avoid bloodshed. The former journalist was known for his oratory. 'What you do here is at the risk of many lives. Before you enter those mills, you will trample over the dead bodies of three thousand honest working men.'

It was to no avail. As Heinde led his men down the gangplank, a group of workers surged to protect the bank and the first shots were fired. Standing upright in their blue-and-white uniforms, the silver 'P's on their buttons glistening in the first shards of sunlight, the Pinkertons unloaded round after round into the crowd. The employees fired back with a motley collection of rifles, revolvers and muskets left over from the Civil War. This first exchange lasted only ten minutes but it saw the deaths of three workers and one agent.

At 8am the Pinkerton guards made their second attempt at a beachhead. When a sharpshooter pierced the forehead of a protester, people erupted in rage. They launched a burning raft loaded with oil-soaked wood towards the barges and then a rail-road flatcar full of flaming oil barrels. Later in the afternoon they fetched hoses and a hand-pump from the fire station and attempted to light an oil slick around the flotilla. Eventually, at 5pm, the detectives surrendered.[1]

The events at Homestead tarnished the reputations of Carnegie and Frick for ever. Carnegie scrambled to distance himself from Frick's decisions, when in fact he had been in continuous telegram contact from Scotland. He even considered paying newspapers to keep stories out of the press. But a phalanx of reporters and illustrators had witnessed the atrocities at first hand and the battle was front-page news across the world. Hugh O'Donnell set up a 'spin room' in an ice-cream parlour to feed journalists stories. Carnegie was labelled a 'moral coward' without a 'grain of decency'. Commentators called for his extradition on murder charges, his club memberships were rescinded and gifts were refused or diverted to the Homestead Relief Fund. Republicans even blamed Carnegie for President Harrison's election defeat by Grover Cleveland that autumn.[2]

Homestead was toxic for Carnegie because it exposed the deep chasm between his external value proposition and the reality of the treatment of his employees. In a series of articles for *Forum* magazine, Carnegie had written of working men's 'sacred right' to 'combine and form trade unions' and praised the labour move-ment's 'triumphant march'. The man who would soon recruit thousands of strike-breakers even set down an eleventh command-ment. 'There is an unwritten law among the best workmen: "Thou shalt not take thy neighbour's job."' In words that must have been excruciating to read back in the aftermath of Homestead, he blamed labour disputes on the 'chairman, situated hundreds of miles away from his men, who only pays a flying visit to the works'.

The hypocrisy was not lost on the international press. 'An avowed champion of trade unions and of organised labour, he now finds himself engaged in an almost ruinous conflict with the representatives of his own views,' noted *The Times*. Another British newspaper underlined the scale of Carnegie's external-relations disaster: 'Here we have this Scotch-Yankee plutocrat meandering through Scotland in a four-in-hand, opening public libraries and receiving the freedom of cities, while the wretched workmen who sweat themselves in order to supply him with the ways and means for this self-glorification are starving in Pittsburgh.'[3]

As the most senior company executive on the ground, Frick was arrested on murder charges which were later dropped. He became notorious across America as a brutal oppressor of the working class and one of the country's most hated businessmen.[4] Carnegie blamed him for the botched operation at Homestead and in 1894 accepted his partner's resignation.

It is impossible to assess how damaging this crisis would have been to Carnegie Steel in the long term. The company was sold shortly afterwards in the largest takeover in US history. But when you consider that both Carnegie and Frick spent the rest of their lives rescuing their legacy through philanthropy, Homestead's staggering financial cost becomes clear. By donating almost their entire fortunes to good causes, worth over $100 billion in today's money,[5] they aimed to 'wipe out every trace of the mischief of the past year'. The glorious Frick Collection and Carnegie's plethora of libraries, concert halls and universities have yet to entirely eradicate that stain.

Hersheykoko

To the east of Homestead, in the county of Derry, Pennsylvania, Milton Hershey was about to reinvent the relationship between business and employees that would create the most successful and loved confectionary brand the world had ever seen. Trust in business had plummeted. Successful businessmen were perceived as 'robber barons' whose wealth was inevitably ill-gotten. 'Trust-buster'

Teddy Roosevelt took the White House in 1901 and led a chorus
of anti-business rhetoric that swept across America. In an age of
vitriolic scorn for business that we would recognise today, Hershey's
success was not only tolerated by the public but warmly embraced.
While investigative journalists hounded Rockefeller and the other
robber barons, Hershey received glowing write-ups. They dubbed
him 'Milton Hershey the Chocolate Man'.[6]

At the centre of Hershey's meteoric rise was a brand built on
his reputation as a progressive employer. In 1,200 acres of cornfield
and pastures, Hershey had constructed a utopian town and factory
that quickly came to symbolise a shift in the way business could
treat employees. They could receive unparalleled benefits, including
insurance, health care, schooling for their children and pensions.
They were offered low-interest mortgages from the Hershey
Trust Bank to buy spacious, detached homes, featuring indoor
plumbing, heating and electricity, luxuries which in 1905 were
available in very few US households.

Milton Hershey sits with orphans on the steps of his newly established
Hershey Industrial School. The school's endowment now exceeds
$9 billion. C.1910.

Hershey built his utopia around a main thoroughfare named Chocolate Avenue, lined with streetlights in the shape of Hershey Kisses. As the town grew, he added a department store, a zoo, a Chinese ballroom and an ice rink. The gardens echoed those at Versailles and the ornate Venetian theatre hosted famous entertainers on its Italian lava floors. All of these facilities were made available to employees free of charge. Just as in Japan's Toyota City, the modern-day equivalent, workers' children were born in a company-funded hospital. The son of the Hershey president was, in 1907, the first to emerge.

While Henry Frick had extorted the last penny from his workers in compulsory, profiteering shops run by the Frick Coke Company, Hershey subsidised the goods sold in his shiny new stores. On Frick's watch, the Pittsburgh area was known as 'Hell with the lid taken off' and steel mill accidents caused 20 per cent of adult male fatalities.[7] In contrast, safety was at the forefront of Milton Hershey's mind when he built his new single-storey factory in fireproof brick, limestone and slate. Its famous twin chimneys became symbols for a new way of doing business.

Hershey's grand experiment mirrored developments on the other side of the Atlantic. In Britain the big players were Cadbury, Rowntree and Fry. These three Quaker families had achieved their dominance by creating a reputation for quality, fairness and purity. At the heart of this reputation was their progressive treatment of employees. By the time Hershey visited, Cadbury had already built a thriving model village at Bournville. This was the spark that inspired Hershey to create something even bigger.

The two brothers at the helm of Cadbury in the late nineteenth century believed business had a responsibility to address social problems as well as commercial ones.[8] Indeed, George and Richard were convinced that the two were mutually reinforcing. Quakers had been attracted to chocolate as a product in the first place because they saw it as an opportunity to wean working-class men off alcohol.[9]

George was appalled by the slums in Britain's new industrial cities and the grim realities of sweated labour. He noticed that inner-city factories were inefficient for fast-growing companies as they quickly ran out of space. His solution was to move production from Birmingham to a purpose-built factory in the countryside. That was in 1879. Some years later, in 1895, he broke ground on a model town for employees. Bournville was designed to 'alleviate the evils which arise from the insanitary and insufficient accommodation supplied to large numbers of the working classes'.[10] As George's son Edward remarked, the company charged affordable rents to 'show that such an undertaking can be a financial success, and not merely an act of philanthropy'.[11]

Like Hershey in Pennsylvania, Bournville marked Cadbury as a different type of company. It was the original garden city, with a fruit tree in every back yard and no end of recreational facilities to entertain and improve the employees. The state-of-the-art factory was highly productive but it was also human: sunlight streamed through large windows, fresh flowers adorned the tables and tea or lemonade was served throughout the day.

Through its innovative compensation packages Cadbury struck just the right balance between incentives and reassurance. The 'piecework' system meant that pay was linked to productivity beyond an above-average minimum wage. The company built loyalty by pioneering paid holidays, pensions and sick pay long before government made these things mandatory. Compulsory morning Bible readings by 'Mr George' or 'Mr Richard' were, in those days, a small price to pay in return.[12]

Win-Win

The chocolate moguls demonstrated that companies can contribute to society with mutually beneficial results. Their progressive approach to employees was central to their success in two ways. First, the brands not only reflected, but were *created* by, their happy employees and wholesome company towns. Second, they understood that employee motivation, loyalty and health all drive financial performance, which in turn improves reputation.

This remains true today. Research by Professor Alex Edmans of London Business School found that companies with superior employee satisfaction, as measured by the '100 Best Companies to Work for in America' list, generated 2.1 per cent per annum better share price performance from 1984 to 2009 than their competitors.[13] Over a decade, that becomes a 23 per cent differential. Edmans also found that it takes four to five years for the market to recognise the value of employee engagement, in part because traditional valuation techniques focus on short-term profit. This implies that it requires leadership to take a longer-term view on the value of engaged employees.

The Cadbury family were entirely comfortable with the morality of gaining commercial advantage from their progressive treatment of employees. 'Win-wins' are at the centre of our connected leadership philosophy, and for this approach to work it is important for business and society to dispel any discomfort. The foreword to Edward Cadbury's book reflects this point of view in its analysis of how the firm's employee initiatives 'distinctly paid': 'I see no reason why we should not be quite frank in the matter – it has been a splendid advertisement. Instead of cynically pooh-poohing it for that reason, I think this is a particularly encouraging fact, and highly creditable to human nature. It shows there is such a thing as consumers' conscience.'[14]

This does not mean that firms can exploit superficial social or environmental activities without 'meaning' them. Edward Cadbury was clear that success required a genuine commitment to benefit society: 'If welfare institutions are carried on purely for the purpose of advertising . . . without sympathy or insight into the needs and feelings of the worker . . . the schemes will be mechanical and lifeless and evoke no true response.'[15] Certainly, no one could accuse his father George of cynicism. He taught for fifty-two

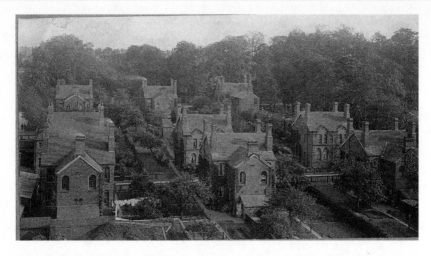

The Bournville model village: affordable rents and a fruit tree in every back yard. 1911.

years at a weekend school for adults located in a working–class district of Birmingham. Similarly, Milton Hershey sought no publicity from his decision to donate his entire fortune to a school that he established in 1909 for orphans and poor boys.[16]

Living the Brand

At the centre of the Cadbury brand was Bournville, whose idyllic setting and smiling employees featured heavily in its advertising and packaging. The Publications Department released books and pamphlets on this unprecedented labour experiment. When mothers bought their children a bar of Bournville chocolate they were investing in a new vision for how business should be conducted.

From 1902, customers had the opportunity to see it all with their own eyes when the company started tours of Bournville. The scene awaiting them in the 'Worcestershire Eden' was 'a garden with a welcome of the sweet breath of flowers and the song of birds'.[17] Cadbury understood that employees are a company's most important ambassadors.[18] The reputational benefit of happy employees was compelling to him: 'This good feeling between employers and employed is of almost inestimable value, both socially and commercially.'[19] By the end of the twentieth century half a million people poured into Bournville every year.[20]

For Hershey, the combination of tours and rapturous media coverage of its methods were so powerful that the company soon halted all billboard and print advertising. For over sixty years the company thrived purely on the back of its reputation as the US's most generous employer.

Milton Hershey had constructed a 150-acre theme park that attracted up to 10,000 visitors to Hershey on a summer's day. Just like Bournville, the employee nirvana represented a brand that connoted goodness, integrity and fun. Millions of Americans passed through each year and found workers full of praise for the company and its home.

Hershey and Cadbury identified the potency of a corporate vision delivered through employees. It is as true today as it was in 1900. A company's external value proposition might be related to service, cost, innovation or quality. If it can build an employee model that not only reflects but also creates that value proposition in the first place, it is likely to enjoy considerable success.

Steve Jobs came to the same insight when he realised that Apple could no longer rely on third-party retailers' employees to represent its brand. By investing in his own network of retail outlets, Jobs defied critics to enable direct contact between customers and employees who embodied the company's offer of innovation. Apple's highly trained 'Geniuses' are at the heart of a revolution in the so-called 'experience economy'. They have helped the Apple Store to generate higher sales per square foot than any other retailer in the US, in spite of the company's established online store. Apple has followed the chocolate moguls' recipe to great effect with its consumer-facing workforce.

Slavery by Another Name

In 1909, London's *Evening Standard* claimed that Cadbury was complicit in the use of slave labour in the Portuguese colony of São Tomé, then the world's largest cocoa exporter. The company's good work and reputation were suddenly at risk. George Cadbury had sent his own investigator to the island and he had identified the practice of indentured labour. However, he was reluctant to tackle the issue directly. He did so through the UK Foreign Office to protect the UK's national interest since Portugal was a significant trading ally. Progress was slow. To the public, it looked like hypocrisy given Cadbury's campaign against indentured labour, 'slavery by another name', in his own newspaper. Cadbury faced a dilemma shared by many big businesses today. He was concerned that if he withdrew not only would the UK be damaged but also his company would be replaced by one that did not care about improving labour standards. Cadbury won a libel case against the *Evening Standard* but the episode demonstrated that having a reputation as a fair employer was now dependent on the treatment of workers in the supply chain, however far away and however difficult to influence. Cadbury survived the crisis with its brand intact by ending its relationship with the São Tomé plantations in favour of the Gold Coast, where the company was able to exert greater control on labour conditions.

Watching all of this was Milton Hershey. When he turned to Cuba to secure sugar supplies during the First World War, he was determined not to repeat Cadbury's error. Central Hershey was established, a Cuban version of his blossoming Pennsylvanian town which brought utilities, health care, education and a racetrack to the impoverished community near Santa Cruz del Norte. Hershey's charming electric railway continues to provide Cubans with mobility and remains one of the best ways to see the island. In the old manager's house, Camilio Cienfuegos, which now serves as a meeting room for refinery workers, locals talk fondly of the former owner. They repeat their fathers' stories of a benevolent employer with a passion for Corona cigars who was happy to repay the value that Cubans provided.

Hershey understood that public scrutiny could easily reach across the Straits of Florida. The distance between Western electronics firms and the huge numbers of Chinese workers who churn out their tablets and smartphones is somewhat greater but no less traversable. A scandal erupted in 2010 amid accusations of poor working conditions at Foxconn, the world's largest contract manufacturer. Foxconn employs over 1 million people in mainland China, turns over $150 billion, supplies most of the well-known consumer electronics brands and is a technology leader in fields as diverse as nanotechnology, heat transfer, wireless connectivity and material sciences. The company attracted widespread outrage following a string of suicides at its vast Shenzhen factory, just across the border from Hong Kong. Shocking images of suicide-prevention netting emerged. A subsequent report by the Fair Labor Association alleged that '14 per cent of workers may not receive fair compensation for unscheduled overtime'.[21]

The implications for Foxconn have been limited. The accepted view in China is that the company's labour practices are a vast improvement on the alternatives. At the very least, the Fair Labor Association's president told reporters, Foxconn's plants are 'no worse than any other factory in China'.[22] While they made for shocking news stories, the suicides appeared to be no more than a statistical inevitability given the huge numbers of employees; the suicide rate among its workforce is lower than that of China overall.[23] But for Foxconn's Western partners the risks attached to such headlines is significant.[24]

Homestead Redux

As progressive as the chocolate moguls were, their record was by no means beyond reproach. By today's standards some of their practices would be considered completely unacceptable. The evening classes provided by chocolate manufacturer Fry and Sons in its Bristol factory sound progressive until you realise that they were put on for child labourers as young as nine. Gender inequality was just as rampant at Cadbury as it was everywhere else at this time.[25] For many years, it was not deemed appropriate to employ married women. When a female worker announced her engagement she would receive a bible, a red carnation and some wise words from a director who would then confirm her departure from the firm. But social mores change. Society's expectations evolve and business must constantly reinvent itself to stay relevant; however, the evidence suggests that companies still tend to lag behind the rest of society. My experience as a gay man in business taught me that even as society became more inclusive, the corporate world generally did not. When it comes to the inclusion of minorities, business has come a long way, but companies continue to be followers rather than leaders.

In the context of the era in which they lived, Milton Hershey and George Cadbury saw the value in being ahead of the curve when it came to external expectations. In their pioneering approach to employees they offered a blueprint for contemporary companies to follow. And yet sometimes it appears that business is destined to repeat history's mistakes.

One hundred and twenty years after the Homestead Strike, the same conflict played out in South Africa's Bushveld. In the winter of 2012, workers at Lonmin's Marikana platinum mine near Rustenburg went on strike to protest against low pay, inequality and dangerous conditions. In the ensuing violence that became known as the Marikana Massacre, thirty-four workers were killed by a police squad that had been called to secure the mine. The similarities with Homestead are uncanny. Both incidents involved a dispute over who fired the first shot and both resulted in murder charges against strikers being dropped after a public outcry. It was the largest use of lethal force by South African security services since the infamous Sharpeville Massacre, one of apartheid's bloodiest days.

If we look carefully, history is dotted with visionaries who pointed towards an alternative relationship, one based on partnership, respect and mutual advantage. Some of their names are still visible in confectionary displays across the world. The chocolatiers demonstrated that reputations are in part defined by the way a company treats its employees and its suppliers, however distant. They understood that authenticity requires an inseparable alignment between brand image and reality on the factory floor. And they showed that engaged, proud and happy workers repay institutions many times over with hard work, loyalty, innovation and results.

3

MEATPACKERS AND MUCKRAKERS

Government and Regulators

Closed Borders

By the time the telephone rang it had been a tough week, even by Daniel Vasella's standards. As chief executive of the giant pharmaceutical company Novartis, he was at the centre of the world's response to the 2009 swine flu pandemic. Countries were scrambling to acquire sufficient vaccines for the winter. So when Vasella recognised the familiar voice of a senior health official, he wondered about the purpose of the call. In any case it was a good opportunity to discuss a sensible plan for dividing available vaccines between countries.

There was a strain in the official's voice as he greeted him and Vasella could tell immediately that something was wrong. His tone was clipped and low. 'Dan,' he said, 'I need this product, I need it now and I can't mess around with quotas.' Vasella tried to explain that he could not bend the rules for one country and not another.[1] He told him what he had told others earlier that day: 'The only way to get you extra vaccines is to put on extra shifts. That will be expensive.' He gave the price for expedited vaccines and the minister exploded. 'Dan, this is not acceptable. You need to know that if you abandon us when we need you, Novartis will not remain on our reimbursement lists.' The threat was clear. If Novartis valued its business in an important market, it had better give them the vaccines they wanted, for the price they named, in the time frame of their choosing. It was a request to which Vasella could not possibly agree if he wanted to treat every country fairly.

Now retired, Vasella looks back on the crisis as one of the more challenging of his seventeen-year tenure. 'That was an extremely difficult period of time for all the executives,' he told us. 'I had angry calls . . . The tone suddenly became very nationalistic. They were not interested in hearing that we had to be fair and responsible across nations.' The company had no choice but to incur the extra expense associated with rapid production in the knowledge that governments would not bear the incremental costs. To make matters even worse, many of the large nations soon realised they had overestimated their needs, and promptly told Vasella they would not be paying for increased supply. 'The governments that exerted a lot of pressure on the industry to deliver vaccines very quickly were the same governments that then said: "We don't want any more of what we ordered," once they saw they ordered too much.' Around half of the fifteen countries that bought vaccines from Novartis cancelled part of their order. France announced that it wanted to cancel almost half its 16 million doses and pay only 16 per cent of the price on cancelled orders.[2]

The story is a reminder of the huge sway that governments hold over companies. 'I became highly aware,' Vasella reflects, 'that in the case of a real health problem, forget about collaboration among countries. Borders will be closed.' Acting in what they perceive to be the national interest, governments have enormous power to create or destroy value for business. The economist Joseph Stiglitz memorably captured two distinguishing features of government: compulsion and universality.[3] *Only* the government can compel people and institutions to behave in a certain way. And government can make these impositions upon *everyone* in the nation. Business takes on government at its peril.

McKinsey estimates that the 'value at stake' from plausible future state intervention amounts to $3.6 trillion per year of EBITDA.[4] Approximately one third of profits are at stake, depending on the industry.[5]

One European utility found that the ongoing value at stake from regulation was €1.5 billion, or about €30 million for every employee involved in handling the company's regulatory and government affairs.[6] Capturing value at stake is not just about protecting downsides such as tax increases; there are also significant upside opportunities to drive growth and profit, including access to new markets and removing barriers to innovation.

Together with McKinsey, we conducted a global survey to track executives' attitudes to external stakeholders.[7] The results show that companies understand the importance of the state. Governments and regulators are second only to customers when firms rank stakeholders in terms of their influence on economic value. In the energy sector, executives perceive government as the most important stakeholder. Keith Trent, a senior executive at the US's largest electric-power company, Duke Energy, told us that 'the single biggest risk we have, outside of a nuclear or environmental disaster, is what we would call "stroke-of-the-pen risk". That means either changes in legislation or a bad regulatory outcome.'

The role of government and regulation is important not only in the traditional utility and heavy-asset industries, but also in technology, data and consumer sectors. The Microsoft CEO Satya Nadella confirms how in a world where so much data is held in the cloud and on mobile devices, 'regulation . . . is clearly the topic of our times. The world is getting pretty complex in terms of regulatory environment because every country does care about digital sovereignty. Governments have a real role to play when it comes to protecting their citizens. And yet you want to have laws that govern how even governments operate so that things that are enduring values like privacy can be maintained. You really need the balance between companies and governments and across governments.'[8]

Although companies understand the power of governments, most remain strangely ineffective in their attempts to do anything about it. Only 21 per cent of firms report 'frequent successes at shaping government and regulatory decisions', a proportion that has not increased over time. The vast majority do not regularly undertake activities that drive successful regulatory outcomes. Effective engagement requires far more from companies than having well-paid lobbyists on their side, yet less than a quarter have organisational structures in place to engage effectively. In part this is down to the common cognitive bias of 'excessive optimism'. Put simply, many executives think that adverse regulation is not something that will ever happen to them even when the evidence suggests otherwise. This was demonstrated in Europe in the 1990s and 2000s when several integrated airport operators and gas companies were so convinced that they would never be broken up that they refused to contemplate the possibility until it was too late.[9]

In this chapter we outline the vast and sometimes underestimated influence governments and regulators have over the companies that operate under their jurisdiction. We illustrate the value destroyed by state intervention and badly made regulation. We also point out the unearned value created when governments set regulation in favour of business. We explore how a handful of firms have adopted a strategy which aligns their own goals with those of society to create mutual advantage. Finally, we visit Japan to examine what happens when proactive engagement becomes regulatory capture.

The Company

Governments can bequeath value just as illicitly as they can withhold it. In the late nineteenth century, while George Cadbury was planning Bournville and Milton Hershey was working in Pennsylvania, Cecil Rhodes was busy expanding his influence in southern Africa. Initially dispatched to Britain's Cape Colony to convalesce on a farm, Rhodes quickly became bored with agriculture and started buying up diamond concessions. Before long, he had established himself as the world's largest diamond miner through a company that would become De Beers. But this was only the beginning. In 1889, Rhodes pulled off the deal of the century.

Together with some aristocratic connections in Westminster, Rhodes persuaded the UK government to award a royal charter to a new corporation, the British South Africa Company. The contents of the charter make for remarkable reading. It grants the 'The Company' the right to colonise the entirety of modern-day Zimbabwe, with implicit permission to extend much further north. The Company is expected to wield 'powers necessary for the purposes of government and the preservation of public order' with the aid of its own 'force of police'. Should that prove insufficient, the British navy and army 'shall recognise and be in all things aiding to The Company and its officers'. The prime minister, Lord Salisbury, was anxious to halt the spread of competing German, Boer and Portuguese interests in southern Africa, but he did not want to pay. The solution was 'outsourced imperialism' in the form of The Company; government in corporate form.

The Company wasted no time as it colonised by force and deception. The principal native leader was King Lobengula of Matabeleland, who the British conveniently assumed also controlled Mashonaland. Together, Matabeleland and Mashonaland make up modern-day Zimbabwe. By 1888, Lobengula had already been tricked into signing a mineral concession that would soon result in complete British dominance. For a brief period, however, he

Cecil Rhodes (centre) stands at the summit of Malindidzumu hill in what was formerly the Rhodes Matopos National Park. It is the site where he is now buried. January 1897.

managed to limit The Company's conquests to Mashonaland, which it seized in 1890. Three years later Rhodes then turned his attention to Matabeleland. The Matabele stood little chance against The Company's Maxim machine guns, and when British Imperial troops entered the conflict to ensure victory, the native army retreated. Shortly afterwards, King Lobengula died of smallpox. The UK government officially recognised the British South African Company as Lobengula's heir, allowing it to 'inherit' his land, cattle and legal authority.

By 1895, just six years after the royal charter was signed, The Company politically and commercially controlled virtually all of modern-day Zimbabwe and Zambia. At the helm was Rhodes, who renamed the territories Southern Rhodesia and Northern Rhodesia. The extent of his power cannot be overstated. Beyond his role in The Company, and his private interests in the De Beers and Goldfields corporations, Rhodes had also become prime minister of the Cape Colony. The Company's dual function as government and corporation was reflected in the motto emblazoned on its flag: 'Justice, Commerce, Freedom'. It had been given all the natural resources and commercial opportunities it could find and in addition the right to raise public revenues. Following the imposition of a hut tax on natives, fiscal income represented 41 per cent of The Company's total revenue.[10]

Commercially, The Company ignored the charter's requirement not to form monopolies. It dominated business in Rhodesia from transport to banking. Its focus, however, was mainly on mining and agriculture, where it operated as a licensor rather than producer. Firms were given concessions to extract Rhodesian resources in exchange for half of their shares. This was 'an enormous' thing, Rhodes told his superiors in London, for it 'practically means we shall get half the minerals in the country'.[11]

The Company's indifferent share performance and measly dividend payments should not mask the enormity of the bounty bestowed upon it by the UK government. There is no better illustration of governments' power to fix outcomes for their favoured corporate interests.

That power remains as strong as ever today. When national interest is at stake there are times when companies can do little but watch as governments make or break their fortunes. But the best firms never wait passively for intervention, whatever the circumstances. If the first half of this chapter demonstrated the awe-inspiring influence of the state, then the second half illustrates the ways in which industry can make its voice heard, both responsibly and irresponsibly.

The Poison Squad

In 1906, Teddy Roosevelt signed into law the US's first piece of federal food and drug legislation, the Pure Food and Drugs Act. It marked the emergence of the government as a gatekeeper to the food and drug market. Contrasting corporate reactions to the Act illustrate the potential benefits available to far-sighted companies that engage proactively with regulators.

Harvey Washington Wiley, who eventually led the forerunner of the Food and Drug Administration, had struggled in vain for twenty years to introduce federal regulation against adulteration. His luck changed at the turn of the century through a mixture of publicity and savvy coalition building. In 1902 Wiley had set up a group of volunteers to investigate the effects of chemical preservatives such as borax, benzoic acid and formaldehyde. These brave young men quickly became known in the press as the 'poison squad' and raised the profile of Wiley's efforts to introduce regulation.

Crucially, Wiley won the support of influential women's groups, who were appalled at the dangers in the food chain. According to one senator, up to 30 per cent 'in value of all the food products

Harvey Wiley watches over the Poison Squad as they dine in the basement of the Agricultural Department. C.1902.

in the United States were either adulterated or misbranded'.[12] Poisonous chemicals, metals and cheap substitutes were used liberally by companies aiming to make a quick buck. Potted chicken rarely contained any chicken. And the patent medicines that dominated the US's drug industry were often laced with alcohol, cocaine and opium.

The tipping point for pure food regulation arrived thanks to the revelations uncovered by 'muckrakers' – investigative journalists. First, *Collier's* magazine published Samuel Hopkins Adams's 'The Great American Fraud', a ten-part exposé of the deadly patent-medicine industry, naming and shaming 264 companies. Soon afterwards Upton Sinclair's novel *The Jungle* was published. He had set out to highlight terrible conditions suffered by migrant workers in Chicago's meatpacking district. But it was the chapter on the meat itself that caused an uproar and sent the book to the top of the bestseller list. As the author put it, 'I aimed at the public's heart and by accident I hit it in the stomach.'

The Jungle painted a grim picture of Packingtown. It described the contamination of meat from diseased animals with human urine, sawdust and rats. In one famous passage, workers fall into steaming vats and are 'overlooked for days, till all but the bones of them had gone out to the world as Durham's Pure Leaf Lard!' Sinclair may have been exaggerating, but commissioners sent by Roosevelt to verify the novel's assertions were unable to dispute much at all. Even before the official report emerged, the public had read enough: meat sales plummeted.

The powerful 'big four' Chicago meatpackers fought hard against regulation. Armour, represented in *The Jungle* by the fictional company 'Durham', tried to discredit Sinclair and considered suing him.[13] In the end they only added to the bad publicity and on 30 June 1906 Roosevelt signed into law the Meat Inspection Act as well as the Pure Food and Drug Act. Far from destroying its business, the new meat regulations helped Packingtown in ways it should have foreseen. Government

Sausage-making in dubious conditions at one of Chicago's major packing houses. C.1905.

certification not only helped regain the public's confidence in meat but also ensured access to European markets that had imposed numerous bans on American produce, particularly pork. An analyst from J.P. Morgan estimated that the Act 'would hurt the packers in the short run, but by providing a "government certificate" in foreign trade, it would reward the packers handsomely'.[14]

The canned-food sector found itself divided in its approach to potential regulation. On the one hand, Harvey Wiley was taking aim at the chemical preservatives that allowed it to prosper. On the other, its reputation had suffered from all the bad press, and piecemeal state regulations stopped it exploiting national distribution systems. Wiley decided to address the canners in person at a trade-association meeting, despite warnings from the organisers that they could not guarantee his safety. Partly through the strength of his argument and partly through the conviction of his oratory, the chemist turned around the angry audience by appealing to their self-interest. 'When the people find saccharin or coal tar sugar in one man's canned goods, they immediately jump to the conclusion that everybody is using it. That one man who does it injures the business of every man who does not.'[15]

One leader who had already grasped the advantage of regulation was Henry Heinz, founder of the company that would become the world's largest ketchup producer. From his early days selling horseradish in clear bottles from his mother's Pennsylvanian garden, Heinz understood the importance of purity to customers. By the time Wiley took aim at ketchup manufacturers for their use of chemical preservatives, Heinz had already ordered his chemists to develop a way of replacing chemicals with natural preservatives. In 1904 Heinz launched the first mass-produced ketchup free from sodium benzoate. While his competitors used benzoate to mask the taste of rotten trimmings they got from tomato canners, Heinz added vinegar to preserve the tastier, ripe tomatoes that went into his product.

He believed that legislation would 'provide a competitive advantage because Heinz's standards for ingredients, production processes and cleanliness were among the highest in the industry'.[16] The company established a Washington office and appointed a full-time executive to focus on regulatory affairs. Wiley later acknowledged the Heinz family's role in bringing pure-food regulation to America. 'I appreciate the loyalty with which your father and all the staff stood by me in the darkest hours of my fight for pure food,' he told Heinz's son. 'I feel that I should have lost the fight if I had not had that assistance.'[17]

By breaking rank with the rest of the industry, Heinz inevitably drew criticism from his peers. They tried to discredit him, claiming that his relationship with Wiley was corrupt and that he was using a 'secret chemical agent' to replace benzoate. But the decision to strike out paid off. As one historian puts it: 'Heinz had positioned his ketchup in such a way that the public good and sales of his product were synonymous.'[18] The company was one of the first to release public-health advertisements, in a successful attempt to educate consumers on the dangers of chemical preservatives. Like Hershey, it opened the doors of its factory to visitors, not to show off its motivated staff but to emphasise its spotless sanitation.[19] Even though the government sanctioned the use of benzoates in very small dosages, Heinz's public-information campaign had transformed consumers' attitudes. Leading competitors crumbled as demand for benzoated ketchup vanished. Heinz doubled its profits within five years, expanded overseas and went on to enjoy a market share of over 50 per cent for much of the next century.[20]

Heinz recognised that regulation can be the friend of well-run businesses. That wisdom would have been beneficial to today's business leaders as they stumbled through their latest crises. The European horse-meat scandal of 2013 and the 2008 Chinese baby-milk-adulteration scare each had enough material for an Upton Sinclair classic.

Proactive regulatory strategy does not have to mean acceptance of the state's decisions. Successful companies are not afraid to challenge the logic of established thinking among regulators if they think they can win the argument. When we asked Lord MacLaurin, the first non-family boss of Tesco, to explain the British retailer's astonishing rise in the 1980s and 1990s, his answer went beyond the usual story of outstanding consumer insight. According to MacLaurin, Tesco's ascent was possible only because of its consistently superior ability to gain planning permission for new, out-of-town superstores. By winning the property battle,

Tesco became Britain's largest supermarket and ultimately the third-biggest retailer in the world.

Today, companies which use the Internet to disrupt traditional industry often run into resistance from outdated regulations. Uber, which connects users with private-hire vehicles, is a good example. Its recent meteoric increase in valuation, which was set to rise to $50 billion in June 2015, is predicated on the belief that it can overcome regulatory obstacles placed in its way by the traditional taxi industry across the world and by those who fear the erosion of secure jobs. Founder Travis Kalanick realised in 2014 that Uber's future depended on its ability to connect with national and local governments. 'Our roots,' he said, 'are technology, not politics – writing code and rolling out transportation systems. The result is that not enough people here in America and around the world know our story, our mission, and the positive impact we're having. Uber has been in a campaign but hasn't been running one.' David Plouffe, Obama's 2008 campaign manager, was hired to provide the talent Uber needs to defend and grow the billions of dollars at stake.[21]

Similarly, home-rental company Airbnb is running up against long-standing laws that were not designed to cope with its people-as-hotels model. As founder and CEO Brian Chesky acknowledges, 'it's probably going to be a fair amount of work to revise some of the laws and rethink the way cities and platforms work together'.[22] A valuation of more than $25 billion and the viability of the sharing economy are riding on this work.

Descent from Heaven

At the extreme end of proactive regulatory strategy is capture of the regulatory process by industry. Of course, there is a big difference between a company that strives to ensure it is treated fairly and one that controls the body that is supposed to be acting in the interests of society. When the regulator is in the pocket of the regulated, society almost always loses out. In the long run industry

Within sight of the Fukushima nuclear plant, police in protective clothing search Ukedo beach for the bodies of victims of the 2011 tsunami. February 2012.

suffers too, even if it gains a significant advantage in the short or medium term. Eventually regulatory capture causes scandals and accidents that result in draconian government intervention.

Perhaps the most shocking modern instance of capture lies in Japan's nuclear power industry. Despite an attempt at liberalisation in the late 1990s, the Japanese electricity generation and transmission market lacks any true competition. Ten utilities enjoy effective monopolies in their respective regions. Tokyo Electric Power, known as TEPCO, supplies the Tokyo area and is the largest of the ten. It also happens to own the Fukushima Daiichi nuclear power plant. In March 2011, in the aftermath of the Tōhoku earthquake and subsequent tsunami, Fukushima went into nuclear meltdown following complete power loss and catastrophic equipment failure. The release of radioactive material into the atmosphere caused universal dread in a country that knows all too well the horrific power of uranium.

As the Japanese came to terms with mass fatalities caused by the tsunami, they also began to ask questions about the nuclear disaster. The answers to those questions revealed a systemic failure by the government to regulate the nuclear industry. At the heart of the failure were the conflicting goals of the relevant government department, the Ministry of Economy, Trade and Industry.[23] It was tasked not only with regulating Japan's nuclear power plants through its agency (NISA), but also promoting the nuclear industry domestically and abroad. As the parliamentary report points out, 'the regulators . . . avoided their direct responsibilities by letting operators apply regulations on a voluntary basis. Their independence from the political arena, the ministries promoting nuclear energy, and the operators was a mockery.'[24] This would be unthinkable in other nuclear-powered economies such as the US and France.[25]

The relationship between the regulator and TEPCO had always been closed and self-serving. It could start as early as university, when future executives and officials would mingle at Tokyo University's department of nuclear physics. The better students would win jobs at TEPCO while their less able peers ended up at NISA.[26] But the bureaucrats could get their own shot at private-sector rewards in a process known as *amakudari*. Translated literally as 'descent from heaven', *amakudari* describes the practice of senior regulators moving into top jobs at regulated companies. These gamekeepers-turned-poachers could provide firms with all the information they need to avoid burdensome regulation. Even worse, *amakudari* meant there was little incentive for officials to rock the boat with their future employers. At the time of the Fukushima disaster, Japan's utilities had appointed forty-five directors from within the ministry.[27] TEPCO even had an unofficial 'reserved seat' among its vice presidents, dating back to 1959, for former ministry officials.[28]

Transfers in the other direction were also common. This is called *amaagari*, 'ascent to heaven'. The complexity of nuclear science means that the regulators became reliant on industry experts to set and enforce the regulations. Eleven of the nineteen committee members responsible for reforming Japan's safety rules were drawn from the power sector's lobby group.[29] This arrangement meant that those taking a seat in parliament could push through policy reforms that prioritised the use of nuclear power before returning to TEPCO. In the immediate run-up to the meltdown, even the Minister for Economy, Trade and Industry was a former nuclear executive.

The parliamentary report into the disaster was eviscerating in its criticism of the 'totally inappropriate . . . relationship between the operators, the regulators and academic scholars' that rendered the nuclear industry 'an unstoppable force, immune to scrutiny by civil society'.[30] It was clear to investigators that TEPCO had 'manipulated its cosy relationship with regulators to take the teeth out of regulations'. The report's conclusion was damning: 'The TEPCO Fukushima Nuclear Power Plant accident was the result of collusion between the government, the regulators and TEPCO, and the lack of governance by said parties. They effectively betrayed the nation's right to be safe from nuclear accidents. Therefore, we conclude that the accident was clearly "manmade".'

Yoichi Funabashi, a former newspaper editor and chair of the Rebuild Japan Initiative Foundation, believes 'a national program to develop robots for use in nuclear emergencies was terminated in midstream because it smacked too much of underlying danger'.[31] Indeed, the head of the Nuclear Safety Commission was a professor whose research included winning social acceptance for nuclear power.

The Japanese people won deserved praise for their extraordinary dignity and altruism in the face of the tsunami's destruction. But the parliamentary investigation laid bare the fact that their political and industrial leaders were propagating a deeply damaging system of collusion.

For many years TEPCO and the other utilities benefited from their control of the regulators and government officials. Not only did they preserve their regional monopolies but they also avoided costly regulations. In the long run, however, this environment has come close to destroying them. Prior to Fukushima, Japan planned to grow the proportion of nuclear-generated electricity from 30 to 50 per cent. In the year after the accident, every single nuclear plant was taken offline until they could be proved safe, and the government announced its intention to phase out the generation of nuclear power entirely. Prime minister Abe's administration has focused on gradually restoring nuclear power to the energy mix. But the devastating impact on the nuclear industry is unquestionable. It lost $20 billion in the first year after Fukushima alone.[32] The government is now working hard to reform the mindset and dynamic of the industry, placing consumers' needs first.

TEPCO would have collapsed without a government bailout; it has only been allowed to survive so that it can pay compensation to those affected by the disaster. The new chairman, Kazuhiko Shimokobe, sums up the damage to the company's reputation: 'For people in society, just the thought of TEPCO's name is disgusting.'[33] When I visited Japan in the immediate aftermath of the accident I met the respected economist and Hiroshima survivor Tadashi Nakamae. For Nakamae, Fukushima represented the moment that the final fraction of trust in authority disappeared from Japanese society.

No stakeholder brandishes as much influence over business as government, and companies must tread a delicate path as they develop their approach. Ignore government and its influence will inevitably catch you off guard; commandeer it and you risk a backlash from society further down the line. Government has unbounded power to create and destroy value in the pursuit of real or perceived national interest. Poorly designed intervention can harm both companies and citizens alike, whereas enlightened firms see the benefits of smart and robust regulation, which keeps business honest and safeguards the reputations of the reputable. The stakes are high.

4

THE LAST NABOB

Developing Countries and Communities

The rise of emerging markets is perhaps the single most dominant narrative in business today. The implications of 1.8 billion more people joining the 'consuming class' are enormous.[1] Of the 7,000 new billion-dollar companies we will see in the next decade, 70 per cent are expected to be based in emerging economies.[2] In the final chapter of this book I explore how these citizens and companies will come to define a new relationship between business and society. In this chapter, though, I follow the declining power of Western companies over the governments of emerging economies. I also examine the more gradual change to the sustained dominance that companies have had over local communities.

Bounty

In a long, dark room in Westminster in 1772, the Member of Parliament for Shrewsbury shifted in his seat to get a better look at his accusers. Lord Clive of Plassey had faced fiercer adversaries than the greying Select Committee of MPs gathered before him to investigate endemic corruption in the East India Company. When proceedings moved on to the issue of 'presents' given by local rulers to Company officials, Clive could endure their unworldliness no longer: 'Consider the situation in which the Victory of Plassey had placed on me. A great Prince was dependent upon my pleasure; an opulent city lay at my mercy; its richest bankers bid against each other for my smiles; I walked through vaults which were thrown open to me alone, piled on either hand with gold and jewels! By God, Mr. Chairman, at this moment I stand astonished at my own moderation.'

Fought in 1757, the Battle of Plassey represented a turning point both for Clive and the East India Company. It was triggered a year earlier when the new Nawab of Bengal had the audacity to react against The Company's domination of his region. The Nawab's forces seized control of the fort at Calcutta and held 146 British captives in an eighteen-square-foot cell. Just twenty-three survived the 'Black Hole of Calcutta' and the incident prompted a ruthless backlash. Clive led The Company's army to regain Calcutta, and after six months of vicious skirmishes and negotiations, came face to face with the Nawab among the mango groves of Plassey, just as the first of the monsoon rains arrived. Three thousand men were pitched against nearly seventy thousand Indians, a French squadron and a herd of armoured elephants, but Clive had no intention of taking on such a mighty ensemble. He had struck a deal with the Nawab's top military commander, Mir Jafar, who agreed to betray his own people in return for the throne. Jafar withdrew his troops and The Company forces quickly defeated those who remained.

The next day, at the Nawab's palace, Clive led the traitorous Jafar by the hand on to the throne of Bengal. Jafar's first act as leader was to open the treasury doors to Clive, literally as well as officially. As he walked through storerooms full of coins and jewels, Clive helped himself to £200,000 worth of 'presents'.[3]

Ever the populist, he also secured at least £1.2 million for his subordinates, the equivalent of more than £12 billion today.[4] It took seventy-five boats to carry the first instalment of the bounty upriver to Clive's fort.[5]

From the East India Company's point of view, the battle removed the last serious obstacle to complete rule in India. Some years later The Company formally accepted the *diwani* of Bengal, establishing it as the revenue collector and administrator of 20 million people.

Clive's view was that 'peace must be made by the sword in this country'.[6] His paramilitary and administrative success were predicated on the violent exploitation of both native rulers and populations. As governor of Bengal he presided over a famine that wiped out one third of the inhabitants. The famine was exacerbated by opportunist company servants who stockpiled six months' worth of food before using native agents to purchase rice by force and sell it at sky-high prices. They made fortunes as people starved in the streets.[7]

Clive's violent streak was apparent throughout his astonishing rise from a childhood of provincial delinquency to the very highest echelons of the East India Company. As a youth in the sleepy town of Market Drayton he set up a thriving protection racket, with local shopkeepers paying up to avoid having their windows smashed.

The parliamentary inquiry into graft at Bengal drove Clive to suicide, but he died having been exonerated of all wrongdoing.[8] In truth, the inquiry was never very likely to find against him. The British state was simply too complicit in The Company's methods and too reliant on its trading role.

At its peak, the East India Company boasted revenue greater than that of the whole of the UK as well as a private army of 250,000 to rule over its subjects, roughly one fifth of the world's population.[9] It thrived, first as a trading organisation and later as a private government. In both incarnations it relied upon the uncompromising subjugation of its Indian hosts. This was apparent from the very start. The first settlement at Surat in 1612 was achieved only after The Company's navy had taken local ships hostage and held them to ransom. As The Company became a public revenue collector, the link between financial success and military expansion became ever stronger. Shares in The Company rose 12 per cent when news reached London that Clive had taken a French outpost at Chandernagore in Bengal.[10] Expansion was achieved by allowing local princes to retain their titles in exchange for a 'subsidy' which, according to company man and future British prime minister, Arthur Wellesley, tended to be 'the whole or nearly the whole disposable resource of the state'.[11]

For successive generations of British men, India was an exotic money-printing factory. The nouveaux riches of the East India Company were known as 'nabobs', a derivative of 'nawab'. As long as they survived the risk of disease, many returned home with enough cash to buy sprawling mansions and, in some cases, a seat in parliament.[12] When they ran out of money they simply went back to India for more, as Clive did before Plassey. It was Clive's sanctioning of *daskats*, passes which exempted Company officials from internal customs fees, which enabled huge private trading fortunes to be made.

For those who could not flourish even under such kind conditions, extortion was the next best thing. 'By the late 1760s,' historian Nicholas Dirks notes, 'there was not an Englishman in Madras who was not seriously on the take, and each new taker seemed to raise the stakes higher.'[13] One George Paterson, dispatched by The Company's London directors to investigate corruption, managed to acquire a fortune of £40,000 despite a salary of only £500 per annum. The MP for Forfarshire wrote of Paterson's homecoming exploits in 1775: 'This Eastern Prince has given a most splendid ball. They continued to drink very freely till five, and then beginning to turn a little riotous they display'd a truly British spirit by demolishing all the decanters, bottles, and glasses, and indeed everything that was breakable in the room.'[14]

For two hundred and fifty years this model of brazen exploitation worked extraordinarily well for the world's first multinational corporation. As long as corporate directors could keep a firm 'boot on the neck' of the odd misguided native who stepped out of line, the cash would keep rolling in. There was no shame in any of this. Colonised nations would not begin to claw back power for another century. But even in this era of complete corporate supremacy, The Company managed to behave so badly that it caused its own downfall.

Mutiny

For all its plunder and conquest during the eighteenth century, The Company on the whole avoided any temptation to rid India of its customs. This was in part a matter of convenience. Local traditions, such as the enslavement of low-caste workers or the flogging to death of criminals by their victims, maintained a cheap and subservient population.[15] Among some Company servants, however, there was a genuine respect and understanding of the native cultures. They enjoyed having their weapons blessed at Hindu festivals and administered temple funds without (always) succumbing to theft. Crucially, they understood the terror of 'pollution' among high-caste soldiers. This sensitivity to an abhorrent system ensured their forces remained well disciplined and mostly loyal.[16]

All of this began to change under the governorship of Richard Wellesley, the brother of Arthur. At the beginning of the nineteenth century there was a drive to instil British values, law and religion in their subjects. This angered peasants, nawabs and The Company's own native soldiers, particularly the infantrymen of the Bengal army, known as sepoys.

A new recruitment policy forced high-caste sepoys to mix with low-caste men. It also required them to serve overseas even though they would lose their caste because they were unable to perform rituals of absolution and cook with wood at sea. Those who crossed the Indus to fight in Afghanistan had been spurned when they returned from war.[17] The Company actively ignored all of this.

The breaking point came in 1857 when it was rumoured that The Company had used pig and beef fat to grease rifle cartridges in an attempt to pollute the sepoys' caste. The design of the new cartridges meant that they would have to ingest as well as touch pig or cow meat when they tore off the top with their teeth.[18] At a large base in Meerut, eighty-five sepoys were sentenced to ten years' hard labour for refusing to use the new cartridges. They were paraded in front of their comrades in chains.[19] By the next evening, Meerut had descended into chaos. Hundreds of sepoys rebelled, torching offices and killing large numbers of Company servants. The Indian Mutiny had begun. Terrible atrocities were committed on both sides as the violence spread. The commanding general forced sepoys to clean bloodstains with their tongues before they were executed, while others were hanged in pig or cow skins according to their religion.

The mutiny, which took eighteen months to suppress, represented an existential threat to British rule. Westminster had seen enough. In 1858 the Crown assumed control of The Company's Indian territories, ending its operational existence. The Company limped on for the purpose of distributing revenues until 1874, when it finally expired. The demise of the East India Company did not amount to a shift in power away from Western companies towards the *governments* of poor countries. Indeed, it flourished under the paradigm of exploitation for a quarter of a millennium. Rather, its death by mutiny suggested that no company could withstand the defiance of its employees, even if they happened to be foreign and poor.

The East India Company's model of corporate colonialism lived on into the twentieth century through its ideological successor, the British South Africa Company (BSAC), which dominated southern Africa on the back of its royal charter. But it too perished because it chose not to connect with the locals as human beings, let alone 'stakeholders', and this time the host government was in no mood to accept the British state in The Company's place.

For years the British South Africa Company got away with behaviour every bit as cruel as the East India's. Its leader Cecil Rhodes was said to have been particularly bloodthirsty as he repressed rebellions, 'taking delight in returning to a scene of fighting to count African corpses with some glee'.[20] As with Carnegie and Frick, it required almost his entire fortune to polish his reputation for posterity. The Rhodes Scholarships he funded for students from colonies to attend Oxford University gilded his name through his generosity and through the recipients' deeds.[21]

Rhodes had died by the time that his company's misconduct finally caught up with it. By the mid-twentieth century, the BSAC had ceded administrative control of its territories to the British state, but retained significant mineral and other commercial interests in Northern Rhodesia. In 1964 an elected government concluded that the treaties under which the British South Africa Company had acquired its country's mineral rights were invalid.[22] The BSAC's leadership accepted an offer of £4 million, net of tax, to be contributed to equally by the British and Zambian governments.[23] The game was up. The carcass of The Company was absorbed into a range of mining firms, including Anglo American. For seventy-five years it had sent dividends back to its shareholders in London on the basis of military conquest and systematised suppression of rulers and peoples. Now, suddenly, the expropriation was happening to them. All over the developing world, companies were about to find out what that felt like.

The Oil Weapon

Within ten years, events in Zambia would be overshadowed by an even more totemic power reversal. In a confrontation that shook the world, oil-producing countries decisively seized back control

of their natural resources from the Western firms that had comman-
deered them with colonial entitlement at the start of the century.

It seems remarkable to our modern eyes that the oil companies
kept their deals going for as long as they did.[24] The prices they
paid for concessions were almost laughable. In 1935, King Ibn
Saud, the founding father of Saudi Arabia, gave the Standard Oil
Company of California sixty years' use of 360,000 square miles
for little more than a series of future loans.

The advent of OPEC (Organisation of the Petroleum Exporting
Countries) and its use of the 'oil weapon' during the embargoes
of 1967 and especially 1973 changed everything. Western governments and companies alike were brought to their knees. In the
years that followed the 1973 energy crisis, the oil firms lost nearly
all of their remaining concessions in OPEC nations and their
assets were partially or fully nationalised.[25]

The shift in power away from Western oil firms towards nation
states had huge implications for the global economy. For the oil
states whose petroleum earnings soared from $23 billion in 1972
to $140 billion in 1977, it meant vast wealth.[26] By contrast, the
developed world was pushed into deep recession by the oil
embargo. Economic output slumped 6 per cent in the US from
1973 to 1974 and declined in Japan for the first time since the
Second World War. Despite the rhetoric emerging from the Gulf
about a 'United South' rising up against historical oppressors, the
oil crisis hit poorer developing countries the hardest. From now
on, the 'third world' would be divided into countries that had
mature hydrocarbon sectors and countries that did not.

As for natural-resources companies, if they wanted to extract
a nation's patrimony they did so as mere licensees. They would
own a piece of paper that gave them rights to convert resources
into money or exportable products under certain strict conditions,
but that piece of paper could be withdrawn at a moment's notice.

The world had changed, and it was not limited to the energy
or mining sectors. After centuries of dominance, Western companies

would not only have to connect with the governments of developing countries, they would also often be forced to do so from a position of comparative weakness. Of course, there would still be occasions when firms lapsed badly in their dealings with such governments. Sometimes they would be punished, and sometimes, particularly in countries without resource wealth, they would not. The overall dynamic, however, had been transformed since the days when Clive of India could stroll unchallenged through the treasury of Bengal, pocketing the state silver as he went.

Barbed Wire

As companies woke up to this new hierarchy, many decided that the solution was to line the pockets of the rulers they had once fleeced. Bribery and kickbacks, already common, became endemic to business in the developing world as executives strove to win

An armed guard stands watch at BP's oil-production plant in Cusiana, Colombia. June 1995.

contracts. The trickle-down economics of newly rich oil states involved plenty of sticky hands at the top of the pyramid. One captain of industry remembers being told on his first day of work in the 1970s to drive a blue Rolls-Royce convertible to the South of France and leave it outside a hotel with the keys under the sun visor. Today, as the scandal with European drug companies in China indicates, bribery remains commonplace, although tough laws and punishments have made it less appealing to British and American employees in particular.[27]

Not much fuss was made about any of this until the 1990s, when NGOs started to shine a light on illicit payments to unsavoury regimes. It was not a great leap from there to a broader question: was it right for multinationals to operate at all in states with questionable records on human rights, corruption or transparency? The conversation had changed. It was no longer about companies exploiting poor countries. Big business had started to become liable for the behaviour of its host nations.

BP learned this the hard way. Actions in Colombia during the 1990s resulted in a crisis that took a decade to fix. It was also the catalyst for an entirely new approach in Indonesia.

In the second half of the 1990s, BP discovered a complex of oilfields, containing billions of barrels of oil reserves, in the Llanos foothills, some 150 kilometres to the north-east of Bogotá, the capital of Colombia. It was a violent and lawless environment in which to operate, a situation which BP did not understand early enough. After a time, programmes to educate and employ the community were established but they were not compelling enough to give the local people an alternative practical vision of the future from that offered by the guerrillas. Meanwhile the company's staff and facilities were under threat from guerrilla groups, dozens of BP's contractors were kidnapped, and many police and military guards were killed. As a result, when it came to developing the oilfields, BP believed it needed to protect itself behind barbed wire, and agreed to pay a small 'war tax' on each barrel of oil produced, which would be used by the government to pay for the military protection we and other companies needed. This series of acts set the scene for BP to be regarded as an unsympathetic foreign exploiter of patrimony, shut away behind its fence. When the leader of a peasant association that had been blockading the access route to BP's facilities was gunned down in his home, BP was inevitably accused of his murder. Accusations were made in Colombia and in the UK that paramilitary groups operating on BP's behalf were responsible for the atrocity. BP was cleared of all wrongdoing by multiple investigations both in Colombia and the UK, but the allegations alone were enough to harm the company's reputation as well as its share price.[28]

When BP arrived in West Papua, Indonesia, it was determined to learn from the mistakes it made in Colombia and not to get dragged into the conflict between the military and separatists. Instead, we trained a security team that was recruited almost entirely from the local area. Offsite police backup and the military made up the second and third rings of protection, but they agreed to stay away unless something truly drastic happened. The local force did a superb job policing a project that involved up to 10,000 workers during the construction phase. They were proud to safeguard a development that was benefiting their community.

It is never a straightforward decision for chief executives when contemplating whether to enter a country with hostile local or national regimes. BP's approach in Indonesia worked well, but it would not be possible in states whose militaries refuse to relinquish control. Every case is different and must be assessed on its own merits. As George Cadbury feared in the nineteenth century, sometimes the uncomfortable reality is that if you pull out of an oppressed nation, less progressive operators will take your place.

Security, of course, is only the beginning. Over the last forty years, big companies have been asked to play an ever-greater role in the progress of developing countries, without being seen to displace governments. Those who have failed to do so have received damaging criticism from NGOs, investors and customers; but there is also an obvious upside for business if it gets this right. Michael Spence, the economics Nobel laureate, once told me that there are two questions to ask when looking at entering a country: 'What is in people's heads and how good are the rules?' Without an educated population and the rule of law, it is very hard to succeed. This echoes F.A. Hayek's articulation of the need for the rule of law, and the distinction between 'a free country' and 'a country under arbitrary government'.[29] For Hayek, the rule of law 'means that government in all its actions is bound by rules fixed and announced beforehand'. Part of doing business in a developing country is to get close to that state and build a long-term sustainable context in which the company can thrive.

Corporate Pigs and Eskimos

So far in this chapter we have seen the pendulum of power swing away from large companies towards the national governments of developing countries. There is, though, another related dynamic that exists between companies and local communities within those countries. Ruling elites regularly deny their populations a share of improved fortunes. And while companies have been forced into a subordinated position with national governments, they have not ceded ground in the same way to communities who often remain at the mercy of business.

There are good reasons for companies to engage sensitively with local communities. First, antagonised local people can physically disrupt vulnerable operations, for example pipelines or remote mines with a single access road. This problem has affected Shell so chronically in the Niger Delta that they have had to leave some areas.[30] Second, when communities organise themselves effectively they will influence central government. Third, NGOs which identify bad corporate behaviour can damage global reputations. However, companies that develop strong local links not only avoid these risks but also build sustainable access to labour and resources. These reasons are all fairly self-evident, but it took many companies a long time to find them compelling enough to take action.

Thanks to one enlightened individual, BP became involved in one of the first effective engagements with a local community. Paradoxically, this occurred in the most developed country on earth, the USA.

Alaska in the 1960s was different from today. Physically separated from the contiguous US, it had only become the forty-ninth state in 1959 and its population, today over seven hundred thousand, was less than half that. More importantly, the indigenous people of Alaska bore all the hallmarks of communities in poor countries that have been exploited. US rule had brought its own injustices, as BP was to find out, but the problems went much further back. Their natural resources had been stolen by small businessmen in two unhappy waves. First came the early nineteenth-century Russian fur traders, followed in quick succession by the Klondike gold miners. These booms ended in busts and did nothing for the indigenous people. They were understandably suspicious when the oil companies arrived.

In the face of rising resource nationalism in the Middle East, BP was desperate for new reserves and had pinned its hopes on Alaska in the 1950s. Yet in 1968, after a decade of false starts and more than $30 million of sunk costs, the decision was made to leave Alaska. The drilling rig was already packed when BP's competitors in Prudhoe Bay struck oil. Further drilling revealed the largest oilfield ever found in North America. Attention quickly turned to the problem of getting all this oil to market, and the only solution was an 800-mile pipeline across Alaska's rough terrain. BP's executives were focused entirely on engineering challenges and project economics. They took their eyes off the wider context and paid a heavy price.

In 1970 the Department of the Interior rejected the application submitted by BP and the other oil companies for a right-of-way permit to build the pipeline. The plans had failed to address how the project would impact the indigenous people of Alaska and the environment.[31] The Native groups had many concerns: land rights, tax rates, damage to their habitat and the speed of oil extraction. By this stage they had a number of representatives in the state legislature and other influential bodies.

BP's man on the ground was Michael Savage. In the early sixties he had been the only employee there other than a secretary and draftsman, and one of only three British nationals in the entire state.[32] Unblinkered and in touch with life outside the corporate bubble, Michael is the kind of person business badly needs. He went on to become managing director of San Francisco Opera and to start a vineyard in the Napa Valley. It was Michael who pioneered the oil industry's approach to the Native Alaskans.

Michael and a small team of BP executives travelled from the east coast to meet Charlie Edwardsen, the radical leader of the Arctic Slope Native Association who was pressing for legal owner-ship of the land around Prudhoe Bay. It was a short meeting and within ten minutes they were heading back to the airport. Edwardsen's message had been simple: 'I don't deal with fucking corporate pigs.' In the car Jim Spence, BP Alaska's chief geologist, said: 'He shouldn't have called you a fucking corporate pig, Michael . . . even if it is true.'

Michael decided that something had to change. He was not willing to be the latest foreign businessman to take advantage of these people. From BP's point of view, it just did not make sense to him for the company to be at loggerheads with the communi-ties in which they aimed to operate for decades.

Michael's first priority was to find community leaders who were willing to contemplate even the idea of partnership. He found an unlikely ally in an Inupiat elder who had every reason to be distrustful. Willie Iggiagruk Hensley grew up inside the

Arctic Circle without electricity 'before Gore-Tex replaced muskrat and wolf skin in parkas, before moon boots replaced *mukluks*, before the gas drill replaced the age-old *tuuq* we used to dig through five feet of ice to fish'. His parents' generation were allowed to attend school only if they were at least 'mixed-breed' and 'lived a civilised life'. They were forced by teachers in state-funded schools to write 'I will not speak Eskimo' hundreds of times on the blackboard. By the time Hensley was ready for school, Native children were still considered wards of the state, and he was sent to Tennessee in a post-war 'civilisation' programme.

Michael Savage's honesty and decency won Hensley over. They worked together with other Native groups to lobby for the landmark Alaska Native Claims Settlement Act of 1971, which awarded 44 million acres of land and nearly $1 billion in federal funding and future oil revenues to the indigenous population. Instead of creating Native reservations, the act distributed shares to all Native Alaskans in twelve regional corporations. Hensley called it 'the

Construction of the Trans-Alaska Pipeline in the Delta River floodplain. November 1976.

most sweeping and fairest Native American land settlement'. The environmental agreement was hammered out over the next two years and in 1973, spurred on by the Arab oil embargo, the Trans-Alaska Pipeline Authorization Act became law.

The oil industry did not receive much credit in the media for its role in the settlement because to outsiders it looked like self-interest: the Act removed one of the main barriers to the pipeline permit. Yet thanks to Michael, a strong working bond had been built between BP and the Native communities. His next move was even more innovative.

His concern with the Settlement Act was that the oil rents would be unearned and therefore unvalued. Michael felt that it was crucial for the locals to have 'skin in the game' and he devised a way to make this happen. In 1979, BP invited Native corporations to participate in the Endicott lease auction, east of Prudhoe Bay. They did not have sufficient funds to pay their way so BP invested on their behalf; but this was an unproven field and in the event of success the Alaskans would have to repay the investment with interest. The risk was, to an extent, shared. Michael also made sure they won contracts for drilling, catering, camp services and security. From the beginning he had engaged Native groups from other areas of Alaska as well as those from the oil regions; they now had an active interest in the industry, both through the service contracts and through ownership of the oil itself. The latter was the more innovative and BP's competitors, and even its own management in Cleveland, at first found it hard to understand why the company should voluntarily surrender an ownership interest in a prospective oilfield for no immediate monetary gain.

Thanks in part to this foresight, oil avoided being the curse it has been in so many other undeveloped parts of the world. The income generated from the commercial partnerships was used mostly wisely by the communities, in contrast to the way the initial rent was spent. BP was rewarded handsomely as it developed the new reserves it so badly needed with the blessing and involvement of the local inhabitants.

I had joined BP in Alaska straight out of university in 1969, and I learned more about community engagement from Michael than from anyone else. The rules were the same regardless of the country's stage of development: compensate for disruption and share rewards that are earned through participation.

In this chapter I have outlined the shift in power away from companies towards the governments of poor countries. Gone are the days when colonial overlords such as Cecil Rhodes and Robert Clive could exploit foreign lands with impunity. Not only must big businesses behave sensitively, but they are now often held responsible for the conduct of their host regimes and the socio-economic development of the countries they enter. At the local level, individual communities in the developing world can remain vulnerable to unscrupulous enterprises. Even here the supremacy of the rich-world company is slipping, however, as local groups and their advocates find ways to punish bad practices and encourage a more collaborative relationship between visitor and host.

5

SILENT SPRING

The Environment and NGOs

Beyond Petroleum

On a bleak English morning in the winter of 2012, half a dozen workers in orange boiler suits and hard hats began work on a drilling rig. At twenty feet, the relatively small size of the equipment was the least unusual of its characteristics. Rather than steel, it was made from cardboard. Instead of the North Sea or the plains of Pennsylvania, this particular piece of equipment was destined for my house in London. The tangerine-clad workers were in fact members of a pressure group, Frack Off, whose mission is to halt all shale gas development in the UK. At the time I was chairman of Cuadrilla Resources and therefore firmly in their cross hairs. Cuadrilla is Britain's leading shale gas explorer, one of only two companies with significant domestic reserves. In Frack Off's view, Cuadrilla was about to unleash the environmental Armageddon depicted in American films such as *GasLand* and Matt Damon's *Promised Land*.

I was asleep as the activists completed their makeshift construction. Their only audience was a confused neighbour who, after pinching herself to make sure she was not still dreaming, called the police. But publicity stunts in the twenty-first century require only a smartphone camera and a Twitter account. Crowds of onlookers are optional. By the time I was having breakfast a handful of political blogs had already picked up the story. Not for the first time, I found myself alongside an NGO at the centre of the debate about the impact of companies on the environment.

I have spent a career balancing trade-offs between development and conservation, and between short-term profits and long-term sustainability. Of all the stakeholders that chief executives must connect with, the environment is the most complex. Unable to speak for itself until it begins to revolt against interference, business has inevitably considered it less important than human stakeholders. The failure of the market to impose costs on companies that harm the environment means that doing the right thing often has no economic value.[1] What is responsible for nature can be irresponsible in the short term for the shareholder. The impact of environmentalists and NGOs has been to provide a reason other than altruism for companies to take the environment seriously.

My journey to BP's helm in the 1990s coincided with the arrival of global environmental challenges at the very top of the political agenda. Most relevant to BP was climate change, and in 1997, on an unseasonably hot May afternoon at Stanford, I became the first Big Oil chief executive to acknowledge the link between man-made carbon emissions and global warming. The successes and failures that preceded and followed that speech illustrate the extraordinary difficulty of the trade-offs facing business leaders as they grapple with the environment.

The pressure to act on climate change ramped up considerably in the aftermath of 1992's Earth Summit in Rio. The idea that greenhouse gases heat up the planet dates back to the Victorians but until Rio it was of interest to few outside the scientific community. Suddenly climate change was front-page news and fingers were pointed, once again, at 'dirty oil'. The *Exxon Valdez* oil spill of 1989 was fresh in people's memories. Society was beginning to determine the future of the oil sector and it did not seem interested in inviting the companies themselves to the table. People were talking about the industry as if it were already dead.

I believed that oil companies, or at least BP, could no longer deny the problem. Something had to be done. But while my belief came from my heart, the last thing I wanted to admit at that point was that it came from anywhere but my head. Ian Hargreaves, editor of the *New Statesman*, asked me whether my change in tack on climate change might be summarised as 'doing the right thing'. My only possible response was: 'You might say that but I certainly cannot.' I had to make sure that BP's approach was seen as rational and analytical.

The board, executive team and employees had to be persuaded that BP was not about to commit commercial suicide. Taking a stance on climate change could make the company a sitting target for NGOs and competitors alike. Sir Robin Nicholson almost single-handedly persuaded BP's board that doing something about climate change was correct. He was its scientific thought leader, an eminent metallurgist, fellow of the Royal Society and former Rolls-Royce director who understood both the science and its business implications. He demonstrated the importance of having committed and knowledgeable non-executive directors.

The board's approval was necessary but not sufficient. Such an important strategic shift required the support of the management and employees. The debate was spirited, to say the least. One division had signed up to an industry association that denied the science of man-made climate change; the head of the business unit was also sceptical, and understandably concerned about the embarrassment of a volte-face. The downstream business was also opposed because it could not see a path from its current position to where it needed to go. In both instances pragmatic approaches were required. The chemicals group was to remain in its industry association and would work to moderate its statements from the inside. The difficulties facing the downstream division inspired the idea of an internal emissions trading scheme: business units able to cut carbon cheaply could sell credits to those who found it more expensive.

Opinion among BP's 100,000 employees was divided. Internal polling suggested that younger workers were more likely to support a proactive position on climate change. This was partly due to a generational change in attitudes to the environment, but it also reflected some difficult trade-offs that confronted the company. While it was easy for new graduates to support a stance they would not have to pay for, senior staff would be the ones tasked with maintaining profitability amidst the new initiatives. Nonetheless, there was a slight majority in favour of the proposals and it was enough to get started. As time went on, the climate strategy had a very positive impact on employee morale and recruitment. An entirely new type of person was attracted to the oil industry.

BP had now opened itself to attacks from all directions by sticking its head above the parapet. Most of the oil industry was furious. The American Petroleum Institute continued to lobby ferociously against environmental legislation through the ironically named Global Climate Coalition. When BP left this group in 1997, the American Petroleum Institute said that it had 'left the church'. While Shell was moving in the same direction as BP, the American majors could not have been more resistant. Relations on various joint ventures began to sour, particularly when BP attempted to introduce carbon-saving initiatives. To an extent, though, the competitors' reaction showed that BP had destabilised them.

While American oil majors railed against BP for exposing the industry to environmental regulation, NGOs voiced concerns that the company was not going far enough. Some, such as Greenpeace and Friends of the Earth, refused to countenance anything other than a complete replacement of the world's hydrocarbon system.

It was extremely hard to engage them in productive debate because their starting point was that BP should not exist. Others, such as the Pew Center and the Environmental Defense Fund, were more realistic but still nervous that the Stanford speech was little more than 'greenwash'. BP worked hard to win their trust and eventually forged excellent working relationships with both groups. They wanted to make sure the company's actions were meaningful, and BP needed their expertise to make that happen. Fred Krupp, the long-standing head of the Environmental Defense Fund, played a central role in the creation of the emissions trading scheme. In the 1970s his organisation had successfully halted the construction of the Trans-Alaska Pipeline; now, twenty-five years on, Krupp was working at the heart of BP as it sought to fix its relationship with the environment.

None of this was easy. It took a lot of senior-management time, required investment and demanded a large exercise in external engagement. But BP also achieved tangible impact in the battle against climate change.

At Stanford, I announced a target of a 10 per cent reduction in carbon emissions based on the 1990 baseline, to be achieved by 2010. BP reached this goal in only four years, saving $650 million in the process, by tightening up valves, halting the venting of gas and improving energy efficiency. This was low-hanging fruit that the company had ignored until the climate programme focused minds and provided the right incentives. Quick wins helped to generate momentum and build belief in the strategy amongst the workforce.

At the centre of the carbon savings was the emissions-trading scheme. Beyond its direct impact on pollution, the development of this market-based instrument also helped BP win a seat at the policy table. When the UK government wanted to develop its own cap-and-trade system, it came to BP for advice. Today, emissions-trading schemes are a crucial plank of climate-change policy across the world.[2] The Clinton administration also began to view

Climate-change talks in California with Tony Blair, Arnold Schwarzenegger and me. July 2006.

the company as a trusted adviser on global-warming solutions, as did California governor Arnold Schwarzenegger.

Most importantly of all, BP changed the debate on climate change. With Shell, it led the oil industry from a position of vehement denial to an acceptance that the status quo was unsustainable. Today every international oil company acknowledges man-made climate change. Instead of arguing with the energy sector over the science, governments and NGOs can now concentrate on working with industry to develop solutions. It was this realisation that Big Oil must move towards a low-carbon world that motivated me to change the firm's tagline to *Beyond Petroleum*.

In hindsight this went further than the public could then accept. It was a mistake to push so hard. *Beyond Petroleum* should have been a subheading, not a main line. The renaming symbolised the shortcomings in our climate strategy. In essence, the company had got ahead of itself and ahead of where industry and government were willing to go at that time. *Beyond Petroleum* was never meant to be literal – not yet, anyway – but there was still too much of a gap between the aspiration and reality, which I now regret. The actions we took were bold, but they could have been bolder. Ultimately that was my fault, and the barriers I failed to overcome provide a useful lesson for today's CEOs as they attempt to change the status quo.

It became exceptionally difficult to keep up the pace of progress. When it became obvious that the race was on to succeed me, some saw an opportunity to moderate the firm's position on climate change. Others sensed a growing hostility to environmentalism among right-wing voters in the US and lobbied hard to stifle coverage of BP's actions. Nonetheless, when I left BP, I spent eight years heading the world's largest 'green' renewable-energy, private-equity fund. The evidence suggests that investment in this area can deliver the returns expected by investors.

In other areas BP was let down by government inaction. When environmental protection requires companies to incur costs, it is up to the state to introduce regulation that creates a level playing field and stops free-riders taking advantage of firms that invest voluntarily. After twenty years of failed UN conferences, governments are still unable to agree an international treaty on climate change. That is not an excuse for business to sit on its hands but it certainly makes it harder to justify investments to lower carbon emissions. BP did allocate time and money for research and development on carbon capture and storage but did not receive sufficient backing from the US or UK to make it an economically viable option. Like Shell, BP was willing to share the results of any breakthrough as a public good, but needed the state to underwrite part of the significant costs.[3]

My developing view of climate change at BP demonstrated why the environment is the most difficult stakeholder of all to connect with effectively. Society was no longer willing to tolerate denial of climate change but neither was it ready to create a context that rewarded a full-blown attempt at a solution. To understand that paradox we need to look to the past.

The Tragedy of the Commons

In *Paradise Lost,* John Milton's seventeenth-century epic poem about man's fall and the ways of God, there is much to be admired about Satan. Steadfast and inspirational, Milton's anti-hero must be sufficiently attractive to tempt Adam from his life of divine leisure. His soaring rhetoric is unsurpassed in English literature. Every now and then, however, Milton reminds us of his subject's villainy. The poet's disgust is apparent for the first time when he describes in visceral language Satan's destruction of the environment during the development of hell's capital, Pandemonium. Deep-rooted suspicion of environmental degradation and of extractive industries pervades many of the world's cultures. In the West, Milton was succeeded first by the Romantic poets of the nineteenth century who bemoaned the impact on nature of the Industrial Revolution's 'dark satanic mills', and then by Joseph Conrad. The Polish-born author records with disdain in *Heart of Darkness* the 'sordid buccaneers' he had witnessed on his travels in West Africa, groups of mining enterprises that tore up the landscape with no regard for the environment or local communities.

China, of course, got there long before the West. In the second century BCE, scholars gathered at the court of the king, to debate philosophy and statecraft. The essence of their conversation was recorded in one of the most important texts of the early Han Dynasty, the *Huainanzi,* 'The Masters of the Huainan'. This criticises five types of wasteful consumption that 'are the source of all disorder': Wood, Water, Earth, Metal and Fire. The text rails against miners who 'exhaust the riches of the earth'. Individual reckless behaviour contributes to the overall depletion of natural resources, a significant threat to China's strength. 'Any one of these five types of wastefulness,' it warns, 'is sufficient to bring about the loss of the Empire.' But this example from early China also demonstrates why environmental problems persist. While the actions of business harm society as a whole, there is no incentive for individual entrepreneurs to stop their damaging behaviour. They receive all of the benefits but suffer only a small fraction of the costs.

This is 'the tragedy of the commons', a timeless concept articulated by Garrett Hardin in 1968. He imagines a pasture open to an entire community but on the verge of collapse.[4] Each farmer weighs up the personal benefit of adding one more animal to his herd against the cost of over-grazing that is distributed in small fractions among all of the users. Rational self-interest tells everyone to add more and more animals even in the knowledge that they will eventually ruin the commons. When companies can externalise the costs they impose on the environment, they have little short-term incentive to desist.

Government intervention to correct this market failure relies on political pressure being exerted on behalf of the environment by concerned citizens; unlike the other stakeholders we have discussed so far, the environment is unable to stand up for itself. That may sound obvious, but it explains why companies have been quicker to engage and respect human stakeholders such as employees or government officials than the environment.

For the vast majority of history, business has been able to exploit the environment without bearing the costs it imposes, safe in the knowledge that nature is a voiceless victim. As humans we have always felt uneasy about the destruction of the physical world but have often perceived the negative impacts as too disparate and too far off to be worth addressing. In this context it is remarkable that any action has been taken at all. The environment's recent emergence as a stakeholder to be respected by industry has been a painfully slow journey that is far from over. The story of this

shift begins, like so many others in this book, in small-town
Pennsylvania at the turn of the twentieth century.

Silent Spring

As a little girl growing up in Springdale, Rachel Carson would
look out of her bedroom window at the plumes of smoke rising
inexorably from the nearby American Glue factory. In 1907, the
year Carson was born into a modest Pennsylvanian family, Milton
Hershey opened his eponymous amusement park for workers on
the other side of the state. Closer to home, Henry Heinz was
celebrating the passage of the Pure Food and Drug Act in his spotless Pittsburgh factory. Andrew Carnegie's infamous Homestead
steel plant was just a short drive away.

The pollution in Carson's home town was particularly grim.
Residents would watch through the gate of the glue factory as
retired horses trudged up a wooden ramp to their deaths. The
pungent smell was so bad that people could not sit out on their
porches on summer evenings.[5]

If American Glue exposed Carson to the negative impact which
companies can have on the environment, her education taught
her that nature was worth defending. Her mother Maria regularly
pulled her out of class and into the countryside to learn about
birds, plants and insects. Carson was brought up in one of the
states that mandated 'nature-study', which aimed to bring science
to life through personal contact with the natural world.

The late-nineteenth and early-twentieth centuries saw the
emergence of a preservation and conservation programme in the
USA that was characterised by a 'fence and protect' approach.
The intention was to seal off areas of outstanding beauty for
recreational purposes and to use natural resources more efficiently.
In 1864, after a decade of local campaigns, President Lincoln
bequeathed the Yosemite Valley to the people of California in a

historic act of preservation. Yosemite would go on to become one of America's first national parks thanks in part to the efforts of John Muir, the nature writer and Sierra Club founder.

This era of selective preservation and conservation came to a shuddering halt on a summer's day in 1962 with the serialisation of Rachel Carson's book, *Silent Spring*, in the *New Yorker* magazine. Its publication changed the way we think about the world and marked the birth of the modern environmental movement. Carson introduced the concept of the delicate balance between the health of the planet and the activities of humans in what she called 'the intricate design of the fabric of life'. She took aim at the chemical companies that were poisoning the environment with pesticides such as DDT. This chemical was used by the US military during the Second World War to shield soldiers and civilians from insect-borne disease. Such was its success that Paul Müller, the scientist who discovered its properties, received a Nobel Prize in 1948. After the war it became the leading agricultural insecticide. Then, slowly and without publicity, a string of studies began to emerge that linked DDT to health problems among humans and animals, noting in particular its propensity to remain stored in their fat.

A collection of academic papers may not have been the likeliest source for an international bestseller, but Carson's great skill was to communicate dry scientific facts to the general public with flair and lyricism. She laid out with clarity the evidence linking pesticides to cancer, infertility and brain damage.

The book begins with 'A Fable for Tomorrow' about an archetypal American town that wakes up one day to a 'strange blight': children become sick, no chicks hatch and the mornings that once were accompanied by the dawn chorus of robins and wrens are now conspicuously quiet. 'No enemy action had silenced the rebirth of new life in this stricken world,' Carson writes. 'The people had done it themselves.' The book's title refers not only to the silencing of nature, but also to society's indifference to environmental destruction. Carson was more successful than she ever imagined in her quest to end that indifference.

The book awoke a sense of the world's vulnerability. This was the decade in which mankind would see itself for the first time from the moon, a tiny blue marble entirely at the mercy of natural forces. Astronauts returning from space would experience and share what became known as the 'overview effect', a feeling of humility and awe invoked by the sight of a fragile dot protected by a wafer-thin atmosphere.[6] Even before the lunar landings, the theorist and architect Buckminster Fuller had coined the phrase 'Spaceship Earth'.[7] Like Carson, Fuller viewed the planet as a finely-tuned system that man could disrupt all too easily.

None of this was easy for business to digest. To some, *Silent Spring* represented the first significant assault on the model of industrial progress as it had developed in post-war America. In the book, Carson railed against an 'era dominated by industry, in which the right to make a dollar at whatever cost is seldom challenged. When the public protests, confronted with some obvious evidence of damaging results of pesticide applications, it is fed little tranquillizing pills of half-truth.'

With echoes of the Chicago meatpackers' attempts to muzzle and discredit Upton Sinclair after his exposé of 1906, the chemical industry immediately declared war on Carson. At first it tried to block publication altogether. A leading manufacturer of DDT threatened legal action against her publisher. When this failed their next step was to smear Carson's character by insinuating that she was a Communist.[8] If industry listened to the likes of Carson, they explained, 'our supply of food will be reduced to East-curtain parity'. Far worse was to follow. Because she was a woman she was variously described as incompetent, hysterical, emotional and unstable. One trade magazine, *Farm Chemicals*, depicted her on its front cover as a witch.

The chemical companies' aim was to convince the public that a ban on any pesticides would destroy businesses, raise food prices and send food production back to the Dark Ages. In fact, Carson made it very clear that she supported intelligent use of chemicals in agriculture: 'I do not favour turning nature over to insects,' she said. For industry, though, it was easier to label her as an extremist. One company released a parody of *Silent Spring*'s opening chapter, in which the world is actually overtaken by insects.

This approach only served to worsen industry's predicament. The publications it failed to gag began to run stories on its heavy-handed tactics. In her speeches, Rachel Carson turned the spotlight on corporate political influence, questioning the tax deductions available for lobbying expenses that 'means, to cite a specific example, that the chemical industry may now work at bargain rates to thwart future attempts at regulation'.[9] Carson was suddenly a major public figure. As *Silent Spring* reached the bestseller list, where it remained for thirty-one consecutive months, CBS

Suffering from cancer, Rachel Carson testifies before a Senate subcommittee. Hearings on pesticide regulation were announced the day after a CBS documentary on *Silent Spring* was aired. June 1963.

produced a one-hour special television programme which aired without the support of its main corporate sponsors.

President Kennedy was so taken with *Silent Spring* that he appointed a Science Advisory Committee to investigate her claims; the panel corroborated the vast proportion of the book and recommended that 'elimination of the use of persistent toxic pesticides should be the goal'. DDT was eventually banned domestically in 1972 once the agricultural chemical industry had developed suitable substitutes.[10] By 1975 each of the dangerous chemicals identified in *Silent Spring* had been banned or restricted by the US government.

Yet *Silent Spring*'s impact went far beyond pesticides. It created widespread public support for the idea that companies' interactions with the environment must be regulated. On 22 April 1970, 20 million Americans took part in the inaugural Earth Day, a diverse set of demonstrations and communal activities designed to spur politicians into action. Earth Day founder Gaylord Nelson, a US senator from Wisconsin, took his inspiration from Rachel Carson. On a trip to California in 1969, he witnessed at first hand the appalling aftermath of Union Oil's Santa Barbara oil spill.[11] Surveying the black slick that covered the pristine coastline, Nelson decided to harness the public awareness of environmental degradation that *Silent Spring* had spawned.

The 1970s were to become the golden age of environmental regulation. Seven months after Earth Day, President Nixon established the Environmental Protection Agency to enforce new legislation related to air and water quality as well as the use of toxic pesticides and the disposal of waste. The Clean Air and Water Act amendments forced companies to alter processes and technologies to higher environmental standards. Big business complained bitterly that the burdensome cost of compliance would silently bankrupt US enterprise. But in the 1970s it was fighting against broad public consensus on the need for government intervention against egregious corporate harm to the natural world. And this was not an era of voluntary regulation or market-based instruments; environmental policy was at this stage conducted under a command-and-control model. This rather blunt approach may not have been popular in the boardroom, but it achieved some impressive results without ever wreaking the economic havoc predicted by industry. Emissions of six major pollutants covered by the US Clean Air Act of 1970 fell by 25 per cent from 1970 to 2001, while GDP grew by 161 per cent and vehicle miles increased by 149 per cent.[12]

Technology helped business achieve what many thought was impossible. At last, the environment had found a voice, however faint. Human-based changes to the natural world had started to interfere with health and happiness. Crucially, the pollution problems identified then imposed local costs on local populations with no time delay. Unlike the diffuse, international and long-term challenges of the twenty-first century, people could see the immediate improvement which followed intervention. The environment was no longer a dumping ground that business could safely ignore.

Birth of the NGO

Today, companies regularly underestimate how much power civil-society groups can wield, while NGOs themselves face questions about their accountability to society and their readiness to campaign responsibly.

Independent citizens' groups have existed for hundreds of years[13] but it was not until 1945, when the newly formed United Nations codified them with the term 'non-governmental organization' and assigned them observer status, that their influence began to rise in fields as diverse as human rights, international development and health. The pollution laws imposed on business in the US and Europe during the 1970s would not have happened without the birth of a new set of environmental NGOs founded in a flurry of activity between 1967 and 1971. In the US, the

Greenpeace's flagship, *Rainbow Warrior*, slips beneath the water in Auckland harbour, New Zealand, after being bombed by French intelligence officers. July 1985.

Environmental Defense Fund and the National Resources Defence Council focused initially on legal action. In an era of new regulation they saw their role as surrogate enforcement agencies, scrutinising companies in the courtroom. They were at the vanguard of 'green' justice; by the end of the 1980s there were 20,000 environmental lawyers who had fought more than 3,000 cases.[14]

Other groups, including Greenpeace and Friends of the Earth, provided an outlet for the anger many individuals felt towards big business's perceived environmental vandalism. They mobilised large numbers of people at events such as Earth Day but also conducted bold direct-action protests that generated significant publicity. In 1985 a Greenpeace campaign ship protesting against nuclear testing in the Pacific was sunk by French intelligence officers, claiming the life of activist Peter Pereira. The ship, *Rainbow Warrior*, gave its name to a generation of environmentalists who were ready to fight government and corporate institutions that mistreated the planet.

Initially, most companies simply ignored NGOs and hoped their unwanted scrutiny would go away. In doing so they repeatedly underestimated the ability of these organisations to harm reputations and profits. For example, Nestlé, the Swiss consumer-goods conglomerate, has endured an NGO-led boycott lasting almost forty years. In 1974 a booklet entitled *The Baby Killer* accused Nestlé of marketing baby-milk formula to mothers in developing countries where widespread water contamination rendered the product lethal. Rather than address the issue, Nestlé sued the authors for libel. Although their claim was successful, the judge warned the company about its marketing methods and the two-year trial generated international attention. From a basement in Minneapolis, four activists calling themselves the Infant Formula Action Coalition managed to trigger one of the largest boycotts in history.

Nestlé was caught off guard. In contrast to the nimble activists, the company waited until 1981 to establish a professional response unit. A senior executive wrote a memorandum to Nestlé's managing director, Arthur Fürer, highlighting the 'urgent need to develop an effective counter-propaganda operation, with a network of appropriate consultants in key centres, knowledgeable in the technicalities of infant nutrition in developing countries, and with the appropriate contacts to get articles placed'.[15] The Nestlé Coordination Center for Nutrition was set up as a 'crisis management task force' with an 'an early warning system and political threat analysis capability'.[16]

Nestlé's mistake was to believe it could win the information war and avoid genuine action. NGOs called off the boycott in 1984 when Nestlé agreed to abide by the World Health Organization's new Code of Marketing of Breast-milk Substitutes, but just four years later they restarted the campaign after it emerged that the company was not actually implementing the voluntary rules. The boycott remains in force today across twenty countries and the International Baby Food Action Network is active in more than ninety markets. Nestlé do not comment on the boycott's financial impact, but it seems that more than three decades of negative publicity will inevitably have impacted the firm's reputation.

At the start of the century Nestlé took steps to take leadership on external engagement with society. This includes commitments on subjects such as nutrition, rural development, water, environmental sustainability, human rights and compliance. These are implemented through various partnerships and the founding of a nutrition institute. And back in the 1970s and 1980s, Nestlé was not alone in its defensive approach to NGO relations. While companies were slow to understand the need to connect with this new type of stakeholder, the fractious relationship was not entirely their fault. Jonathon Porritt, who ran Friends of the Earth from 1984 to 1990, was refreshingly self-critical when we asked him why business took so long to work constructively with NGOs. 'Let's be honest: a whole bunch of people who joined the environmental movement in the seventies were pretty extreme. They wanted to end capitalism and live out some sort of alternative, hippy existence. So if the starting-point premise for NGOs was the dismantling of market economies, most companies thought: "Is this going to be a worthwhile conversation?" and the answer was clearly no.' Even today, it is worth remembering that NGOs do not necessarily represent the views of society as a whole.

The modern NGO is an entirely different animal in its attitude, sophistication, size and wealth. In the last two decades the non-profit sector has seen extraordinary growth, and the quality of personnel in the upper echelons of NGOs is also greatly improved.

Many NGOs now work with, rather than against, business to drive change. For Rocky Mountain Institute's Amory Lovins, who's been doing this for four decades, it is the only practical attitude to adopt because firms have a unique ability to take big changes to scale and an intimate knowledge of the systems that must change: 'If you're not part of the problem, how can you expect to be part of the solution?' Fred Krupp of the Environmental Defense Fund (EDF) has advised Walmart, McDonald's and FedEx as well as BP. In Krupp's view 'capitalism and markets have proven to be the best way to organise society and get entrepreneurs innovating on behalf of things that people want'. His organisation is not afraid to use the levers of capitalism to achieve environmental results. When Kohlberg Kravis Roberts, Texas Pacific Group and Goldman Sachs launched a $45 billion takeover bid for the Texas utility TXU in February 2007, the Environmental Defense Fund did not campaign from the sidelines. It hired an investment bank which made EDF a central player in history's largest private-equity deal. In return for its blessing, it secured an agreement that prevented eight out of eleven new coal-fired power plants from being built.

Not everyone supports this model of corporate-NGO partnership. There are, of course, risks for NGOs that lend their credibility to big business. Jonathon Porritt recalls the discomfort felt inside Forum for the Future, the charity for sustainable development, when its work with BP exposed it to criticism in the wake of the Macondo oil spill.

Yet the current spectrum of environmental NGOs seems to provide just the right balance between constructive cooperation and hard-edged scrutiny. There is an undeniable benefit to all parties when partnerships between companies and NGOs thrive. Business gets expertise and happy stakeholders while society moves closer to its goals without unnecessary regulation. Like all partnerships, there will always be some level of uneasiness on both sides. General David Petraeus, the former commander of United States Central Command, draws the parallel between environmentalists working inside companies and journalists embedded in the military: 'It may not feel comfortable for either of you but it's just the smart thing to do in the twenty-first century.'

Business-minded NGOs can get on with their corporate programmes safe in the knowledge that campaigning organisations such as Greenpeace and Friends of the Earth will hold big business to account with absolutely no danger of corporate capture. Their single-issue focus enables an agility that can catch ponderous large firms off guard. Companies may be wary of these more pugnacious groups, but "if you have nothing to hide you should have nothing to fear". The existence of aggressive, scientifically literate campaigning drives up corporate standards.

At a time of declining confidence in authority, NGOs are the most trusted institution in many countries across the world.[17] It is crucial that they use that position of trust wisely and responsibly. At the moment some organisations are failing to do so, for two main reasons.

The first is a casual attitude towards accountability. At one extreme are organisations that raise money by promoting a popular cause – sweet-looking animals tend to go down well – and then spend it on something for which the general public would never knowingly dip into their pockets. Then there are groups that fight campaigns to please donors even when there is no clear benefit to society. In the case of 'Golden Rice', for example, a genetically engineered crop fortified with Vitamin A that has the potential to reduce child mortality and blindness in poor countries, it is difficult for me to see the objective case for NGOs' opposition.

The second concern is a continued tendency among some NGOs to indulge in dogma at the expense of results. This brings us back to where we started this chapter: fracking and unconventional oil and gas. This issue will provide a stern test of environmentalists' readiness to choose pragmatic solutions over unrealistic ideology. NGOs have a responsibility to campaign based on objective facts in the pursuit of realistic solutions. To achieve the changes required by society they must eschew a default position of opposition to big business. In the words of John Muir: 'Not blind opposition to progress, but opposition to blind progress.'

Sell the Sizzle

We have embarked on the third age of environmentalism, following the 'fence and protect' conservationism of the early 1900s and the age of command-and-control local pollution regulations triggered by *Silent Spring*. This third age is characterised by global, uncertain and often intangible issues such as climate change, biodiversity and resource scarcity, with impacts that are dispersed both in time and geography. These issues are likely to increase public demand for more government action. However, business leaders should not expect any sudden regulatory certainty that would enable better long-term planning.

We are already starting to see what a changing climate might look like. Although scientists are loath to link specific natural disasters to man-made climate change, it is widely accepted that extreme weather events will increase in frequency unless we control greenhouse gases. Insurers estimate that in 2012 just two US disasters, Hurricane Sandy and the Midwest drought, imposed costs of around $100 billion.[18]

While rapid economic growth in developing countries will impose unprecedented strain on the planet, it will also create new demand for environmental protection. McKinsey predicts that by 2025 an extra 1.8 billion people will join the world's 'consuming class', individuals who attain the $10-per-day threshold that defines their ability to purchase white goods such as televisions or refrigerators.[19] If the largest emerging-market economies even come close to the per-capita ecological footprint of the West, the planet will face a worrying future.

As incomes rise, however, people have the time and inclination to worry about the environment. At least that is the theory behind the Environmental Kuznets Curve, a hypothetical graph that plots environmental degradation against income. The inverted U shape of the line suggests that environmental degradation increases up until a certain level of GDP, at which point it falls as emerging middle-class citizens demand change. This has been borne out for local air and water pollutants such as sulphur dioxide but not, so far, for greenhouse gases. That could change once climate change begins to impinge on the quality of life in developing countries.

When it comes to local pollution, we are already starting to see a response. During the 1990s local air pollution took 5.5 years from average life expectancy in northern China.[20] Face masks are a fact of life in Beijing, where children escape the thick smog to play sport in filtered air domes. In 2013 Shanghai residents were confronted with the sight of nearly 9,000 rotting pigs in one of the rivers that feeds their city's water supplies. This was the last straw for some. Chinese micro-bloggers posted messages inviting bureaucrats to swim in their filthy rivers. One local environment official declined an offer of more than £20,000 to do so.[21]

Every environmental movement has a figurehead, and in Ma Jun, China has found a twenty-first-century Rachel Carson. Travelling the country as the *South China Morning Post*'s environmental correspondent in the 1990s, Ma was shocked by the near-universal defiling of waterways. His 1999 book, and call to arms, *China's Water Crisis*, is seen by many as the successor to *Silent Spring*. In 2006 Ma founded the Institute of Public and Environmental Affairs (IPE). This enlists an army of online volunteers to produce air and water pollution maps from a vast collection of previously indigestible government data. Thanks to its efforts, companies that previously escaped sanction are now forced to mend their ways. His team have exposed 97,000 instances of non-compliance and pressured over 500 companies to publicise road maps to greener practices.[22] Trust in NGOs among China's 'informed public' has catapulted from 53 to 84 per cent in the last six years.[23]

As companies grapple with the third age of environmentalism there are three areas that will determine their success and society's ability to solve its ecological challenges. First, they must be better at exploiting the easier 'win-win' solutions. Second, they need to address long-term threats posed by unsustainable behaviours, even if there is no incentive to do so in the short term. Third, they should provide the innovation that makes a greener economy attractive and exciting.

It is clear that firms need a far more professional approach to win-win resource efficiency opportunities. NGO leaders such as Amory Lovins have been making the business case for green programmes for forty years. Executives have been slow to respond, in part because of a deep-seated suspicion of 'tree huggers' telling them how to run their businesses. As 100 years of commodity price decreases were wiped out in a single decade to 2008, they started to wake up and take notice.

To solve challenges such as climate change, society will need to ask companies to go beyond win-wins, but the low-hanging fruit can take us much further than many observers realise. A recent project conducted by the World Wildlife Fund and the Carbon Disclosure Project[24] suggested that the US corporate sector can meet the 2020 carbon-reduction targets required to keep global temperature increases below 2°C entirely through cost-negative measures. By boosting energy-efficiency initiatives and adopting more low-carbon energy sources, companies can cut emissions by the necessary 3 per cent per year while saving $190 billion annually.

Combining the profit motive with humanity's imperative to save itself could achieve remarkable results. That is why people like Fred Krupp are so keen to harness big business to create change above and beyond what is required by law. While the Environmental Defense Fund does not accept donations from Walmart or any other corporate partner, it has set up an office in Bentonville, Arkansas, to facilitate closer links with the world's largest retailer. Walmart's eco-savings programme highlights both the power of win-win opportunities and the potential for impact through its supply chain. Since 2006 it has reduced greenhouse-gas emissions from its stores and distribution bases by almost 20 per cent and saved billions of dollars in the process.[25] Renewables supply 24 per cent of the company's electricity at prices that meet or beat traditional sources, and it has encouraged over 100,000 suppliers to do the same.[26] By shrinking all packaging by 5 per cent

Walmart has also generated annual savings of $3.4 billion, the equivalent of its 2010 third-quarter profit.[27]

That all of this happened by chance demonstrates the need for business to apply a more rigorous approach to resource efficiency. Former Walmart CEO Lee Scott only started to think carefully about sustainability when he was introduced to river-guide-turned-consultant Jeb Ellison, a man who has spent a third of his adult life sleeping in a tent on riverbanks across the world.[28] Back in 2005 Walmart was pilloried by environmentalists as well as unions and small businesses. As it moves towards its targets of zero waste and 100 per cent renewable energy use, the company has not only saved significant money and carbon but also transformed its relationship with the outside world.[29]

Finding and implementing win–win solutions is step one for business. The second area of this modern age of environmentalism is more challenging. It is the ability of companies to confront issues of long-term industry viability without the certainty of short-term returns. How does the energy sector, for example, address the fact that some of its core products are simply not compatible with the low-carbon world of 2050, in the absence of any significant incentives or requirements to change its business today? In 2012, the International Energy Agency estimated that to have a 50 per cent chance of limiting temperature rises to 2°C, only one third of the world's fossil fuel reserves can be burned by 2050.[30] The oil and gas industry assumes, with some justification, that this means that the more carbon-rich sources, such as coal, will be affected disproportionately. Investment in technology that reduces or captures and stores carbon emissions could alter this conclusion. Yet as I discovered at BP, investing in potentially game-changing technologies such as carbon capture and storage often contradicts public companies' requirements for short- and medium-term profitability. Government has a role to play in research and development for high-risk activities which serve the common good, but the main onus lies with business.

There are no easy answers, but one thing is certain: avoiding these conundrums now will only make them harder to answer in the future.

A handful of chief executives, led by Paul Polman of Unilever, are making difficult investment decisions in the name of long-term survival. Polman has halted quarterly reporting in an effort to elongate his company's time horizons. His 'Sustainable Living Plan' aims to double the size of the business while lowering its environmental impact, including a 50 per cent reduction by 2020 in its ecological footprint.[31] Polman is part of a small group of CEOs putting their own jobs on the line for sustainability. Their plans are bold and not all of them will succeed. Crucially, though, they are driving structural changes. This means that when a visionary leader leaves a company it makes less sense for the successor to rip up the sustainability strategy. Instead of a reversion towards the mean, the average is gradually rising. When Lee Scott retired as chief executive of Walmart, the 'simple math' of his green initiatives meant incoming boss Mike Duke was never going to scrap them. 'When we use less energy that's less energy we have to buy, and that means less waste and more savings,' Duke said.[32] It would be surprising if Duke's replacement, Doug McMillon, changed course.

Dealing with issues of long-term viability would be far less complex for companies if tomorrow's regulatory landscape was clearer. That is why business should support governments' attempts to introduce an international climate-change agreement. If a company does not believe it can thrive under legislation that has been anticipated for years on the back of a clear societal problem, then it has not prepared itself to survive even into the medium term. Companies cannot afford to repeat the confrontational attitude their predecessors adopted in the 1960s and 1970s.

The final theme of the new environmental age is the most exciting. Business needs to position itself at the centre of trans-formative solutions that make the low-carbon world an attractive destination. For too long, governments, NGOs and companies have tried to shame people into taking action through scaremongering. Research shows that people switch off when they hear the words 'carbon dioxide';[33] and what psychologists term our 'finite pool of worry' explains why long-term, intangible environmental causes cannot compete for attention with the mundane urgency of daily life. Ed Gillespie, expert on sustainability communications and co-founder of Futerra, tells the story of Elmer Wheeler, a US hot-dog salesman whose first rule of marketing was: 'Sell the sizzle, not the sausage.' It is business that holds the key to an aspirational vision of low-carbon life. In 1939, General Motors's Futurama exhibition allowed New Yorkers to touch with their own hands the exhilarating world of expressways, helping to inspire demand for an entirely new, car-based infrastructure.[34] Companies must lead today's consumers towards equally compelling versions of the future.

They will also need to pioneer the innovations that make such a future possible. Firms at the leading edge are making tentative steps towards a 'circular economy', creating products that can be recovered and regenerated at the end of each serviceable life. Meanwhile, technological advances in big data, mobile connectivity and smart grids will soon allow companies to provide personalised information on environmental choices, from product provenance in the supermarket to energy usage at home. However, studies of human behaviour tell us that really smart technology needs to be able to override our consuming instincts. Stanley Jevons identified 150 years ago that efficiency goes hand in hand with growing consumption, as we enthusiastically get through more for our money. Smart meters that highlight energy-saving behaviour are no use if people reward themselves with a second refrigerator in the garage, or an extra degree on the thermostat.

If it can address these three themes, business has the potential to thrive in the third age of environmentalism and meet society's demands for a liveable planet. The environment, for its part, is likely to emerge once and for all from its role as silent victim to become perhaps the most important stakeholder of all. Increasingly complex environmental challenges amount to a voice that will boom out across the world's boardrooms and parliament buildings.

6

QUEEN AND SERVANT

Technology

Three Days in Taksim

'My friends, welcome to Turkey. We wanted the Europeans among you to feel at home, so we organised the rain. But we are the most hospitable nation on earth, so we went the extra mile. We even arranged some protests!'

The date is 15 June 2013 and I am at a hotel in Istanbul to chair the annual edition of an unusual event. The Performance Theatre is a pop-up think tank which brings together a select group of CEOs, public servants and spiritual leaders in the quest to realise 'a new kind of growth', founded on long-term value for society as well as shareholders. The idea is to expose executives to fresh voices. Sitting in the audience today is General David Petraeus. Bob Thurman, one of the world's foremost Buddhist thinkers and father to actress Uma, is to his left.

Each year this event happens in a different city. For the past two weeks, this year's venue has been rocked by protests against the government. A dispute about the construction of a shopping centre and army barracks near Taksim Square has escalated into nationwide demonstrations. Suddenly, the conference's opening

The eviction of sit-in protestors from Taksim Gezi Park in late May 2013 sparks anti-government unrest across Istanbul. June 2013.

address by a senior Turkish official has taken on unexpected significance.

His attempt to make light of the uprising goes down badly in the room. A smattering of guests laugh nervously, but most shift uncomfortably in their seats, averting their gazes out through the golden window frames on to a rain-soaked Bosphorus. It does not improve when he becomes serious. The protests, he assures us, do not reflect the will of the Turkish people. They are the work of 'terrorists supported by outsiders'. The official blames unnamed foreign powers intent on destabilising Turkey. 'I don't want to tell you who are to blame, but we know exactly who they are.' His words are intended as much for the television cameras positioned at the back of the hall as they are for the invited guests.

Only a few years ago, speeches like this would have been the only version of events available to ordinary Turks. Social media has changed that for ever. While the speech continues on the stage, members of the audience are surreptitiously tweeting critical comments under the tables. An activist involved in Egypt's 2011 demonstrations said: 'We use Facebook to schedule the protests, Twitter to coordinate, and YouTube to tell the world.' Everywhere you look in Istanbul, people are glued to social networks, using them to arrange physical events, express an opinion or simply receive uncensored news.

A protestor uses her phone to report the latest news on unrest around Istanbul's Taksim Square. June 2013.

The next day we drive the short distance from our hotel to Taksim Square. Overnight the police have stormed the area, clearing out protestors gathered for a concert using tear gas and water cannon. An uneasy calm hangs over the place. Riot police lie asleep underneath the verandas of sweet shops, resting after a hard night's fighting. One group of workmen sprays away debris with giant hoses while another crew plants mature flowers in the colours of the Turkish flag on a mangled central lawn. They are literally papering over the cracks. The sound of protestors chanting is audible in the distance over the din of early-morning traffic.

Back at the conference, the CEO of a global company voices a thought that has crossed the mind of most delegates. 'In Egypt, people used the Internet to bring down an unpopular government in two weeks. Imagine how fast a company could fall.'

The advent of widespread Internet connectivity and social media has allowed outsiders to scrutinise companies like never before. This is the first of three lessons we are to learn in Istanbul about the way technology shapes the relationship between business and society. Technology-driven transparency is shifting the balance of power away from traditional institutions such as governments and companies towards individuals. Companies need to learn how to adapt to these new sources of scrutiny.

Since 1995 the number of Internet users has increased almost 200-fold to over 3 billion in 2015. By 2025 that number will likely double.[1] Ten years ago there was no such thing as Facebook, Twitter or Instagram. Today, well over a billion people have Facebook accounts and social media has redefined the way we interact with the world. Crucially, an ever-increasing proportion of online activity is happening on mobile devices,[2] including in emerging economies such as China, where in 2012 mobile Internet access overtook PC-based access.[3]

Vint Cerf, Google's 'Chief Internet Evangelist' but more commonly known as one of the 'Fathers of the Internet', remembers using a production model of the first commercial mobile phone in 1983. 'It was this huge brick called the Motorola DynaTAC. I was fascinated by it so I rang its inventor, Martin Cooper, using the DynaTAC, to find out more.' This was around the time that the Internet went into operation, 'but we had no idea that our two inventions, the Internet and the mobile phone, would combine in the future to such great effect'. It would be another twenty years before the creation of the smartphone. Today there are almost 2 billion smartphone users.[4] Former Intel CEO Andy Grove's dream of a billion connected PCs has been surpassed by Mark Zuckerberg's vision of 5 billion connected mobiles. These

Martin Cooper makes the first public call from a cell phone while walking around New York City. April 1973.

developments mean that individuals no longer require groups to hold companies to account. A single voice can be heard across the world.

The technological advancements that took us from Martin Cooper's oversized Motorola to Steve Jobs's iPhone have generated a step change in the way people relate to companies. It is not the first time that technology has done this. The invention of the steam-powered rotating printing press in the mid-nineteenth century enabled the mass production of books and newspapers.

Without that mass production, many of the world's worst business practices would never have been eliminated. Ida Tarbell and her muckraking journalist colleagues would not have defeated the monopolies of America's robber barons. Upton Sinclair's *The Jungle* would not have precipitated regulation of food and drugs. Rachel Carson would not have launched the environmental movement with *Silent Spring*.

The impact of the Internet and social media has been to democratise the publication process, causing an exponential increase in the number of public voices. While Rachel Carson needed a publisher and a TV station to communicate her message, individuals today just need a phone. Facebook's chief operating officer, Sheryl Sandberg, is proud of this contribution. 'We give ordinary people a voice, which gives them extraordinary power,' she told us. 'In previous generations, business execs had a voice, you could own a TV station and have a voice, but an average person couldn't get on NBC and tell their story. You had no channel, no distribution, and no voice outside of maybe your town hall. The promise of Facebook is that it helps shift the balance in ways that I think are very healthy.'

Even though they still try, it is now impossible for companies to control the flow of information that defines them. Low-level employees have access to critical data before management, and can easily embarrass the company on social media. Regulators in one country find out about legislation in another instantly and can move quickly to copy it. Activists' reports of corporate behaviour that might be acceptable in one part of the world can instantly cause outrage elsewhere. In a crisis, companies face online humiliation or simply scrutiny from any number of sources. They need to accept that digital technologies have taken some of their power and given it to society. Companies need to adapt and they can do so through engaging radically, something we explore in detail in Chapter 11. In return, technology has given them significant benefits, helping them not only to connect better externally, but also to increase productivity internally by enhancing knowledge sharing and collaboration.[5]

Don't be Evil

Back in Istanbul, two titans of secret intelligence are leading a panel on the other big news gripping the world in June 2013. It is two days since the US charged Edward Snowden with espionage after he leaked the existence of PRISM, a sprawling online surveillance program run by the National Security Agency. The panellists are General David Petraeus, the recently retired CIA director, and Sir John Scarlett, the former director general of Britain's MI6. As in the media, the debate in the room is focused on the role of large technology companies which are alleged to have shared users' private data under court orders obtained by the US government. Petraeus and Scarlett remind the audience that the companies were legally bound to provide the NSA with answers to specific requests, and that they were also obliged to remain silent on the details of those arrangements.

A third member of the intelligence community is less diplomatic. Referring to Google's famous 'Don't be evil' slogan, he asserts that 'it is unrealistic for a company that possesses the world's data not to be evil sometimes'. Many of the Silicon Valley leaders we interviewed for this book had a complacent attitude towards privacy. 'By its very nature,' said one, 'email works by computer programs reading what you write. People will get used to that idea.' Surveys do not agree: 45 per cent of Americans feel they have little or no control over the personal information which companies gather about them online.[6] Attitudes to privacy are likely to evolve differently in the security-conscious USA and civil-liberties-focused Europe. However, the issue is only going to become more important. Digital technology has clearly got ahead of the public's understanding and willingness to accept it. The Snowden affair reminded us all of the ethical issues at stake.

Public suspicion of digital-technology firms is rising as they make the transition from Californian start-ups run by plucky kids to global superpowers that can predict when our love for another person will end. Scale and concentration of power are important here. If a local video store loses or mishandles its customers' personal data, only a few hundred people care or even notice. For Facebook, with over 1 billion users, the consequences would touch a huge proportion of the world's population. As a result, these companies have allocated significant time and resources to protect privacy.

Our second lesson from Istanbul is this: the perception that technology has increased companies' leverage to inflict harm is at the centre of today's fractured relationship between business and society. Lloyd Blankfein believes that this concern is the major difference between the current anti-business wave and previous eras of discontent. As CEO of Goldman Sachs he is forced every day to confront the fact that 'people fear the power that technology places in the hands of large institutions, whether public or private; and fear very quickly breeds resentment'. Like many of our interviewees, Britain's former foreign secretary, David Miliband, points to a perceived excess of power as the cause of society's distrust of business. Clearly, digital technology has augmented that power.

Our trust of technology itself tends to be very strong. It is companies' use of technology that rings alarm bells. People may be suspicious of the bosses running banks, yet they entrust their life savings to the IT infrastructure behind the scenes. Sebastian Thrun, the inventor of Google's driverless car, is consistently surprised by how quickly people adjust to his creation. 'After about ten minutes they gain complete confidence that the system works perfectly and they are perfectly happy to be distracted as the car drives itself. Compare that to the amount of time it takes to trust a new teenage driver.' Even when volunteers experience 'insane' speeds on racetracks, they rapidly become totally relaxed. 'Human beings trust machines enormously,' Thrun concludes, offering machine-controlled elevators and auto-piloted aeroplanes as further examples of our willingness to put our lives in the hands of computers.

So it is the abuse of technology by business that we really fear, rather than technology itself. The most obvious way companies can hurt us is through physical injury. Before the era of nuclear power, it was impossible to imagine that a single accident could kill hundreds of thousands of people. The use of the atomic bomb at Hiroshima and nuclear bomb at Nagasaki changed the world's frame of reference. Civilian nuclear power has generated constant (and irrational[7]) dread ever since. The environmental movement of the 1960s and 1970s helped to inculcate in the public conscious-ness an awareness of the post-war industrial system's unprecedented potential for harm. Whether through radiation or chemical poisoning, companies now had the ability to harm entire populations with substances whose invisibility rendered them all the more terrifying. In a television interview in 1963, Rachel Carson talked of mankind acquiring 'a fateful power to alter and destroy nature'.

Workplace deaths have actually decreased drastically in the past century, not only because fewer people in developed countries work in dangerous industries, but also because those industries have become much safer. Since 1900 the fatality rate in US mining has fallen over 3,500 per cent.[8] Technology and regulation have made accidents less likely and responses more effective. A 1947 accident in Texas City killed 576 people when a boat full of chemicals set alight and destroyed every piece of local fire-fighting equipment, leaving the town defenceless when a second vessel caught fire. In contrast, a very similar accident in 2013 claimed twelve lives. Any loss of life is appalling, so the progress made in recent decades on reducing the number of accidents and their cost to human life should be applauded.

Technology has, in fact, helped to reduce the risk of death across almost every activity. As Dan Gardner illustrates in *Risk:*

The Science and Politics of Fear, we are the safest humans in history.[9] Yet no amount of statistical analysis will rid society of the sense that modern industry is more lethal than ever before. The images of Chernobyl, Bhopal and Fukushima remind us that technology can unleash destruction on an apocalyptic scale.

The rise of digital technology has added two major new fears beyond the purely physical. One, as we have discussed, is the misuse of personal data. The other is the fragility of hyper-connected financial systems. The recent crisis made people angry as they began to see the risks of integrated and digitally connected systems; wherever you were in the world, you could not escape the fallout from mistakes made by bankers on Wall Street. 'Lehman Brothers touched everyone,' says Andy Haldane, chief economist at the Bank of England. 'And the only way I can make sense of why it touched everyone is because we are now hyper-connected. When the "big one" comes, hyper-connectivity is no longer a friend; it's a foe because it spreads the bad stuff.' Lloyd Blankfein sees this as a watershed moment in the modern perception of big business. 'Being confronted with the possibility of systemic financial events that could tear down huge banks introduced an element of fear that was every bit as damaging as the anger.'

Silver Bullets

Our third Turkish lesson about technology and the relationship between business and society is far more positive than the first two. Technology may shine a light on corporate wrongdoing; the power it offers companies may render people deeply uneasy. But technology is also the greatest force available to business as it struggles to respond to society's needs. Whether it is major break-throughs or gradual progress, technology offers companies the chance to do the right thing by the world and is the core engine of economic prosperity.

I am reminded of this fact in Istanbul when I receive a phone call telling me that the UK government is ready to come out in support of unconventional – or shale – gas development on home soil. It is perhaps the most significant milestone in the early stages of a nascent and possibly transformative British industry.

That potential exists thanks to the efforts of pioneers in the US, where the technological efforts were made in a gargantuan display of persistence. The story of US unconventional gas and oil demonstrates how technology in the hands of the right type of business can meet even society's most insatiable requirements. It is a story that is all the more remarkable because it is about one man.

In the three decades following the OPEC oil embargo of 1973, the overwhelming consensus among industry insiders and external observers alike was that US domestic production of oil and gas was doomed to inexorable decline. Simultaneously, and in apparent disregard of that consensus, the US public steadfastly continued to expect nothing other than rock-bottom fuel prices. Very few analysts saw how those prices could continue to remain low given the US's growing reliance on increasingly expensive imports. George Mitchell, the son of a Greek goatherd and shoeshine-shop owner, refused to accept that it was beyond the capabilities of enterprise to fix this problem.

As the boss of his own independent firm, Mitchell Energy & Development Corp, in the 1970s he started a journey that would span four decades. His self-imposed challenge was to find a way to commercialise the enormous hydrocarbon reserves trapped in shale rock underneath Fort Worth. US government research had confirmed the presence of a huge 'play', known as the Barnett Shale, but most serious observers agreed that extraction could never be economical.[10]

In the end, it was two different technologies that helped Mitchell overcome his challenge. The first was hydraulic fracturing ('fracking'), the injection of fluids at high pressure to release oil or gas from the shale rock. The second was the drilling of horizontal wells to reach significantly more reserves. Mitchell invented neither of these techniques. Fracking was developed by Amoco (now part of BP) in 1947 and by Mitchell's time, there were few oil men who had not tinkered with it in shale only to give up in despair. Both the Russians and the Americans tried at one point to use nuclear explosions to fracture shale rock.

Mitchell's genius, like many of the great entrepreneurs, was in the application of technology, not in its invention. First, he made the inspired decision to combine hydraulic fracturing and horizontal drilling. It was this combination of the two processes that made large-scale extraction possible. Second, he was willing to persevere with his experiments year after year. In *Outliers*, his popular study of winners, Malcolm Gladwell notes that people achieve world-class performance in their chosen field after 10,000 hours of practice. George Mitchell makes that look lazy. He drilled over 10,000 wells. 'I never considered giving up,' he told reporters shortly before his death in 2012, 'even when everyone was saying: "George, you're wasting your money."'[11] Finally, he was willing to change direction. In 1998, as he neared his eightieth birthday, he agreed to replace many of the expensive chemicals in the fracturing fluid with water.[12] This slashed the costs of production, increased efficiency, and triggered a race to develop the US's giant reserves of shale gas and its sister, tight oil.

The subsequent energy revolution that has swept across the US is the one of the most significant events of the new century. Shale gas went from less than 10 per cent of natural-gas production in 2007 to almost 40 per cent in 2014, and production of crude oil increased by 70 per cent over the same period.[13] Fuel costs for consumers and industrial plants have declined substantially. Energy independence, the holy grail of US politics, no longer looks like a pipe dream. It is now entirely plausible that the US could meet the vast majority of its energy needs from domestic production together with imports from Canada and Mexico. As unconventional production of oil and gas has risen, there have been significant macroeconomic and geopolitical implications. And if the US chooses to rely less on the Middle East for oil, China's influence in the region may grow as it obtains greater security of supply. A substantial rebalancing of global trade could occur if the US continues to outperform China in its exploitation of its hydrocarbon reserves. At their peak in early 2011, oil imports accounted for around two thirds of the US trade deficit, but by early 2015, they accounted for just over one quarter.[14]

The environmental implications are no less significant. Technological advancements in shale-gas production offer probably the most realistic opportunity to make an immediate dent in greenhouse-gas emissions.[15] Of course the oil industry will not get the chance to use shale gas to address humanity's global climate-change concerns unless it alleviates the local environmental fears associated with 'fracking'. Often new technology solves one societal complaint only to trigger a new one.

George Mitchell understood that business could not maximise the impact of shale gas without dealing with its environmental critics. His son, Todd, spoke of the 'Mitchell paradox' to describe a man who spent his career immersed in hydrocarbon production and yet spent his spare time in rural conservation. Mitchell Sr was, however, absolutely clear on the need for sensible regulation of the wildcat operators who have hurt the industry's reputation with unnecessary environmental damage.[16]

It is technology, of course, that can ensure that damage is minimised. US enterprise boasts a rich history of technological innovation unleashed in response to the environmental issues of the day. Fred Krupp, president of the Environmental Defense Fund, recalls the progress on sulphur emissions made by heavy industry in the 1990s when acid rain caught politicians' attention: 'The common wisdom was you couldn't possibly mix more than ten per cent low-sulphur coal from the Rockies with the

Eastern high-sulphur coal because the burners would go out. When we got the emissions-trading scheme through Congress, people realised there was profit to be made so they started tinkering. They tried twelve per cent. It worked, so they tinkered some more and they managed fourteen, and eighteen and so on until eventually seventy per cent of the low-sulphur coal could be successfully mixed. This wasn't a big, "gee whizz" technology breakthrough,' he says. 'It was humans on the shop floor discovering a profit centre and it got their juices going to solve the problem.'

The same pattern of small, incremental changes adding up to game-changing progress has occurred in transportation. One by one, lead, MTBE, ethanol and benzene have been systematically removed from gasoline. Despite howls of protest, auto manufacturers have transformed fuel efficiency and exhaust filtration. Compared to twenty years ago, today's cars resemble mobile air-scrubbing machines or itinerant iPads that have used technology to become cleaner, safer and more efficient.

The Montreal Protocol on ozone-depleting substances is widely regarded as the only truly successful example of an international environmental agreement. In 1987, less than two years after the ozone hole had been identified, all major countries committed to a phase-out of the offending chemicals. By 2005, emissions of ozone-depleting chemicals had fallen 95 per cent and by 2050 the ozone layer should return to its 'natural' level.[17] Economists marvel at the unprecedented show of cooperation. The era's biggest environmental challenge to business was dealt with swiftly, efficiently and with remarkable consensus among nations that usually have wildly diverging interests. In reality, though, the hard work had been done by the time the delegates sat down in Montreal. DuPont, the leading producer of chlorofluorocarbons, had already developed substitute chemicals for use in refrigeration, air conditioning, packaging and aerosol propellants. Business was ready to act and so society's problem was fixed.

The contrast with climate change is stark. In 1990 the US Council of Economic Advisers estimated that the elimination of chlorofluorocarbons and halons by 2000 would cost only $2.7 billion. The same report advised that the UN's latest greenhouse-gas targets would be 150 times more costly than that.[18] In 1992 the Senate unanimously passed a resolution supporting faster CFC phase-out. In 1997 it voted 95–0 for a resolution stating that the US should not participate in the Kyoto climate protocol.

At its best, technology allows business to address society's concerns and demands in a relatively painless way, without bearing unsustainable costs. Deploying a new technology is far easier than asking consumers to change their behaviours or being forced to rethink your business model. It is with that in mind that producers of fatty foods and sugary drinks are turning to the world of science as their role in the world's obesity pandemic places them in the spotlight. Shortly after her arrival as Pepsi's CEO, Indra Nooyi launched a programme to find new ways of eliminating sugar, salt and fat. Under Mehmood Khan, recruited from a senior role at the Mayo Clinic, a new department has strived to help healthier versions of unhealthy products pass the taste test. It has developed low-sodium potato crisps that retain a salty flavour, and offered up Pepsi Next, a 'diet' cola that is more appetising than previous versions of the genre.[19] Meanwhile, its competitor Coca-Cola has introduced Coca-Cola Life, which contains a third fewer calories and a third less sugar than regular Coke.

The search for a natural zero-calorie sweetener that really works goes on. Nooyi is caught between politicians who are unimpressed with the industry's progress and investors who are losing patience with Pepsi's preoccupation with the trend in health consciousness. The problem with technology is that it does not work to order. Nooyi must hope that it soon starts delivering some practical results. In the long term, it is only technology which can keep the purveyors of sugar syrup on the right side of society in a way that does not destroy their business.

Queen and Servant

Economists like to say that there is no such thing as a free lunch. Technology is the exception to that rule. Major technological advances such as the steam engine or the Internet make everyone better off, generating increases in output that are disproportionate to the cost of development. They tend to be non-rival (one person's use does not preclude another's) and long-lasting in their impact.

Professor Robert Jensen showed what technology can do in a study of the southern India state of Kerala.[20] Before the advent of mobile phones, sardine fishermen had no way of anticipating how much demand there was for their sardines at the various markets dotted along the coastline. If a market was oversupplied, the fishermen who chose it would be forced to accept low prices or even to throw away their catch. It would be too late and too costly to move to another market with less supply. Customers in those undersupplied markets would have to pay high prices for sardines. Prices fluctuated wildly and a good proportion of the

A Keralan fisherman makes a call to coordinate with nearby boats as they close in on a large shoal of fish. April 2004.

daily catch was dumped. It was an unsatisfactory situation for business and for the local communities.

The introduction of mobile phones in 1997 enabled what can only be described as a miraculous change in fortune for Kerala. Without any intervention from the government or major investment on the part of the fishermen, a new technology simultaneously increased their profits and reduced consumer prices. Fishermen were able to phone ahead to find markets offering the best possible price. This eliminated waste, boosting their profits by 8 per cent on average. The removal of waste increased the overall supply of sardines, which meant that Keralans paid on average 4 per cent less for their daily staple. The increased profits, the reduced prices and less waste were persistent changes rather than one-time gains, for business, society and the environment.

Facebook's Sheryl Sandberg has seen this phenomenon play out in many different locations: 'Across the developing world, cell-phone technology, Facebook and YouTube give people more transparent access to markets and prices, empowering both consumers and producers. Whether that's the ability to monitor food prices in India or the ability of fishermen to send their catches to the markets with the best possible prices, this is changing people's lives.'

As Tim Berners-Lee, the inventor of the World Wide Web puts it, 'technology and business are so interrelated that one can't exist without the other'. It is critical to success for many reasons, but one of the most important is that it shapes the relationship between business and society. Technology is the 'queen and servant' of that relationship. It is the servant of companies who use it to communicate more effectively with the world and to solve society's weightiest problems. It serves society as a tool with which to scrutinise business. Yet technology is also the queen. It never stands still. Ground-breaking new technologies have consequences that are unpredictable and far-reaching. And if mishandled, innovations that have the potential to help society can end up harming instead of improving it. If badly presented, even beneficial new technologies can look bad.

The right approach is one that fosters early and open engagement with the public, using trusted, independent scientists and academics wherever possible. Business has to accept that new technology is hard for people to understand and ripe for sensationalist media coverage. Sheryl Sandberg, Facebook's COO, likes to tell a story which shows how timeless this problem is. 'In Britain, when the car was invented, they passed a law saying that you needed two people to operate a car: one to drive and one to walk in front with a red flag. When caller ID was invented, California tried to pass a law banning it because it was seen as a huge violation of privacy. When you change things quickly, you have to deal with uncertainty and fear. That means helping to explain fully what your product is and how it is used.'

Biological sciences that modify naturally occurring life forms challenge deep-seated beliefs and can be particularly controversial. When US companies attempted to bring genetically modified (GM) food to Britain in the late 1990s, their over-simplified advertisements left people feeling patronised and confused. They had not taken the time to understand society's concerns. A newspaper backlash ensued and 'Frankenstein Food' was off the menu for the foreseeable future.

According to Sir Paul Nurse, president of Britain's Royal Society and a Nobel laureate, 'the corporate and scientific communities failed to win the argument on GM because they failed even to understand the basic questions people were asking, let alone answer them'. At the time, as chair of a 'science in society' committee, Nurse was involved with research to identify some of those questions. 'Often, when companies or scientists want to hear the views of the public, they go to NGOs,' he says. 'But NGOs are not the public. So we went to speak directly to people across the country. And the striking thing was that they wanted answers to questions which we had never thought of. The most common concern was:

"We don't like GM foods because we don't want to eat foods with genes in them." Now, that is not anything that a scientist or business person would even think about because obviously all food has genes in it.'

Nurse believes that business and science leaders share a common responsibility to explain the impact of new technology. 'Both could do much better,' is his verdict.

Technology defines the nature of the connection between business and society. Its advances have both shattered trust in enterprise and allowed companies to provide things humans really want. Some of the most important technologies have done both of these things in quick succession. Our visit to Istanbul called to mind three ways in which technology shapes how the world perceives business. First, it provides tools for civil society to scrutinise corporate behaviour. The paraphernalia of the digital age, from smartphone cameras to social networks, have done more for transparency than any other innovation since the steam-powered printing press. Second, we tend to fear the apparent leverage for harm that disruptive technologies give large companies. Finally, technology offers great opportunities for the private sector to meet the ever-increasing demands with which society presents it. All of this means that the way business uses technology will go a long way to determining the future of its relationship with society. It must be handled by companies as a cherished and complex agent of connection.

7

THE RESERVOIR

Reputation

Reclaiming Reputation

Who cares about reputation? Not chief executives, apparently.
'Reputation' and 'trust in business' were sixth and tenth on the
list of priorities ranked by leaders in a recent Conference Board
survey.[1] Rather, they were more concerned about human capital,
operational excellence and regulation.

These leaders are both right and wrong at the same time. They
are wrong because reputation is vital. It has the power to make
or break a company. But they are right to view reputation as
something that cannot be 'managed' separately from the fundamental business. Reputation is an outcome, not a construct. It is
the result of a company's basic approach, products and activities;
it is about connecting with people based on who you really are.
This has been clear to thinkers as far back as Socrates, whose
view was that 'the way to gain a good reputation is to endeavour
to be what you desire to appear'.

Over the last twenty years 'reputation management' has been
appropriated by spin doctors and public-relations operatives. To
them it is about press releases, lobbying and talking points. When

we see a company's CEO on television using strange, mellifluous management-speak, we sense immediately that we are receiving a version of the truth rather than the actual truth. Alastair Campbell, Tony Blair's former director of communications, told us that he believes the type of polished spin which once served his old boss so well is no longer effective in a world which values authenticity so much more highly. Campbell is struck by the glaring lack of authenticity among most CEOs.

Business leaders should think about reputation every day, not as a construct to be created, but as an indicator of their company's viability and overall performance. One of the clearest lessons from the first six chapters of this book is that reputation is determined by how well a company meets society's demands in its everyday business activities. Companies that integrate external engagement into their core strategy and operations are likely to acquire a strong reputation, and are more likely to survive long into the future.[2]

We think of reputation as a reservoir of goodwill that must be filled up over time from many deep sources, not artificially engineered for last-minute use. It is tested during times of crisis; a well-stocked reservoir can be drawn down to give a company the opportunity to make its case and set things right. When the reservoir runs dry, an accident or scandal (even if it happens far down the supply chain) can derail or destroy even the largest company. A prominent Australian regulator summed this up in a wonderfully blunt way: 'When the day comes that you screw up – and believe me that day will come – I have two choices. If you have behaved well up until that point, I can slap you on the wrist. But if you have messed people around I will have no option but to punch you in the face. The public will demand it.'

As a result, much of this chapter is focused on crises. First I examine how companies such as Johnson & Johnson and Toyota recovered from reputation shocks thanks to large stocks of goodwill. Next I tell the story of BP's Gulf of Mexico disaster to explore what happens when that goodwill runs low. For Arthur Andersen in the wake of the Enron scandal, the consequences were terminal. Finally, I try to explain companies' potential to induce fear and dread, even when the evidence suggests they did little wrong.

Deep Reserves

We owe the concept of reputation as a reservoir of goodwill to the late Jim Burke, who led Johnson & Johnson for thirteen years until 1989. Burke presided over and survived the worst crisis in the company's history. In late 1982, seven people died in the US after taking J&J's market-leading painkiller, Tylenol. As news emerged that Tylenol capsules had been contaminated with cyanide through deliberate acts of sabotage, a national furore erupted. Almost 100 million Americans took the painkiller, which suddenly became a suspect whenever someone died. Burke recalled one of the most dramatic scares: 'A driver was found dead in the cab of his truck alongside of the road, with a bottle of Tylenol that had been opened, that he'd used. He was taken to the hospital, tested positive for cyanide, and was ascribed as another poisoning victim, in another part of the country. It had nothing to do with Chicago. Now, it took us a while to sort out the fact that when you test for cyanide, you're testing to see if a person is cyanotic. Heavy smokers are cyanotic. This man was a heavy smoker who had a heart attack and just happened to have taken Tylenol.'[3]

Analysts were forecasting a dark future for the company. Tylenol represented almost 10 per cent of J&J's sales, and a larger share of its profits.[4] In the days following the first deaths, Tylenol's market share collapsed from 37 per cent to below 7 per cent.[5] J&J's value fell by 14 per cent. The *Wall Street Journal* noted that 'as time passes without a suspect being caught or a motive for the seemingly random killings assigned, damage to the Tylenol name is mounting'.[6]

Yet, almost miraculously, by the end of November more than half of the lost market share had been restored.[7] By spring the comeback was almost complete; Tylenol regained its dominance and J&J was widely praised as a model company. The way in which J&J handled the crisis was undoubtedly impressive, but it was the state of the company before the crisis that enabled such a fast recovery.

People tend to treat companies as they do other human beings. If we trust someone and believe them to be of good character, we are likely to forgive them when they make a mistake. But if that person has bad history, we might not even give them the chance to explain. As it happened, J&J had 100 years of good history. Burke remarked at the time that 'we are sensing a tremendous reservoir of goodwill and trust towards Johnson & Johnson and the brand. All good consumer products develop this reservoir, but I don't know any product out there with a greater reservoir than Tylenol.' He felt that this reservoir 'among the public, the people in the regulatory agencies, and the media . . . was of incalculable value in helping to restore the brand'.[8]

Three years before the poisonings Burke had taken steps to ensure that J&J would not fritter away its hard-won reputation. He had been rereading the company credo, written many years earlier by R.W. Johnson Jr. This makes it clear that 'our first responsibility is to the doctors, nurses and patients, to mothers and fathers and all others who use our products and services'. It was the work of a man who understood that business operates in a wider context. Johnson goes on to make commitments to a host of stakeholders, from employees to the environment, before concluding: 'When we operate according to these principles, the stockholders should realise a fair return.'[9]

Burke felt the company was in danger of forgetting its roots. With a copy of the credo on the table, he called in his senior team. 'If we're not going to live by it,' he began, 'let's tear it off the wall. We either ought to commit to it or get rid of it.'[10] The credo was relaunched as the code by which the business would actually be run. When the crisis hit, J&J was a company that understood what lay beneath its reputation. 'All of the previous managements who built this corporation handed us on a silver platter the most powerful tool you could possibly have – institutional trust,' Burke reflected.[11]

The culture that had built up this valuable stock of goodwill also ensured that J&J naturally did the right things in the heat of the crisis. The company's response was orchestrated not by a team of PR advisers, but by the existing leadership who knew what to do and how to communicate. Burke planned meetings with his most trusted executives every morning at eight and again in the evening. In reality they spent most of their lives around his desk for six weeks.[12] Their response to the poisonings reflected three characteristics that had defined the company's reputation for many years.

First, they put customer safety and reassurance before short-term self-interest. As soon as the first fatalities occurred in Illinois, J&J withdrew the entire batch under suspicion, shut down the related plants, and warned physicians against the use of Tylenol capsules. As the death toll mounted, Burke became convinced of the necessity for a national recall of all capsules, whatever the cost. He travelled to Washington DC to meet the directors of the FBI and FDA. Neither felt that a recall was necessary at that stage, but Burke pressed on. The withdrawal cost more than $100 million. It sent a message that the company would always prioritise its customers over any narrow commercial interest. Burke summed up this philosophy as: 'Johnson & Johnson is relatively unimportant in this. Society is very important.'[13]

Second, J&J adopted a position of radical openness. From the first day, instead of circling the wagons, they were completely transparent as they handled more than 2,500 calls from journalists. Before long the headlines started to focus as much on J&J's openness as on the poisonings. From the very first death, they set up toll-free numbers for concerned customers to phone. The lines were manned by volunteer employees who were instructed to be as candid as possible.[14] Here, there is a vitally important lesson for today's companies. Transparency cannot be jettisoned in a crisis.

The new reality of Internet-driven scrutiny means companies simply have to be open or face immediate and inevitable accusations of a cover-up. Transparency should be active as opposed to passive. It is often necessary and reasonable to 'curate' the information you communicate to the world. However, you will be held to account against a standard of authenticity.

J&J's third response was innovation. Presented with a flaw in their packaging, J&J turned to technology to meet society's evolving demands. Just forty-two days after the crisis started, they announced the launch of triple safety-sealed packaging that would discourage tampering and make any attempt at contamination obvious.[15] In the light of that action it would have been easy to blame a less respected company for previously having taken inadequate precautions. It was J&J's good reputation that meant it was perceived as a victim.

J&J enjoyed a healthy reputation reservoir *and* an aptitude for crisis management. To understand why the former is a more

Toyota's president and CEO, Akio Toyoda, bows in apology to customers at a press conference in Beijing, captured by the world's press. March 2010.

powerful force than the latter, we turn to the corporate pride and joy of Japan, a country perhaps more concerned with reputation than any other. Toyota's unexpected recovery from the depths of its unintended acceleration crisis proves that a good reputation trumps inadequate crisis management.

Substance Over Style

The trouble began in August 2009 when a Lexus driven by an off-duty highway-patrol officer suddenly accelerated out of control on Highway 125, north of San Diego. As the car hurtled along at a speed of over 100 miles per hour, one of his passengers dialled 911: 'We're in a Lexus and our accelerator is stuck . . . We're in trouble, there's no brakes . . . We're approaching the intersection. Hold on. Pray, pray.' Moments later they crashed into another vehicle and burst into flames, killing the driver and three of his family.

As with the Tylenol crisis, critics were quick to predict lasting damage as further incidents related to unsecured floor mats and sticky pedals emerged. Unlike Johnson & Johnson, however, Toyota (which owns the Lexus brand) was about to provide an extended demonstration of how not to react in a crisis. The company's indecisiveness ensured an open-ended flow of negative headlines and gave the impression it had lost control of events. It paused before announcing a recall and then lurched through a succession of incremental recalls, withdrawals and conflicting safety statements that went on for months. Internal memos shared with a US congressional committee investigating the issue appeared to show that some executives were more interested in avoiding costly recalls than guaranteeing customer safety.[16]

Rather than accepting responsibility, Toyota's stance was defensive. It snarled at the *Los Angeles Times,* which had broken many of the accident stories, and told customers that there was 'no defect' despite recalling more than 4 million vehicles. This earned a public censure from the regulator, and the US transportation secretary was quoted as saying: 'If anybody owns one of these vehicles, stop driving it.' It took the newly appointed CEO, Akio Toyoda (grandson of the founder) a month to apologise for the initial accident in California. He did so at a press conference in Japan. Part of the problem was that the company lacked a recognisable public face in the US. By the time Toyoda apologised in stilted English to an angry congressional committee in February 2010, many Americans perceived a lack of contrition. The company that bears his name had lost $35 billion of its market value in the preceding month.[17] In 2011 it slipped behind General Motors in global sales, having toppled its American rival in the race for the top spot in 2008.

Toyota made almost every mistake in the book. But it endured. By the first quarter of 2012 it had regained its crown as the world's largest auto maker and that year it sold a record number of vehicles. Its measures of brand loyalty surged back past GM and Ford for the first time since the start of the crisis.[18] The Toyota reputation for quality was powerful enough to absorb not only a crisis but also a sloppy response. It is striking that it is a reputation based on the most fundamental, tangible part of a business: manufacturing. Driven by its purpose to make Japan proud, the 'Toyota Production System' made lean, just-in-time operations famous. It persuaded consumers that Japanese cars could be as well constructed as their German equivalents, an achievement no one thought possible.

Toyota may not have excelled in its PR and communications efforts. But its reputation for quality protected the company at its lowest ebb. It will be interesting to see if Volkswagen's reservoir of goodwill is deep enough to allow a similar recovery following its emissions crisis.

Running on Empty

I began this book in Texas in the aftermath of BP's Macondo oil spill. Watching oil pouring into the deep water of the Gulf of Mexico was one of the more painful experiences of my professional career. I had to look on as the company's reputation reservoir appeared to empty out on television.

Macondo was a reminder that reputation matters. It demonstrated the damaging consequences of going into a crisis when the company's stock of goodwill has run low. And it illustrated the problems created when the response to the crisis does not satisfy the expectations of a critical world.

BP's market value fell by more than $100 billion in two months following the accident, a loss of over 50 per cent. The damage lasted. In the twelve months prior to Macondo, BP's share price had outperformed Shell's by 15 per cent. Three years on, it was down by 25 per cent while Shell was up 30 per cent. In the language of two Oxford academics who studied the impact of corporate catastrophes on shareholder value, BP looked like a 'non-recoverer'.[19]

In July 2015, BP agreed an $18.7 billion settlement with US federal authorities and five Gulf states, taking the total bill for clean-up, damages and penalties to $54 billion.[20] This places the cost of the accident at over $11,000 per barrel, more than 130 times the market value of a barrel at the time. An unprecedented divestment programme was launched to pay for all of this. Three years on from the accident, BP had sold $65 billion worth of assets and was planning a further $10 billion in asset sales by the end of 2015. The entire direction of the company has changed. Beyond the financial and strategic implications, perhaps the most worrying impact of the reputational crash might be on employee recruitment and retention.

It is possible that the scale of this damage was driven by the slow erosion of BP's reputation. Public and political anger encouraged US authorities to push for severe punishments. While Johnson & Johnson was given the benefit of the doubt over Tylenol, BP was considered guilty before proven innocent. It lacked a sufficiently deep reservoir of goodwill to draw down. In the years leading up to Macondo, a series of accidents and cultural changes left the company without American friends when it needed them most.

Despite an overall improvement in safety, the end of my tenure as CEO was marred by two significant incidents. First, in 2005, there was the severely tragic Texas City refinery explosion in which fifteen people lost their lives and more than one hundred and seventy were injured. Then, in 2006, pipeline corrosion led to a small oil spill on Alaska's North Slope and a very high-profile decision to cut back production until the source of the leak was repaired. The events were a reminder that no operation is risk free. Independent panels were appointed, recommendations were made, lessons were learned and a former safety executive was appointed to run BP America. Strained relationships were being repaired

To the incoming Obama White House, BP was, however, an accident-prone foreign entity. So it was no surprise to hear President Obama's threatening language in the aftermath of Macondo, as he assembled a team of 4,500 government officials to investigate.[21] Obama insisted on using the old name, British Petroleum, to emphasise its outsider status. The new CEO, Tony Hayward, in an address at Stanford about a year before the spill, set out a 'back to basics' agenda. 'We had too many people that were working to save the world,' he told students. 'We'd lost track of the fact that our primary propose in life is to create value for our shareholders.'[22]

BP's reservoir of goodwill was being drained and the company was in a situation that no single executive was likely to be able to turn around. Johnson & Johnson had a skilled communicator at the helm as they entered the Tylenol scare. But because it was the first large corporate crisis to play out in real time across TV, online and social media, BP lacked the right skills for this type of media frenzy. Every movement and every statement was seized upon.

Tony Hayward later made it clear that communication was not his strongest suit. 'If I had done a degree at the Royal Academy of Dramatic Art rather than a degree in geology,' he told a BBC documentary, 'I may have done better.' When the world's spotlight fell on him in the summer of 2010, he felt 'completely overrun and just not prepared to deal with the intensity of the media scrutiny'.[23] His infamous remark to the TV cameras, 'I'd like my life back,' was borne of understandable tiredness and frustration. But the comment was perceived as disrespectful to those whose lives had been turned upside down or even lost because of the event. As Hayward told the *Financial Times*: 'There was no way in a million years that I was ever going to connect with the citizens of Louisiana and Texas. I needed to have a role, but not the leading role.'[24]

Boats attempt to tackle the blaze at BP's Deepwater Horizon rig in the Gulf of Mexico. April 2010.

BP did manage an extraordinarily effective technical response. Strong long-term relationships with suppliers helped the company develop engineering solutions to an unprecedented challenge; thanks to intensive work with them, the well was eventually capped. BP also managed the clean-up proficiently and the damage to the environment was far less serious than many anticipated. This was also partly due to local conditions. Although an issue with a well in deep water was everyone's worst nightmare, the characteristics of the Gulf of Mexico were more favourable than for the *Exxon Valdez* spill: light oil in a warm ocean generally dissipates faster than heavy oil in cold water.

The financial arrangements in the face of this existential threat were very impressive. Dev Sanyal, then group treasurer, highlights two reasons for this success. First, BP identified the risk to its finances before anyone else did. In the immediate aftermath of Macondo, BP's creditworthiness, measured by its credit-default spreads, remained largely unaffected. BP's treasury seized the opportunity to raise much of the capital they knew they would soon need. Just a few weeks later the spreads had widened from 50 to 1,100 points; well into 'junk bond' status. At this point many banks would not have extended credit to the company. But BP had been cultivating excellent relationships with its financial partners for decades. It was always active in the commercial paper and bond markets in less turbulent times. These partners had a deep understanding of BP's sources of value and its strength. They did not hesitate to stand by the company. This is Dev Sanyal's second reason for the robust financial defence. Whereas fractured bonds with Washington and the American people hampered the reputational effort, long-standing relationships underpinned the successful technical and financial responses.

The Macondo oil spill illustrates the consequences for businesses that have insufficient goodwill upon which to draw. In this instance, though, the effects are unlikely to be terminal. By taking responsibility and committing funds to the clean-up operation, BP has already begun to repair some of the damage to its reputation. It will still be marked by the episode for years to come but it will not perish. Its reservoir had not emptied entirely. When that happens it is almost impossible for a company to stay alive. Arthur

Andersen, for example, collapsed overnight in 2002 when its involvement in the Enron scandal emerged.

The world's second-largest accounting firm was accused of enabling Enron to hide huge losses through off-balance-sheet vehicles. At the time, Enron was the biggest bankruptcy in history; people were shocked and enraged. Andersen had been implicated in three serious accounting frauds in preceding years, so the Department of Justice was uninterested when it tried to end the latest scandal with a fine. As one judge put it, Andersen had displayed a 'callous, reckless disregard for its duty to investors and the public trust for decades'.[25] In March 2002, the department charged Andersen with obstruction of justice. The firm's lead Enron partner, David Duncan, later admitted that he set in motion the destruction of over two tons of documents and 30,000 emails in order to hide wrongdoing.[26] Andersen's Houston office had to commandeer extra paper shredders, such was the scale of Duncan's enterprise.[27]

When Andersen was convicted three months later,[28] a reporter called the CEO for his comment. He offered just three words: 'Andersen is dead.' In truth, the accounting giant had died the day that the indictment was served; the trial was irrelevant. News of the criminal proceedings was enough to destroy the company's reputation for ever. Andersen's major clients abandoned it immediately, without waiting for the jury's verdict. A global powerhouse of 85,000 staff was reduced to a team of 200 left to administer lawsuits.

What do the stories of the darkest hours of Johnson & Johnson, Toyota, BP and Arthur Andersen tell us? First, that reputations shape the destiny of major companies. Second, that the size of the reservoir of goodwill determines whether a company makes it through shocks. Third, that these reservoirs are built up over time by a company's ability to integrate society's demands into its core activities. Fourth, that crisis management matters, but cannot overcome an existing reputation deficit.

This leaves the question of the incidents themselves. If reputations are built on responsible underlying commercial activity, then that should preclude scandals and accidents. It is not quite that simple, however. Patently illegal or immoral actions along the lines of Arthur Andersen are obviously avoidable; depending on their seriousness, transgressions of this nature can destroy even the most respected company. But accidents are impossible to eradicate entirely. As long as humans are involved, there is the risk of error, even when sound systems exist. If you replace humans with machines the risk becomes one of malfunction. A deep reservoir of goodwill offers companies that err the chance to make amends.

Fear and Dread

So far we have focused on the things that companies do to create a good or bad reputation. But reputation, like beauty, is partly in the eye of the beholder. It is important that firms understand how people arrive at their judgements. To do so, they should delve into the murky and now very popular world of behavioural economics.

Decades of research into cognitive bias – patterns of irrational thinking – by psychologists, cognitive scientists and economists has been brought to life in recent years by authors such as Malcolm Gladwell, Daniel Kahneman, Richard Thaler and Cass Sunstein. Words such as 'nudge', 'blink' and 'anchor' have taken on new meaning at cocktail parties around the world. For our purposes, one particular cognitive bias will help to explain how it is that companies can engender feelings of fear and dread even when there is little or no evidence of wrongdoing.

In 1973, Kahneman described the human tendency to over-estimate the probability of events that are easily called to mind, as the so-called 'availability bias'.[29] Visceral, emotional events are more available and so we tend to misjudge their likelihood. This explains, for example, why people think the chances of dying in an accident are fairly high when in fact they should be far more concerned about heart disease. In his 2012 report, David Anderson, Britain's independent reviewer of terrorism legislation, highlighted the warped influence of the availability bias on public policy. He noted the incessant creation of counter-terrorism legislation despite the fact that fewer people die each year as a result of terrorism than drown in the bath.[30]

Politicians and regulators often make irrational decisions both because they respond to citizens' misplaced fears and because they are susceptible to cognitive bias themselves. The effect on business can be very damaging. The ash cloud from the 2010 eruption of Iceland's Eyjafjallajökull volcano caused European governments to ground aeroplanes. With no evidence except belief, government ministers imagined that engines might be snuffed out and aeroplanes would fall out of the sky.[31] This action diverted passengers into their cars and significantly increased the risks of fatal accidents.

The reputation of a company or an industry that has done little wrong can rapidly deteriorate when intense and oversimplified media coverage of unverified safety or environmental events triggers irrational perceptions of risk. Facts quickly become irrelevant. Academics call this the 'availability cascade'. The advent of the twenty-four-hour news cycle has accelerated the speed at which these cascades unfurl. The media enable explosive amplification of every action at a pace that many companies are unable to match.

In 1995, as the first signs of this new media landscape emerged, Shell unwittingly sparked an international boycott over its decommissioning of Brent Spar, a North Sea oil storage buoy.[32] After two years of detailed analysis in conjunction with the UK government and environmental experts, it was agreed that the 'best practicable environmental option' would be disposal in deep water. Then, without warning (Shell's stakeholder engagement was, according to then-chairman Sir Mark Moody-Stuart, insufficient[33]) Greenpeace launched a large-scale campaign against the plan, occupying the plant and calling for a boycott of Shell's petrol stations.

A Greenpeace boat approaches Shell's disused Brent Spar oil platform in the UK's North Sea. The NGO was able to change Shell's decommissioning plan – ultimately to the detriment of the environment. May 1995.

Playing the role of 'availability entrepreneur', the NGO fed television stations with emotive footage and questionable reports, asserting that 5,500 tonnes of oil would be dumped.[34] All too eager to maximise a compelling news story, many media outlets repeated incorrect information. The news organisations later apologised, as did Greenpeace, but the damage had been done. Shell was forced to adopt a decommissioning solution that it knew to be environmentally inferior. Meanwhile its reputation had taken an underserved battering: sales plummeted by 20 per cent in Germany, where its petrol stations were firebombed by protestors.

The effect of an availability cascade can be even stronger when human safety is involved. We discussed earlier the reprehensible circumstances that led to the Fukushima nuclear accident. While the event was inexcusable, the reality is that it highlighted just how safe nuclear power really is. A nuclear meltdown in an old plant, overseen by a lax regulator, in the aftermath of a mammoth tsunami and earthquake, caused no deaths. The generation of nuclear power, when measured on a unit of energy produced, leads to fewer fatalities than all other major energy sources.[35] It is more than 200 times safer than hydroelectricity. George Monbiot, the outspoken environmental journalist, reassessed the facts after Fukushima and reversed his long-standing opposition to nuclear-power generation. Understandably, the reaction in Japan was less measured. The decline of nuclear power's reputation in other countries as a result of the Japanese accidents showed all the signs of cognitive bias. Just as insurance sales spike in the aftermath of an earthquake, anti-nuclear sentiment rises following an accident, even if the risk of another accident is no greater than before.

Companies are not necessarily powerless to control unfair reputational damage. It is important, though, to understand that society does not always perceive corporate actions rationally. When citizens develop irrational fear it is futile to hope that logic will prevail. Toyota, for example, clung to the fact that driver error and poorly positioned floor mats caused unintended acceleration rather than inherent design defects. They failed to engage with the reality that, rightly or wrongly, many people had become wary of Toyota cars.

Reputation is a slippery concept. In extreme circumstances the outside world can quickly create a version of a corporate reputation with almost no basis in fact. But companies cannot achieve the same feat. It is a mistake for them to treat reputation as a construct to be managed rather than as an outcome of fundamental activity. That outcome, the reservoir of goodwill, is one of the most precious assets a business possesses. It determines competitiveness and, in a crisis, viability. It must be built up painstakingly over time.

Part Two

The Four Tenets of Connected Leadership

8

HISTORY RHYMES

Connected Leadership

History Rhymes

'If men could learn from history,' wrote the poet Samuel Taylor Coleridge, 'what lessons it might teach us!' In sifting through the wrecks and glories of 2,000 years' worth of commercial endeavour, there is one lesson in particular that stands out: society has never been truly comfortable with business, despite its role as the engine of human progress.

History provides us with the context we need so as to understand contemporary anti-business sentiment. The Occupy movement in the US represents the extreme end of a more widespread dislike of large companies. The global financial crisis has made villains of bankers once again and the slow recovery has been punctuated with scandals that encompass food adulteration, tax avoidance and oil spills.

Many of the CEOs we interviewed believed that the scrutiny and pressure directed towards modern business leaders is unprecedented. Hank Paulson, the former US treasury secretary and Goldman Sachs boss, argued that 'the job of CEO is far more difficult now than it was five or ten years ago, when it was exponentially harder than twenty years ago. Chief executives are just raked over the coals these days.' Part of this is down to the new world of rolling news and intense transparency; but there is also a sense that society demands more than ever from business. Large companies are expected to solve major economic, environmental and social problems while international institutions stutter and government budgets shrink. The challenges are indeed daunting and the bitterness towards discredited companies is undeniably ferocious. History tells us, though, that there is nothing intrinsically new about this climate of distrust. The cycles of anti-business sentiment are driven by cycles of antisocial corporate behaviour. When South African police in 2011 used what turned out to be lethal force against striking mine workers, they were standing in the bloody footsteps of the private security guards called in by Henry Frick during the Homestead Strike. The 2013 European horse-meat scare and the 2008 Chinese baby-milk scandal were borne of the same short-sighted greed that characterised Chicago's meatpacking district at the turn of the twentieth century. BP enraged the American public with its pollution of the coastline just as Chinese iron miners faced hatred in the first century BCE for scarring rural mountaintops.

Regardless of how bad or how familiar the consequences of its transgressions against society are, business fails to learn lessons. To understand how this can be possible, we must turn again to behavioural science. Psychologists have unearthed a simple but compelling reason to explain why we are prone to repeating errors: overconfidence. As Kahneman puts it, 'most people genuinely believe that they are superior to most others on most desirable traits'.[1] This superiority complex engenders an irrational conviction that reasonably expected events will never happen to us. Newly wed couples believe the chances of divorce are zero, even if they are on to their second marriage,[2] while smokers massively underestimate their personal risk of lung cancer.[3] Institutions are just as susceptible to this optimism bias. A study of global rail projects between 1969 and 1998 found that projected passenger use was overestimated more than 90 per cent of the time. The growing body of evidence did nothing to improve planners' predictions over the five decades.[4]

The German philosopher, Georg Hegel, remarked that what 'history teaches us is that people and governments have never learned anything from history'. For Hegel, this failure to learn was justifiable because 'each period is involved in such peculiar circumstances, exhibits a condition of things so strictly idiosyncratic, that its conduct must be regulated by considerations connected with itself, and itself alone'. It is an argument picked up by modern thinkers, from Kahneman to Nassim Taleb, who caution against narrative fallacies, oversimplified explanations of essentially random past events. 'Hindsight,' Kahneman says, 'perpetuates the illusion that the world is understandable.' Sometimes, though, what you see really *is* all there is. The details of how innumerable companies have shattered their relationship with society may differ, but the pattern is unmistakable. To paraphrase Mark Twain: the history of corporate misbehaviour does not repeat itself, but it does rhyme.

Even the companies which manage to identify that something is not right often struggle to act on that insight. There are three reasons for this. First, CEOs who have themselves presided over unsatisfactory relationships with external stakeholders have a strong incentive not to highlight their shortcomings. The Oxford academic Vincent Crawford cites 'career concerns' as the 'single biggest obstacle to executives learning from mistakes'. Second, corporate culture is inherently resistant to change, which means that leaders who actually want to alter the status quo have great difficulty doing so. Third, there is a tacit resignation to the inevitability of anti-business sentiment among the more historically aware bosses. Some, notably in the financial sector, have long since given up trying to fight what they regard as the inevitable bloodletting that accompanies an economic downturn. This resignation is wrong-headed. One of the clearest messages emerging from the past is that companies stumble and sometimes perish when their connection with society fractures. The chief executives who either miss this warning or wilfully ignore it are risking the very survival of their organisations and rejecting a crucial opportunity for differentiation.

History tells us that success over time is only possible when companies connect effectively with external stakeholders and contribute positively to society. The past is littered with the carcasses of firms that broke these rules. Intriguingly, the life expectancy of a leading US company has plummeted in the last century, from sixty-seven years in the 1920s to fifteen years today.[5] Richard Foster, a Yale professor and former McKinsey director, estimates that by 2020 more than three quarters of the S&P 500 will be currently unknown firms.[6] 'Sustainability' is one of those words meaning everything and nothing at the same time. For us its meaning is simple: it is about companies surviving and prospering over the long term by creating value for business and society. Paul Polman defines sustainability as 'the right to produce profit long into the future, given to firms who contribute to human progress'.

Three positive constraints keep business on a sustainable path. Purpose ensures that companies and products continue to meet society's needs; reputation is a natural check on poor behaviour since it ultimately determines the appeal and acceptability of companies; and regulation restrains commerce within a civilised box when the first two constraints fail. Without purpose, reputation and regulation, business serves only self-interest and ignores the common good; eventually it fails. The problem for business is that it so often sees these constraints as an unwanted obstacle rather than a guide to success.

So business needs a system to govern its relationship with the world. For the past twenty years that system has been Corporate Social Responsibility, or CSR. This has, however, failed to bridge the divide between companies and society. It is used as an excuse to avoid meaningful regulation, it treats reputation as an artificial construct and it is disconnected from the firm's core purpose and activity. The original idea of connecting with the world through CSR is dead.

The Death of Corporate Social Responsibility

CSR became the standard system for major companies to handle the connection between business and society in the twentieth century. It arose from largely good intentions as an acknowledgement of the need for business to be a responsible citizen. It has done some good. Companies mostly consider the external world more carefully than they did in the late twentieth century, and annual CSR reporting has enabled the growth of the ethical-investment industry. In absolute terms, the scale of corporate philanthropy is vast, even if the amounts are less impressive compared to profits. Large US companies made philanthropic donations of almost $20 billion in 2011, improving hundreds of millions of lives; 85 per cent of these firms have a charitable foundation.[7] In terms of benefits to business, the consensus among our interviewees was that CSR's main impact was on employee morale. For Hank Paulson, this was the primary driver when he ran Goldman Sachs: 'Looking back, a lot of what we did with stakeholders, like the community programmes, was about the employees. These things kept our people happy and persuaded others to join the firm. Sometimes we did things in places where we were not doing a lot of business, like in Chile with the national park, but the staff really loved it.' When companies connect effectively with external stakeholders they trigger a virtuous circle as employee motivation increases, driving performance and ultimately improving reputation.[8]

Despite these positive effects, CSR – or 'Environmental, Social, Governance' (ESG), as it is known in the investment community –

has failed in its main purpose of building a stronger relationship between business and society. It has proven to be irrelevant to a company's reputation in the face of corporate scandals. It is a small, uninspiring answer to a problem that requires a big-picture solution. Inside business, executives view CSR as a fluffy, largely irrelevant cost centre. For civil society groups, it is meaningless propaganda that fails to achieve their goals. Neither side is satisfied. As one of the earliest CEO proponents of CSR, I feel well placed to call for its final demise.

None of the CEOs we interviewed felt that CSR was sufficiently effective, either for their companies or for the outside world. 'If it doesn't build the business,' commented Unilever's Paul Polman, 'I think it's unsustainable.' This scepticism was matched by the NGO leaders we met. Amory Lovins, co-founder and chief scientist of the Rocky Mountain Institute, insists on engaging with CEOs and corporate boards. 'We rarely work with the CSR or environment teams,' Lovins explains, 'because they can't really drive broad and durable change, and don't always make the best business and strategic case.' Fred Krupp, head of the Environmental Defense Fund, agrees: 'Normally, the CSR function is a ghetto that's been established for PR reasons, promoting tiny contributions – vaccines they've donated, say, or playgrounds they've built – but ignoring the impact of the day-to-day business. We have not seen big change driven through partnerships with CSR officials so we have insisted in our work with companies that we meet with the CEO.'

The criticism from people inside and outside business centres around one crucial shortcoming: CSR is fundamentally disconnected from a company's core commercial purpose and activity. This approach has four main flaws. First, CSR ambitions are rarely realised because they lack the active participation of the big-spending commercial functions such as production and marketing. Second, centralised CSR teams tend to take too narrow a view of the relevant external stakeholders. Managers on the ground have a much better understanding of the local context, who really matters, and what can be delivered. Third, CSR focuses too closely on limiting the downside. Companies often see it only as protecting their reputations, perhaps to get away with irresponsible behaviour elsewhere. Finally, CSR programmes tend to be short-lived. Because they are separate from the commercial activity of a company, they survive on the whim of senior executives rather than the value they deliver. These programmes are therefore vulnerable when management changes or costs are cut. Paul Polman paints a discouraging picture of the status quo. 'This is how CSR works in most companies – and I'm not trying to be cynical because it's better than not doing it at all. The typical CSR executive is fifty-five; he wants to work for another three years on something less stressful. There are some good projects going on in the company which make it into the first three pages of the annual report. They maintain relationships with some very safe NGOs. It's about giving an ambulance away,' he says, 'it's about opening a hospital and it's about linking it a little bit to the business. But it's merely post-rationalisation. It's definitely not the business model. In reality it's very much separate from the business.'

The disconnect between CSR and commercial operations means that companies with superb CSR records can also be hugely damaging to society. Howard Davies, the chairman of Royal Bank of Scotland, cites a handful of investment banks which, in the run-up to the financial crisis, 'had very good CSR on the one hand but who had completely lost touch with what the core of their business was doing for the economy and for society'.

An even more damning indictment of CSR is the story of Enron, the energy company which collapsed in the US's largest-ever bankruptcy and corporate corruption scandal. Up until the moment that allegations emerged of concealed debts and exaggerated profits, Enron was widely lauded as a CSR champion. While top executives were busy defrauding shareholders and undermining global trust in US capitalism, Enron's CSR

(Left) Enron's former CEO Ken Lay is led into Federal Court in
handcuffs in Houston, Texas. July 2004. (Right) A framed copy of
Enron's code of ethics sits as a reminder on a former employee's
desk. June 2015.

team was performing admirably. It won six awards in 2000
alone, including one from the Environmental Protection Agency.
It had previously been honoured with a corporate-conscience
award from the Council on Economic Priorities. Since the
launch in 1999 of its Social and Environmental Responsibility
Program, Enron was ticking all the boxes. In 2000, its newly
established Corporate Responsibility Annual Report dutifully
set out its impact on the environment and recounted a wide
range of philanthropic activities. By following the carefully
chosen principles of 'Respect, Integrity, Communication and
Excellence', Enron would 'integrate human health, social, and
environmental considerations into our internal management
and value system'.[9]

The absurd hypocrisy of all this is reflected in a story told by a senior energy executive who began his career with Enron. On his desk sits a framed copy of Enron's corporate values. He recalls with a wry grin the elaborate ritual that accompanied the firm's quarterly earnings report. The entire staff would leave their desks at Enron's Houston headquarters and file into a local theatre for a presentation from the founder and chief executive, Ken Lay. Lay was a larger-than-life character who knew how to work a crowd. His presentation would always begin with an impassioned account of Enron's work in the community, how it was changing the world and why it was the only company worth working for. By the time he was ready to reveal the financial data, he had whipped the audience into a frenzy. People were on their feet, whooping and cheering every word. Then, without fail, Lay would announce yet another quarter of record profits. 'With hindsight,' our interviewee says, 'the numbers were all made up.'

Enron demonstrated in dramatic fashion just how irrelevant CSR really is. Its initiatives not only masked a deeply rotten core, but also represented the type of indulgence that gives succour to the economists who claim that companies which stray outside purely commercial activity are effectively stealing from investors. Lay was the unofficial mayor of Houston, using Enron funds to pay for the Astros' new baseball stadium and throwing the first pitch at the inaugural game.

It was exactly this sort of frippery that Terry Leahy sought to avoid when in 1997 he became chief executive of Tesco.[10] As he built the company into the third-largest retailer in the world, Leahy 'could not see the sense in CSR, by which you look for some other social contribution other than the business you were engaged in'. Leahy's preference was to get on with the job you were paid to do and behave morally: 'My natural instincts were to do things which were worthwhile,' he says. 'Almost in an innocent sense that I didn't come from a business background, so I was influenced by other things in terms of what was important: school, religion, things like that. You brought those motivations to work, and you felt there was a right and a wrong way of doing business which drew on these broader moral codes.'

Leahy felt passionately that Tesco could be of most use to society by concentrating on its role as the provider of quality food and products at affordable prices. Tesco's tagline, 'Every little helps', was 'really a summary of how we were, in some small, not overly claimed way, trying to be beneficial to lots of ordinary people in their lives'. In its early days, the company asked staff to operate under the twin pillars of service to customers and respect for each other.

For many years Tesco was able to thrive by meeting this commitment to its customers. It had a purpose, after all, that was very obviously useful to society. By focusing on customers alone, however, it eventually hit trouble. Its impact on a wider group of stakeholders began to cause serious reputational damage. The retailer eventually over-reached in its eagerness to expand its out-of-town footprint, and created conflict with suppliers who complained that Tesco's insatiable quest for low prices and high profits was driving them out of business. Suddenly, Tesco was a public villain and Leahy was a sitting target for journalists. 'I couldn't go on the BBC without getting a grilling, and it wasn't an interview, it was as if I'd been a criminal. You had to get through a list of ten things: "How do you sleep at night?" would often be the opening phrase. "You close shops, you ruin farmers' lives, and people are committing suicide."'

In an effort to quell the storm, Leahy expanded Tesco's CSR activities, with an emphasis on communities. Swimming pools were built and amateur sports teams were sponsored. Unsurprisingly, this did little to appease the critics; Leahy had been correct from the beginning to be sceptical of CSR. Yet an absolute focus on delivering value for customers at the expense of everything else had not worked either. Something was missing. It is abundantly obvious that the world needs a system to fix the relationship between business and society, but it is also clear that CSR has not been fit for purpose.

Connect

The problem identified in the first half of this book is a weighty one. I have argued that for more than two millennia business has consistently failed, with only a few notable exceptions, to connect successfully with society. To fix this problem corporate leaders need to rethink their place in the world. They must map the world in which their firms operate and seek to exist in harmony with that context rather than in opposition to it. To achieve these lofty goals, business must do something easy to describe but much harder to achieve. It must integrate societal concerns deeply into commercial strategy and operations at every level of the company. This is connected leadership. The idea, as Andrew Mackenzie, CEO of BHP Billiton, describes it, is for 'every single employee, contractor and supplier to take responsibility for social issues'.

The logic is simple and compelling. The success of a company depends on its relationships with the external world, not just customers and investors but also employees, regulators, politicians, activists, NGOs, the environment and technology. Choices made throughout the business, from the boardroom to the shop floor, affect that relationship. For the company to be successful, decision-making in every division and at every level must take account of those effects.[11]

Without leadership, concepts are meaningless. Enron's Ken Lay made all the right noises when he talked about 'incorporating environmental and social considerations into the way we manage risk, govern our projects, and develop products and services' to 'help us maintain our competitive advantage'.[12] Yet he was not remotely interested in delivering on those fine words.

Strong leaders armed with a persuasive concept need a set of directions to turn ideas into actions. Many understand the need to change their relationship with society but most do not know how to achieve it. Without a clear plan, they lack the confidence to allocate money and talent to an area which may make a difference to the business. The second half of this book represents our attempt to deliver that plan through what I call 'connected leadership'. We have reviewed both our own successes and our failures, scoured the lessons of history and interviewed more than seventy CEOs, politicians and leaders of civil society. I conclude that in order to transform their connection with society, companies must do four things: 'map your world'; 'define your contribution'; 'apply world-class management'; and 'engage radically'. In the chapters to come I illustrate why each of these four tenets of connected leadership is so important.

THE FOUR TENETS OF CONNECTED LEADERSHIP

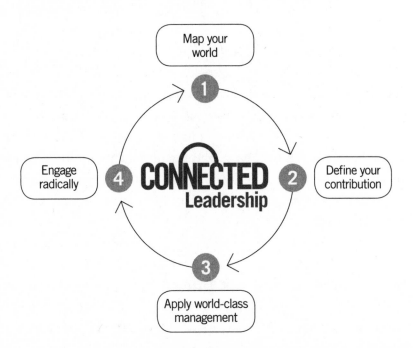

Chapter 9 examines the first two tenets: 'map your world' and 'define your contribution'. It sounds obvious, but it is absolutely critical to understand the trends that are shaping your context, and to quantify the value at stake. Effective marketing relies on detailed knowledge of the preferences and resources of consumers. Effective societal connection is the same but for stakeholders. That means discovering, on an individual and institutional level, what stakeholders want, when they want it, how much they are prepared to negotiate, how your activities affect their goals, and what resources and influence they can bring to bear.

A well-defined contribution matters because businesses must somehow meet societal needs to create value over time. The greatest companies explain with great clarity how the fulfilment of their purpose benefits society. This has been Paul Polman's quest as CEO of Unilever. 'We are finding out quite rapidly,' he told us, 'that to be successful long-term we have to ask: "What do we actually give to society to make it better?" We've made it clear to the organisation that it's our business model starting from the top.' It is vitally important to focus on issues which are most relevant to the firm's core commercial activity. Companies can only 'win the game' in a limited number of societal and environmental areas. In other, less applicable areas they should only 'play the game' by meeting basic standards. By defining their contribution, companies enable themselves to set a clear engagement strategy. For every topic, firms must choose which combination of the '3 Cs' of engagement strategy – contest; concede and lead; and collaborate – is most appropriate.

Chapter 10 explores the third tenet of connected leadership, 'apply world-class management'. The management of the connection between business and society is rarely done as professionally as other parts of a business. Companies should manage it like any other corporate function, using the four core tools of management: creating capability; organising to win; establishing processes; and measuring outcomes. Leadership is as important as management (the two are not the same), and, like Peter Drucker many years ago,[13] I believe the role of CEO must continue to change in order to focus more on the issues that define and enact the company's core purpose. The relationship with society is one of the most important of those issues.

The final tenet, 'engage radically', is about a new era of transparency and advocates complete openness. To earn trust and credibility, the private sector should engage the external world on the front foot, building lasting relationships which are based on regular, authentic negotiation rather than public-relations propaganda, brinkmanship or passive silence. This is the focus of Chapter 11.

I have seen extraordinary feats achieved by companies that excel in each of these areas. There are few, if any, that have managed to combine all four at the same time. When they do, the potential for human progress and corporate success is limitless.

The New Frontier of Competitive Advantage

Connected leadership is an approach that has the potential to produce mutual advantage for business and society, to realise the 'Square Deal' between the two that Teddy Roosevelt dreamt of in 1903. Society can only benefit if it is able to set the extraordinary power of enterprise on an honest path. Arthur Page, a pioneer of corporate ethics who was part of the management team of AT&T in the 1920s, understood just how forceful a lasting mutuality between business and society could be. 'Idealism,' he told a conference in 1927, 'is to find out the place where our interest and the public interests coincide.'[14]

Crucially, connected leadership can do more than generate mutual advantage for society and the private sector as a whole. It can offer competitive advantage to individual companies which connect most effectively with the world, as well as improve the standing of an entire industry.

Given the diminishing traditional sources of competitive edge available to companies today, this is big news. In *The End of*

Competitive Advantage, Columbia Business School's Rita McGrath depicts a commercial environment 'in which advantages are copied quickly, technology changes, or customers seek other alternatives and things move on.' Michael Porter of Harvard Business School describes the 'cycle of imitation and zero-sum competition' that erodes enduring outperformance: 'Facing growing competition and shorter-term performance pressures from shareholders, managers resorted to waves of restructuring, personnel reductions, and relocation to lower-cost regions, while leveraging balance sheets to return capital to investors. The results were often commoditization, price competition, little true innovation, slow organic growth, and no clear competitive advantage.'[15]

Connection with society is the new frontier of competitive advantage. It can crush firms that ignore it and provide a means of success for the companies that address it effectively. Terry Leahy, Tesco's former CEO, vividly describes this force: 'I always felt a sense of power and politics going beyond just the formal structures of business, that actually there's a struggle for power for everything that's worthwhile and valuable in society. There's almost an informal battle for who actually controls a business like Tesco or BP. It's not a case of "Let Tesco run their company as they will,"' he explains. 'Unions want to have control, politicians and regulators want to have control, NGOs want to have control, and the media wants to have control. You're into negotiating for power, and as part of that negotiation you have to articulate those ambitions to do good – "This is how we behave, this is how we do good; the benefits outweigh the costs." That's mainly what you end up spending your time doing as CEO, I've found.'

A good relationship with society is not a vague objective that is nice to achieve if possible. It is a key determinant of competitiveness, and companies need to start treating it as one. In our survey of more than 2,000 executives around the world, less than 20 per cent reported frequent success in influencing state and civil-society decisions. Yet McKinsey's research finds that the value at stake from plausible government intervention alone represents approximately one third of corporate profits.[16] This highlights the vast opportunity for competitive advantage, especially considering how companies struggle to raise their operational performance just a few percentage points above their peers.

Connecting effectively can set companies apart in numerous ways, from new revenue streams and reduced regulatory risk to reputational enhancement, market access and lower resource costs. In the next few chapters I highlight companies at the leading edge which are winning because of their relationship with society. In the low-margin world of retail, Walmart has increased its cost advantage over competitors through a range of eco-efficiency measures. A single initiative to reduce packaging waste increased profitability by 25 per cent.[17] The Dow Chemical Company returned $7 billion on its $1 billion investment in energy efficiency thanks to a programme created by a factory-floor manager.[18] Novo Nordisk, Scandinavia's most valuable company, has achieved a 60 per cent share of the insulin market in China after a long-term effort to build clinics and educate regulators, physicians and patients about diabetes. Today, we label companies that aim to make money by solving societal problems as 'social enterprises'. In the future, 'social' will become implied; companies which do not understand how to respond to society's demands will fail.

A perfect storm of colliding trends means that competitiveness will increasingly be determined by the ability to connect. In an era of constrained state budgets and record wealth among top companies, big business will be expected to solve more of the world's economic, environmental, and social problems. Moreover, as citizens' expectations increase, so do their powers of scrutiny. Digital communication has enabled individuals and NGOs to observe almost every activity of a business, to rally support against it, and to launch powerful global campaigns very quickly at almost no cost. High expectations and scrutiny are here to stay. Successful companies must be equipped to deal with them.

As Mike Duke, former CEO of Walmart said: 'More will be expected from market leaders and globally successful companies, and those companies who are most involved will be most successful, creating an upward spiral.'[19] Jonathon Porritt, co-founder of the charity for sustainable development, Forum for the Future, singles out Unilever's Paul Polman as someone who 'knows that neither capitalism nor his specific organisation can thrive without changing the ground rules'.

Like other realistic leaders of civil society, Porritt understands that there is no room for squeamishness at the idea that companies can do well by doing good. CSR failed primarily because serious executives viewed it as commercially irrelevant. For business to change so radically there has to be a financial rationale. The reason leaders are excited about the concept of connected leadership is that it is based on hard-edged commercial logic. Without that, the whole idea would be unsustainable.

Taking Care of Business

It is in everyone's interest to restore trust in business. At a very basic level, we need to reassess the way we think about business. There is a tendency in many countries to presume that all big business is bad. This type of lazy thinking lumps the good in with the bad. Teddy Roosevelt's Square Deal required citizens to recognise the businessman who 'honestly endeavours to do right'. The world may never get to a point where it adores commerce, but it can surely come to respect it. Business feeds, employs, cures and entertains us; people outside as well as inside the corporate world should do more to take care of it.

Government, the most direct guardian of business, has a huge role to play in facilitating a reformed relationship between industry and society. There are many areas where companies should require no incentive to solve societal challenges. The win-win opportunities are significant and, as the Environmental Defense Fund's Fred

Krupp puts it: 'Who wants to go deal with the government, if you don't have to?' There are times, though, when addressing humanity's problems imposes costs on companies. It is then critical that government acts to create a level playing field. There have been instances when government has failed to do so despite demands from some businesses – for example, in the case of climate change. When we asked Tony Blair for areas in which politicians must do better, the former British prime minister highlighted governmental inaction on carbon policy. 'If you get the key governments together,' he said, 'marching in the same direction, you will create an unstoppable momentum behind this and then you will find people will be investing in these areas and the intellectual ecosystem that is necessary to drive the change will happen. You know, I'm confident it will but I do think you need the strong signal being given by governments that they are still fully behind this.'

There are some issues that are much better dealt with by government than by companies. Tax is one such issue that recently caused outrage in the USA and Europe. Multinationals including Google, Amazon and Starbucks faced criticism after it was reported that complex transfer-pricing systems enabled them to pay almost no corporation tax in countries in which they generated billions of dollars of revenue. The responsibility to set the rules for tax lies with a host government. Yet does the recent dramatic growth of multinational cross-border business demand an agreed multilateral approach to tax? Governments must construct the box in which business operates. Companies cannot be expected to decide the socially acceptable rate of tax, as Starbucks did in the UK with their offer to pay a fixed amount of £10 million per year regardless of profits.[20]

It is in the long-term interests of both society and business to have effective, proportionate regulation. History demonstrates that without intelligent but firm rules, the human instinct to exploit lawlessness drives business to uncivilised behaviour. Too often, such behaviour has been allowed to take place by the neglect and inefficiency of the state. We can, and should, point fingers at the immoral executives who take advantage, but we should also demand more from our governments.

Hank Paulson's description of the confusion that awaited him upon his arrival in Washington as the Secretary of the Treasury is chilling. 'I got to DC one year before the financial crisis and I could not believe how outmoded the structure was. There were about five safety and soundness regulators. It was just as bad at the Office of Thrift Supervision which had oversight of AIG, IndyMac, WaMu, you name it – I mean, these guys were basically not regulated.' Paulson observed a regulatory system that had been completely outgrown by the financial markets. Banks could essentially choose their own oversight authority. If a regulator made a mistake it sided with industry to avoid admitting its errors.

Paulson, who played poacher and gamekeeper at the very highest levels, is adamant which side carries the most blame for what happened. 'Since the beginning of history, if you really get down to the fundamentals, every financial crisis has been caused by flawed government policies.' He worries that regulators have still not caught up with the complexity of modern finance. Peter Hancock, the post-crisis AIG chief executive, shares Paulson's diagnosis of a regulatory framework that badly failed society, and has his own concerns about remaining weaknesses. 'The three-trillion-dollar municipal-bond market is unbelievably under-regulated today,' he points out. 'You can go over a year without filing reports.'

Taking their inspiration from Singapore, some of our inter-viewees feel the solution is higher pay to attract better regulators and an end to the corrupting effect of the revolving door between watchdogs and industry. Both changes would be welcome. They would help to build supervisory structures strong enough to stand up to the companies whose fierce lobbying blocks so much legis-lation in the US. But this is not just about big business. Hank

Paulson notes with exasperation that small businesses get away with avoiding taxes (for example, by paying in cash) and damaging the environment (for example, by polluting rivers and logging irresponsibly in Latin America) because it is politically unpalatable to target them.

Tough regulation is crucial if government is to set a framework that encourages socially useful corporate activity. It is equally important, however, that the regulation is intelligent. Sir John Vickers, who was chair of the UK's Independent Commission on Banking, said of his time at the helm of the Office of Fair Trading: 'I learned that markets worked less well than I thought they did. I also learned that government worked less well than I thought it did. The extent to which government worked less well than I thought it did was, however, far greater than the extent to which markets worked less well than I thought they did.'[21]

Many policy responses to the financial crisis illustrate governments' propensity to legislate without considering unintended consequences. The EU's cap on bankers' bonuses is an example. Rather than ensuring that bonuses reflect outcomes that benefit both the bank and the economy, the intervention will simply increase the proportion of fixed salary in compensation packages. If the aim was to stop financial institutions rewarding poor performance, the policy could not have been more badly designed. Governments simply have to be more intelligent if they are to help business play a more useful role in the world.

9

ON PURPOSE

'Map Your World' and 'Define Your Contribution'

Map Your World

In February 1975, officials in Haicheng, north-east China, decided to evacuate the city of 1 million inhabitants. This bold decision followed reports of unusual changes in groundwater and land levels as well as peculiar animal behaviour. A few days later, a magnitude 7.3 earthquake struck. Because of the officials' pre-emptive action an estimated 150,000 deaths and injuries were avoided.[1] From rigorous scientific tracking to a keen awareness of their social surroundings, Haicheng officials showed the breadth and depth of sensitivity needed to avoid disaster. This is a useful lesson for business. You need intelligent processes and systems to listen to the world around you and you must be willing to act on the signals distilled from the external world.

'Map your world' is the first tenet of connected leadership. It is about watching for and interpreting changes in the context in which a company operates. That context is affected by changes in, amongst other things: the macroeconomic environment; attitudes towards an industry; expectations of stakeholders and employees; and the company's actual behaviour. These changes need to be identified early. They not only affect the value of the company directly, but also indirectly since stakeholders may change their behaviour too.

Companies must be sensitive to the changes in the world around them and overcome their own tendency towards cognitive biases such as excessive optimism, anchoring and confirmation. For example, 76 per cent of executives of global companies told a McKinsey survey that they believed that regulators would rate their companies' reputations as positive. Yet less than a quarter said that their companies frequently succeeded in influencing regulatory decisions. It is vital to challenge entrenched internal beliefs and complacency by asking questions such as, 'Why would anyone listen to us?'[2]

A company should quantify the value at stake by examining how external changes affect the specific influences on profitability, and establish priorities for action. Translating societal issues and interventions into monetary estimates imbues connected leadership with the necessary rigour.

Sean Rooney of Shell's International Government Relations team explains how that company conducted an exercise in 'mapping your world'. The team identified ten major external influences ranging from carbon dioxide targets to renewables subsidies to the risk of asset expropriation. For each of the ten drivers, it estimated the value at stake for itself and society along three horizons: near-term financial impact, long-term financial impact and reputation. This 'value at stake' assessment identified upside opportunities as well as downside risks, and helped guide the company in its actions.

Once the first tenet is accomplished, companies can then act on the second tenet, defining their contribution.

The Hundred-Billion-Dollar Identity Crisis

At the heart of every good relationship is reciprocity. An observer looking on without any reference point might therefore assume that all is well between business and society. Business provides the goods and services we need and want. It offers employment, innovation and a sizeable portion of government tax revenues. In return, society provides capable workers, the rule of law, infrastructure and natural resources, not to mention billions of eager consumers.

Somewhere along the way, however, companies forgot to define their contribution. They began to focus too much on what they could take – cheaper inputs, higher prices and weaker regulation – and lost sight of what they were giving. That sort of company becomes something to be despised. If, on the other hand, a chief executive can confidently outline exactly why society needs her company, she has every reason to expect success.

IBM and Unilever are two very different titans that managed to reframe their positions in the world by thinking deeply about purpose. It is no coincidence that both organisations had, to varying degrees, lost their way. They each suffered identity crises that triggered periods of self-reflection, ultimately leading to transformations of reality and perception. Their stories illustrate why defining your contribution, the second tenet of connected leadership, is so vital.

For IBM, the journey started in 2002 with Sam Palmisano's appointment as CEO. Lou Gerstner had pulled off one of history's great corporate turnarounds in the 1990s but the company's future direction remained uncertain.[3] If mainframes were yesterday's business, what was tomorrow's? Palmisano was sure about two things: IBM needed to innovate and it needed to stand apart from its competitors. In 2004, three years before the iPhone was first launched, Palmisano took the fateful decision to sell IBM's PC business to Lenovo. It was a significant gamble, predicated on the belief that PCs would become increasingly commoditised. IBM was waving goodbye to a consumer base of 100 million. Never again would an individual consumer buy a product with an IBM logo. At the same time, the company began a flurry of acquisitions, pushing itself further away from hardware towards business-to-business software, data, analytics and consulting. 'I was convinced that in tech it is impossible to be a consumer-electronics firm and an enterprise player,' the now retired Palmisano asserts. 'We had to choose.'

Yet these changes left the outside world confused. Clients, employees, politicians, and even members of Palmisano's own family did not know what IBM stood for any longer. People would come up to him and say: 'I never thought IBM would quit computing,' or 'I heard you bought PricewaterhouseCoopers Consulting – so you're a consulting firm now?' By 2008, IBM was performing well, with revenues exceeding $100 billion and steadily improving earnings. But for many, both outside and inside the company, the identity of one of the great American companies was no longer clear.

Palmisano realised that something had to be done. He turned to Jon Iwata, the newly promoted chief marketing officer, and challenged him to clarify the meaning of the IBM brand, to define clearly what IBM contributed to its clients, to technology, and to society. Iwata examined what set IBM apart historically. 'The one constant through nearly a century of change was the purpose of the company – what we believe, what we stand for. We believe that technology can improve business, society and the human condition. It starts with the customer, but it's the whole range of constituents that make choices about you: whether they should work for you; whether they should allow you to operate in their town or nation; and whether they should invest in you.'

Iwata commissioned his team to identify modern examples of IBM delivering what it believes through case studies defined not by revenue or profit, but by client impact. The most powerful examples related to a trend that was by now dominating the agenda of the company's research department. As early as 2003, IBM's Global Technology Outlook report had predicted what we describe today as the era of big data. Computing would become so economical and physically small that it would eventually be embedded in everything and everyone. The research foresaw not only the proliferation of mobile devices but also the 'instrumentation' of cars, appliances, roadways, power grids and medical devices with sensors and RFID tags. The 'Internet of things' would generate unprecedented volumes of data which if mastered could revolutionise the effectiveness of natural and man-made systems.[4]

In the spring of 2008 it became clear to Iwata that IBM was beginning to make this science fiction a reality. The most exciting aspect of the fledgling projects was that IBM was now optimising and transforming its clients' core activities, not just their back offices. Instead of improving police-force payroll management, IBM employees were helping front-line officers use data to predict where crime would happen. The Memphis Police Department, for example, used IBM's predictive technology to reduce serious crime by 30 per cent and violent crime by 15 per cent.[5]

All of this spoke to the wider purpose for IBM: using technology to improve how the world functions. Working with one of IBM's leading thinkers and writers, Mike Wing, Iwata tried to sharpen his thoughts in a five-page essay. As spring turned to summer, the two men bounced the text back and forth until, eventually, an idea began to take shape. Iwata describes a meeting in June 2008: 'Mike was in his own world, bashing away at his laptop and totally ignoring the presentation. Then, out of nowhere, he taps me on the arm and says: "I think I've got it: smarter planet. IBM is building a smarter planet." Straight away I knew it summed it all up perfectly – not just a way to describe these big-data projects, but also the purpose of IBM as an entity. 'Smarter' was a simple way to describe the beneficial impact of technology on a company, a power grid, a health-care system, a city. It was the modifier that connoted IBM itself.'

A week later, Iwata was trawling through items of business in his monthly one-on-one session with Sam Palmisano. As the boss prepared to leave, Iwata slid a copy of his essay across the boardroom table. 'I think this scratches your itch about the meaning of IBM.' Palmisano, a bear of a man who grew up among a large

Italian–American family in Baltimore, slid his trademark horn-rimmed glasses back on and began to read. 'And then,' Iwata recalls with a smile, 'Sam just jumps right out his chair. "This is it! This is IBM."' Palmisano told Iwata to circulate his paper to the top seventy-five leaders in the company and solicit their opinions. The feedback was overwhelmingly positive, but it was the very personal reaction of three or four in particular that stood out for Iwata: 'Several of them wrote to me saying: "I took the liberty of sharing this with my children," or "I asked my husband to read this too, I hope you don't mind." And what they were hearing was music to my ears. "Now I understand why you work so hard. Now I understand why IBM matters." I tell you,' he says, 'more than any market research, more than any study we could have done, those little snippets from family members meant the world. They were hugely important in building our confidence that this was important, because it meant that they understood why IBM was relevant to the things they care about.'

Smarter Planet encapsulates why IBM is relevant to the world. Its public launch at the height of the financial crisis generated what Sam Palmisano describes as a 'mind-blowing' response. 'I've never seen anything like it. Business had earned the right to be targeted and suddenly here was a storied company that was managing to connect with the world again. People respected that. And once a newly elected Barack Obama got behind the idea, it just took off.'

At one level it is a lucrative new revenue stream that combines profitability with societal impact. Over the past six years, the company has undertaken 25,000 client engagements on the Smarter Planet platform, on target to exceed its goal in 2015 of $7 billion of incremental revenue.[6] Customers who know about Smarter Planet are significantly more likely to do business with IBM.[7] Between 2008, when Sam Palmisano launched Smarter Planet, and 2013, IBM's brand increased in apparent value by almost $20 billion, or around one third.[8]

Beyond the specifics of individual projects, the Smarter Planet idea has also managed to crystallise exactly why it is that society needs IBM. Ginni Rometty became CEO in 2012 with the aspiration to make IBM 'essential to each of our vital constituencies'. The power of Smarter Planet is that it defines, in a universally appealing and memorable way, exactly how IBM will achieve that aspiration. 'Very concretely,' Jon Iwata says, 'in our time as custodians of the IBM identity, we are going to be essential to our clients and societies by building a smarter planet.' From the growing number of entrepreneurs who choose to be acquired by IBM, to the employees who want to feel good about their work and the mayors whose cities have been wired for the future, the full range of stakeholders understands once again what it is the company stands for. Investors get it too; after ignoring IBM and technology stocks in general for fifty years, in 2011 Warren Buffet took a 5 per cent stake worth over $10 billion. Of course, the actions IBM took to connect with society do not mean they are a perfect company in general. They will still need to predict and then react to changes in digital technology and their business environment. But IBM knows what it stands for in the world again, and so does society.

The Outsider

In January 2009, two months after Sam Palmisano launched Smarter Planet at a speech in New York, Dutchman Paul Polman became the first outsider to take the reins at Unilever. Like Palmisano earlier in the decade, Polman inherited a business in flux. The consumer-goods giant, which reaches 2 billion people each day with brands such as Dove soap and Lipton tea, had seen revenues fall from €52 billion to €40 billion. The business had lost its focus on consumers and their world. It had become preoccupied with the transition from a conglomerate model to a composite model, and with the decision to have one chairman rather than two. It had also been slow to react to two crucial societal trends. According to Polman, it 'was behind Nestlé and other competitors on the obesity issue and lost market share as a result' and it 'failed to adapt quickly enough' to the growing importance of emerging markets. 'So not being in tune with society,' the incoming CEO realised, 'had cost us dearly.'

Polman's solution was to place not only consumers but society as a whole at the heart of Unilever's business model. In other words, to focus not only on how to sell more products to customers, but also on how to sell more products that are good for customers, in a way that benefits suppliers and does not destroy the environment. In 2010, Unilever announced its Sustainable Living Plan. This would redefine the company's purpose and vision: to double the size of the business while helping 1 billion people to improve their health and well-being, halving the environmental footprint, and enhancing suppliers' livelihoods. Each of these three goals is directly related to Unilever's core business activities and they all provide potential win–win opportunities for the company and society. By using its Lifebuoy brand to improve hygiene habits, the company sells more soap and helps to cut in half the number of people who die from diseases such as diarrhoea. By investing to reduce carbon emissions and water usage, it lowers costs and minimises its exposure to water scarcity, an issue that poses a serious risk to consumer–goods firms in many parts of the world. And by providing hundreds of thousands of smallholders with better training and equipment, it receives better yields and greater certainty of supply. Unilever sets out targets to achieve its overall vision and each year it publishes an unvarnished appraisal of progress.

The Sustainable Living Plan, and Unilever's relentless commitment to its implementation, has established Polman as a leader in the movement to connect business with society. It is unusual to hear the head of one of the world's largest companies explain to journalists that capitalism needs reframing and that the Occupy movement has a point.[9] Perhaps even bolder was his decision to end quarterly profit reporting and earnings guidance, and 'discourage' hedge funds from short-term investment in Unilever, while encouraging longer-term shareholders. This all happened as soon as he became CEO, 'because they couldn't fire me on my first day'. Polman points to the fact that the average time US equities are held has decreased from seven years to seven months over the last four decades. 'Are they really my shareholders if they own my stock for a nanosecond or a few months?'

Polman's concern about the behaviour of short-term investors is one shared by many CEOs. This behaviour and the resulting impact is a long-standing cause for complaint. Not much can be done about it directly. The consequences of it can be heavily moderated by the company's strategy and performance. The emerging success of his Sustainable Living Plan demonstrates that this is the case. Companies can thrive by integrating sustainability into their core strategy. Polman, who describes himself as 'a hard-core business person', has generated healthy shareholder returns and grown revenues from €40 billion to €50 billion while making an important difference to society.[10] There have been times such as the 2013 sales warning when the pressure ratcheted up on him. But the test of the CEO in those circumstances is how he will maintain focus on the long term.

To ensure that his new strategy is 'hard-wired into the business', Polman has 'asked every brand to have a social mission that is linked inextricably to its product mission and economic mission'. It is easy to see how this sends a powerful message both internally and externally. The Lifebuoy soap brand, for example, takes on a whole new significance for employees, customers, NGOs, and governments when commercial and societal objectives are combined. The brand managers are on track to educate 1 billion people in over 100 countries about the benefits of hand-washing. The soap has become 'a movement to improve lives'.[11]

Polman speaks passionately about the motivation his workforce gets from Unilever's purpose. 'The energy that people derive from improving lives creates a high-performance machine that's unstoppable. We were sinking so we had to freeze salaries for three years, we had to ask people to work harder than ever and yet our engagement scores are way off the charts when compared with the benchmark of eight thousand firms.' It is not just employees who have been won over. The director of one formerly critical environmental NGO told us that Polman 'is doing more to change the dial on the world's challenges than any politician I can think of'. For all the external plaudits, however, the most revealing thing about Polman is his personal business philosophy. It may not sit well with economists, but the former trainee priest is unrepentant about his priorities: 'I'm here to run a business with purpose,' he says. 'This is a company that has such a broad influence on global society, being in all the countries with all the consumers, and is able to influence things for the better – that's what drives me. That's one of the reasons I like working here because I think just to grow market share or make more money has never really interested me; although of course you want to be successful. So I get a kick out of that personally. This comes down to the deeper purpose of why we live in the world, to make a difference and to touch people for the positive.'

Polman also says things that are uncomfortable for corporate executives. He understands, at a very deep and very personal level, that the results of business are largely ephemeral, as forgettable as the annual reports that announce them, when compared to the enduring contributions to society made by the great industrialists. 'Nobody remembers what happened to the profits when previous leaders were in charge. Nobody knows what happened to the market share or what was acquired or divested. People have forgotten all of that. But what they still talk about is what our founder Lord Leverhulme did in Victorian Britain when he invented bar soap and brought hygiene to the country.' In a very humble way, he has set out to follow in Lord Leverhulme's foot-steps. It was Lifebuoy that Lord Leverhulme used to help slash infant mortality in Britain and the parallels are clearly a source of pride both to Polman and more broadly to Unilever.

Unilever is by no means the only corporate behemoth with a rich history of distinctive contributions to society. India's largest company, the Tata Group, was established in the nineteenth century by Jamsetji Tata to fulfil his nationalist vision of Indian develop-ment. In the US, at the turn of the twentieth century, Target's founder George Dayton aimed to maintain 'the higher ground of stewardship' according to his strict Presbyterian beliefs, while in 1943 Robert Johnson announced in a guiding 'credo' that Johnson & Johnson's 'first responsibility' would always be to those who used its products. A few years earlier, in 1939, HP's founder Dave Packard noted that 'many people assume, wrongly, that a company exists simply to make money'. For Packard the crucial thing was to 'make a contribution to society, a phrase which sounds trite but is fundamental'. This was a view shared by a handful of pioneers in Europe, where many of the leading confec-tionery firms were as interested in alleviating social ills as they were in making money.

The deep-rooted sense of purpose that characterised these organisations' beginnings partly explains why many have stood the test of time. Japan, home to over 20,000 companies that have existed for more than a century and some that have survived a millennium, has a word to describe commercial greybeards: *shinise*. Professor Makoto Kanda, an expert in *shinise*, notes that they tend to possess a central credo not based solely on profit.[12]

A truly great corporate purpose is rarely evident from the moment of a company's incorporation. It is often the result of protracted deliberation among a company's leaders, and is revealed by a company's successes and failures over years of operation. Facebook was not founded for its current purpose of 'connecting the world', but its runaway success enabled it to aim higher. Many companies respond to periods of poor performance by developing a new purpose, and often emerge stronger as a result. It would therefore be a mistake to force companies to define their contribution to society from the moment of incorporation, as some commentators have suggested.[13]

Excellent companies respond to new circumstances: they grasp the big challenges of the day and set about solving them. They are aware that they exist in a context more important than themselves. Hershey's succeeded not only because it represented purity and quality in an era of adulteration, but also because it attempted to resolve society's most pressing problem. It mastered the developments of the Industrial Revolution, from mass production to national distribution, and at the same time addressed the era's exploitative underbelly by pioneering employee rights and benefits. Hanging in Milton Hershey's office was a sign with a straightforward message: 'BUSINESS IS A MATTER OF HUMAN SERVICE.'

The '3 Cs'

When a company understands its contribution to society it can then set its strategy for engaging the world. That strategy requires focus. Every company should aim to 'win the game' in the one or two dimensions where its actions genuinely make a difference. In other dimensions it should simply 'play the game'. It might make sense, for example, for pharmaceutical companies to prioritise actions to make drugs more accessible to poorer countries while ensuring they simply adhere to minimum legal standards on issues such as climate change or quality management and use of water.

The '3 Cs' – contest; concede and lead; and collaborate – are three ways of enacting different priorities in a strategy. Walmart's actions, which I will examine in more detail in the next chapter, illustrate these different behaviours. 'Contesting' is about correcting misperceptions and pushing back against unfair or illogical regulation which threatens to harm citizens as well as business. Sometimes government and public opinion gets it wrong and business must be able to stand up for itself. Walmart, for example, felt they were being targeted wrongly for their treatment of employees. They used academic studies to establish a fact base. These compared their wages favourably to other non-union firms.

'Concede and lead' means admitting when the industry has got things wrong and leading the way in finding solutions. 'Concede and lead' does not come as naturally to most companies, and it requires an enlightened, long-term view of success. It requires business to take responsibility for its negative impacts and to identify steps to improve its performance for the benefit of society. Walmart adopted a 'concede and lead' strategy on sustainability, accepting that its environmental impact was significantly negative and pushing managers to make the company a leader in eco-efficiency.

'Collaborate' is an imperative, always required when things involve other participants in industry, government or civil society. This was crucial for Walmart as it sought deep reductions in emissions and waste. Without collaboration with suppliers and green NGOs, it would never have achieved its targets so rapidly. There are many instances when it is logical for companies to act alone, notably when an early move will gain competitive advantage, or when the rest of the industry is refusing to acknowledge an issue that concerns society. Martin Glenn, former CEO of the BirdsEye frozen-food brand, emphasises the healthy competition that drives the best firms to outdo one another in this arena: 'For big initiatives which you want to own, you'll take a risk, and then you will seek advantage from that.'

Sometimes, though, it is wise to seek safety in numbers. McKinsey's Sheila Bonini and Lenny Mendonca set out the relevant scenarios: 'Collaborating with others makes more sense when being the first mover might put the company at a competitive disadvantage, when collaboration will create gains that no single player can achieve individually, or when collaboration on standards and regulation provides the basis for industry-wide reform.'[14] Perhaps the most important reason to come together is the potential for weak links to destroy the entire sector's reputation. When that happens, no amount of individual good work is enough to prevent collateral damage. Ex-Goldman Sachs CEO Hank Paulson calls this 'distinction without a difference'. Despite what he felt was an ambitious programme of government engagement and ethics training, Paulson's bank was caught up in New York Attorney General Eliot Spitzer's campaign against Wall Street. 'I knew we were different but it became clear we weren't going to convince Spitzer of that,' he recalls. 'You see it all the time. Regulators catch an outlier who says: "We are all alike," and the regulators sweep up the whole industry in their net. The shit splashes on you if bad things happen to your competitors.'

Partnerships between rivals, of course, are never easy. They require mutual interest, patience, and people who trust each other. Paulson's successor, Lloyd Blankfein, acknowledges the value of partnerships, but reminds us of the diverse business models that can cause divergent regulatory goals. Goldman's biggest competitor, J.P. Morgan Chase, is a very different bank because it has a large consumer arm. Nonetheless, Blankfein agrees that a more concerted attempt by the financial sector to join forces could yield better outcomes.

For the most complex societal problems, business has to be prepared to strike up strategic coalitions outside the world of commerce. For example, a beverage company cannot hope to solve the problem of water scarcity in Southern Africa without involving regional and national governments, NGOs and local inhabitants. Even when BP was the third-largest company in the world, it was powerless to make solo progress on issues such as transparency on state oil revenue. When BP acted unilaterally to publish its payments to Angola, the only reward was the unmoved wrath of the host government. Later, with the full support of the British Foreign Office as well as activists such as Global Witness,

BP helped to develop the Extractive Industries Transparency Initiative. Now boasting thirty-two compliant countries the EITI has become increasingly difficult for corrupt regimes to ignore.

More and more companies are beginning to see themselves in the context of a broader world. Even when other parts of the system, such as NGOs, are focused on a single issue, it is up to business to piece together the bigger picture when confronting the planet's most pressing challenges.

The choice of which mode of behaviour to use is important but must not cut across the company's core purpose.

Send for the Anthropologist

The past decade has been a particularly rich one when it comes to corporate misbehaviour. Technology firms have disregarded privacy, pharmaceutical companies have bribed doctors, and supermarkets have sold everything from horse meat to fake baby milk. None of them seem to pay much tax, if you believe what you read in the newspapers. Yet amidst all the scandal and corruption, it is the banks that have been the dominant objects of public scorn. The financial crisis insulted people in ways that miscreants in the production economy simply could not, however much they tried. The damage to society was deeper, the ill-gotten gains unimaginably larger and the hatred accordingly fiercer.

I explored earlier the deep-seated distrust of finance that has pervaded many of the world's cultures for centuries. 'Bankers,' Hank Paulson assured me, 'will never be beloved.' The specific errors of the latest banking crisis were unique, however, and they are worth revisiting. If there is common ground among the analysts who have studied the crisis, it is that banks became divorced from their social purpose. While that was certainly true in certain parts of the industry, the overall picture is more complex. In our estimation, the problem was not that bankers had *no* social purpose; it was that they had the *wrong* purpose and often no ability to understand how damaging their activity was to the real world. It is not enough to define your contribution to society; you must make sure it is actually made.

In his *Theory of Moral Sentiments*, Adam Smith describes the 'impartial spectator', an imaginary figure who helps humans to behave in a manner of which external observers would approve. In some parts of finance, the only metric by which people felt judged was their remuneration. They behaved accordingly. A pernicious combination of perverse incentives and moral hazard led some front-line staff to issue substantial sub-prime mortgages that they knew could not be serviced, and others to package up and sell those mortgages in the derivatives market. The remuneration structures in some institutions were so distorted that it was more profitable for individuals to initiate a mortgage than fulfil it. Allied to this was the common belief that the US government would simply bail out a bank if anything went wrong. It was, as IBM's Sam Palmisano puts it, 'the casino economy aided and abetted by the government'.

What most commentators choose to ignore, however, is that there was a perfectly benign rationale behind the government's support of the sub-prime mortgage industry. There was a genuine desire to expand the availability of mortgage credit to low-income families. Howard Davies, founding chairman of the UK Financial Services Authority, believes this desire was shared by a significant proportion of senior bankers. 'Quite a few of them really did think they were doing the world a great service by enabling poorer people to own their own home for the first time. The popular portrayal of bankers who lost their purpose is somewhat facile. Many of them were misguided rather than wicked.'

The over-extension of mortgage credit was not the only aspect of the sub-prime financial disaster that was predicated on a misguided sense of mission. The architects of complex credit derivatives such as mortgage-backed securities believed fervently in the 'risk dispersion creed'.[15] The idea was that banks would use these new products to reduce their exposure by hedging against default risk, and investors would be able to choose bespoke risk profiles. The innovation would improve the liquidity of markets, they assumed. Bankers talked in reverential terms of 'market completion'.[16]

Of course, these concepts soon came crashing down.[17] The derivatives products designed to reduce risk increasingly came to be used for outrageous gambles. By 2005, their sheer complexity and opacity rendered markets less, not more, liquid. And the grand plan to offer mortgages to America's least creditworthy individuals spectacularly failed.

The obvious question is why did the banks not see this coming? One of the most important reasons was their inability to keep a clear line of sight from their core activity to the needs of society. Howard Davies summarises the exotic chain of connections that was established: 'The original borrower seeking a mortgage in Florida would typically deal with a broker, who was remunerated essentially on commission. The broker might have been funded by a local bank, but that bank immediately securitised the loans and through an investment bank they were then sold on to somebody else – be it in the US, Germany or wherever. And at some point in this chain between the borrower and the broker, the local bank, the investment bank, the securitisation process and the end investor, the connection between the end lender and the original borrower was completely lost.'

For many actors in the chain it became impossible to see through the thick crowd of intermediaries. They were no longer able to track back to the ultimate user, assess the quality of the borrower and the underlying assets and consider the actual utility of the product. It was assumed that those involved knew that unless they were providing a service of value to society, they would go out of business. That assumption led regulators to believe that these markets could be self-policing. As it happened those assumptions proved to be wrong. If bankers had taken the trouble to observe what was happening outside their corporate bubble, the signs were there. They would have seen, for instance, a socio-logical trend that eventually caused the system to snap. Prior to 2000, Americans defaulted on their debt in a very specific order: first, their credit cards; second, their cars; and finally their homes. By 2006, that order had been completely reversed.[18] In the twenty-first-century US, a credit card and a vehicle were more important for survival than a home with no remaining equity. Almost none of the financial models picked up on this.

This was not the only failure to stay in touch with reality. Even after clear indicators of severe stress in 2007, senior bankers continued to gamble. By then, the inter-bank market had begun to seize up and in Britain, Northern Rock had been forced to accept a government bailout. Yet still RBS pressed ahead with the takeover of ABN AMRO, loading itself up with debt and in the process reducing core Tier 1 ratios to low levels and drawing upon wholesale funding which then dried up. Sir John Vickers, chair of the UK's Independent Commission on Banking, points to a 'complete misunderstanding of how bad things could poten-tially be, and indeed turned out to be. These institutions were allowed to leverage forty to fifty times their capital – a completely crazy thing to do. And even now the international community is talking about a backstop of thirty-three times. It's just not a sensible way to run capitalism.'

There were, of course, bankers who never lost the all-important line of sight from product to need. Pär Boman runs the Swedish bank, Handelsbanken. Before the crash, Handelsbanken was given the opportunity to invest in mortgage-backed securities that offered high returns of around 9 per cent with apparently very little risk. The agencies had given the securities their top 'triple A' rating. Boman, ever cautious, took his team to New York and asked to see the paperwork for the underlying mortgages. That, the investment bankers on the sell side told him, was not possible. Undeterred, Boman got on a plane to California and inspected a selection of the houses in person. What he saw shocked him. 'Then it was very clearly nothing for us.'[19] Handelsbanken thrived through the economic slump. Non-performing debt represented just 0.4 per cent of its loan book by the end of 2012, less than a tenth of the level held by many of its peers. It was the best-performing European bank in the years surrounding the crisis, in 2012 having the highest return on equity.[20]

Gillian Tett, the *Financial Times* columnist, explains why Pär Boman's grounded societal awareness was the exception, not the rule. As an anthropologist, Tett is trained to look across the broadest possible spectrum to get to the truth. Her diagnosis of the financial crisis centres on the notion of silos. Over lunch, using small tapas plates to represent the fragmented blocs of the financial ecosystem, Tett set out her theory. 'On the one hand, you had this complete social silence whereby credit derivatives were considered too boring, unimportant and complex for outsiders such as journalists and regulators to understand, let alone investigate.' This created what Tett calls 'cognitive silos'. Just as important were 'structural silos' within the banks themselves. 'On the other hand, you had these gaping divides inside financial organisations that meant the risk-management and corporate functions were either unaware of the risk-taking that was happening on the CDO (Collateralized Debt Obligation) desks, or too weak to intervene.' In her research, Tett cites an interview with a director of a major bank, given shortly after his institution had announced huge losses related to 'super-senior' CDOs: 'Frankly, most of us had not even heard the word "super-senior" before the summer of 2007. We were just told by our risk people that these instruments were triple A, like treasury bonds. People did not ask too many questions.'

Not asking too many questions was a fatal flaw leading up to the crisis. By failing to investigate whether its espoused mission was actually achieving benefits for the wider world, the industry allowed itself to be accused of having no purpose at all. A significant minority of bankers undoubtedly deserve that criticism but many do not. The financial sector is critical to economic development and so it is essential that it define again its contribution and regain trust. The sector's importance was demonstrated once more by the credit crunch that followed the banking crash. 'The abrupt drying up of credit, from both banks and the so-called shadow banking system, coupled with the massive destruction of wealth in the forms of houses, stocks, and securities, produced what you might expect: less credit, less buying, and a whopping recession.'[21] There have been some notable efforts to restore values to banking. The jury remains out but there now does appear to be a willingness to do things differently.

The Ratepayer Fallacy

At the most basic level, a company's societal contribution begins with the value it brings to consumers. Rarely is the business–society relationship scarred more than when firms forget this fundamental truth. The corporate scandals that truly shock the public are the ones that involve blatant disrespect of users. This tends to happen when a quirk of the market means the consumer is not a customer in the traditional sense.

Keith Trent, formerly the chief operating officer of the US's largest electric-power company, Duke Energy, pinpoints where his industry errs with a single word. 'Historically, a typical utility referred to its customers as 'ratepayers'. That might give you a bit of a clue as to how they're viewed, as opposed to being someone you want to really please, someone you recognise as critical to your success.' In the US, many states do not enforce competition among utilities. And even in states with competition, the effort associated with switching suppliers plays into utilities' hands. The result is often a complacent attitude towards customers, who feel they have no choice but to accept skyrocketing prices and patchy service. But it is a dangerous attitude to take in a market that is otherwise highly regulated. Globally, less than a quarter of people trust their utilities.[22] Eventually, consumer anger forces politicians to act.

In the UK, switching has been uncommon in spite of deregulation, and although the UK has some of the lowest energy prices in Europe, utility companies now have the worst reputation of all industries.[23] When the then-leader of the UK Labour Party, Ed Miliband, wanted to demonstrate in 2013 that he was on the side of the people, he did so by positioning himself against the utilities. In his conference speech, he announced that a Labour government would freeze prices for two consecutive years. It is not just politicians who will punish utilities. The introduction of smart grids will trigger a wave of new products and services; consumers will look beyond traditional energy suppliers if the relationship continues to deteriorate. When an Australian utility distributed free iPads to help customers track their energy use, a significant minority sent them back, apparently believing that it was a trick.

A second example of an industry seemingly losing sight of customers lies in pharmaceuticals. These are companies that, perhaps more than any others, should be universally celebrated for their contribution to society. Yet the term 'big pharma' has negative connotations in many Western countries. The sector has been beset by a seemingly endless stream of deviant behaviour: bribing physicians, conducting biased or harmful clinical trials, and mis-selling drugs. Part of the problem is the division that health-care systems create between pharmaceutical producers and individuals. The patients may be the consumers, but they are not the customers.

Novo Nordisk, Scandinavia's most valuable company and the world's biggest producer of insulin, has striven to overcome this division. It has sought to place patient service at the heart of its purpose. It has developed new tools to measure the societal value it generates as it sets about its vision of defeating diabetes. One of its priorities – along with several of its competitors – is to expand access to care and improve medical capabilities in developing countries. Governments and patients are less likely to react adversely to the commercial advantages such programmes bring when they know that the company genuinely cares about the social benefits. Novo Nordisk's longevity in this arena has won over the sceptics. Its impact in China has been significant. Arriving in 1994, it invested heavily in clinics and education, helping patients and physicians understand how to treat diabetes. In just four years between 2006 and 2010, Novo Nordisk trained 55,000 doctors and 280,000 patients.[24] It is now the leading player in China's growing diabetes market. Chief operating officer Kåre Schultz views 'shared value' strategies as a long-term investment. 'It can take many years to create a sustainable business in these countries, but once the economy allows for proper diabetes care for the population, doctors and health authorities will remember that we were there for them when the going was tough. That's our experience.'[25]

So in utilities and pharmaceuticals, there are two examples of the perils facing companies which fail to persuade even their customers that they are contributing something useful. Unfortunately for big business, pleasing your customers is only the starting point. You have to be good for them, too. When society decides that the fulfilment of your purpose as a company harms consumers, the repercussions can be enormous. It does not matter if those consumers are willing participants. Consumer-goods companies face highly complex challenges as the propensity for obesity and diabetes expands. The global economic cost of obesity is roughly $2.0 trillion or 2.8 per cent of global GDP, roughly equivalent to the GDP of Russia.[26] The medical evidence suggests that obesity is a problem of many constituent contributing factors and no single-point solution. However, the big food and drink companies are at risk of being made the only contributing factor. They are an easy target.

Presiding over a city where more than half of adults are overweight or obese, former New York mayor Michael Bloomberg declared war on the producers of fatty foods and sugary drinks. His interventions may well spread to other parts of the US and beyond. Companies need to act quickly to assess the value at stake from these interventions and accordingly change direction. As we discovered earlier, Pepsi CEO Indra Nooyi is ready to make that change but only when food science catches up with society's demands. It remains to be seen whether or not time is on her side.

Purpose is the litmus test of sustainability in business. Contribution to society over the long term is the only thing that guarantees survival and enables success. Some companies make a contribution but forget how to communicate it. Others think they are helping but in reality they are not. The worst companies allow themselves to become a menace to society. The very greatest companies place human progress at the heart of their purpose. They do so based on a firm understanding of their place in the world.

10

PROFESSIONAL ERA

'Apply World-Class Management'

Pink Gin

Until about forty years ago, the *Mad Men* stereotype of clueless executives enjoying liquid lunches while their creative staff dreamt up hit-or-miss ad campaigns was fairly accurate. The only professional thing about some marketing departments was their commitment to alcohol. I remember observing a marketing colleague who spent his days drinking pink gins in BP's senior dining room. He seemed to symbolise the amateurism of the job in those days. As John Wanamaker once joked: 'Half the money I spend on advertising is wasted; the trouble is I don't know which half.'[1]

Eventually, in the shadow of a new millennium, CEOs became exasperated with the inability of marketers to put hard numbers to their work. With no way of justifying their investments, companies started to cut back marketing budgets. Faced with further marginalisation in the corporate hierarchy, the best proponents started to smarten up. A combination of data and improved IT processing power enabled a much more scientific approach.

Consumer insights became increasingly data-driven and detailed; key accounts were prioritised and managed with greater rigour; and, perhaps most important of all, companies significantly improved their use of tools such as Return on Marketing Investment to measure outcomes. The balance swung decisively in favour of science over art, a trend which continues today with the emergence of the ability to collect and process 'big data'.

Consumer-goods firms such as Procter & Gamble, who had done the best work in the old era, now embraced the new approach. From ethnography (embedding anthropologists in developing-world households to understand consumer behaviour) to netnography (trawling the Internet for insights), they rapidly sharpened their analytical capabilities. Investments were tracked with more precision. Airlines, credit-card companies and supermarkets reinvented direct marketing, tailoring offers based on customer habits and launching loyalty schemes as a means of individualised insight and promotion. As the world of marketing started speaking a more commercial language, grounded in proper analysis, CEOs became interested again. Indeed, in recent years a realisation has dawned that the responsibility for marketing extends throughout the organisation. As McKinsey's Tom French puts it, 'the best firms know that customer service, in-store experience or the product itself are forms of marketing. We're all marketers now.'[2]

The professionalisation of marketing was a swift and important milestone in the history of commerce. It provides a valuable lesson for societal connection which, were it to achieve a similar transformation, would revolutionise the relationship between business and society and generate huge opportunity for the most proactive companies.[3] The race has begun to promote the last remaining business function yet to achieve consistent standards into the professional era.

Applying world-class management here has the potential to set companies far apart from their peers. Many of my successful activities at BP would not have been possible had I not directed BP's well-oiled commercial machine at this area. The transformation of a 'two pipeline' British company into the first genuine global 'super major' and the third-largest company in the world was based on the ability to enter new, often troubled territories, and that required consistently exceptional understanding and management of societal issues.

The construction of the Baku–Tbilisi–Ceyhan pipeline was one of BP's more important accomplishments during my time as CEO. The pipeline, which originates in Azerbaijan's Caspian Sea and arrives in the Turkish Mediterranean via Georgia, reintegrated vital oil supplies from the Caspian with the rest of the world for the first time in a century. It was one of the great engineering endeavours of the new millennium; but the real hurdle was politics. BP had to secure the support of over one hundred different ethnic groups across three countries, to say nothing of the Americans and Russians. One of the treaties took two days to sign because it required seventeen thousand signatures. The BP team tasked with delivering the project applied all of the analytical rigour and project management that they had learned in exploration, production and finance, and as a result they achieved their goal. Conversely, the biggest setbacks of my tenure, both in terms of reputation and share price, occurred when the management of the connection between society and BP slipped below the highest standards. That was as true of the controversies in Colombia as it was of the Texas City fire and the dispute with the Federal Trade Commission over BP's takeover of Arco.

Today there are only a handful of companies that proficiently manage the connection with society. This represents an opportunity to explore a new frontier of competitive advantage. Less than a quarter of the 2,000 companies McKinsey surveyed for this book have the management resources, talent and processes required to engage stakeholders effectively.[4] Bloomberg chairman Peter Grauer is adamant that the 'traditional approach to managing this part of enterprise needs a dramatic overhaul. This is likely to become a key differentiator as the pressures on business increase.' The previous chapter discussed the importance of a purpose, which defines a company's contribution to society, and of a compelling strategy to connect with society. This chapter is about turning that strategy into action. It starts right at the very top.

The 'Palmisano Shift'

The professionalisation of societal connection can only take place with a fundamental reappraisal of the role of CEO. The requirements for the top job are changing. Sam Palmisano, who led IBM from 2002 to 2012, believes his time at the helm coincided with a palpable shift in the criteria used to evaluate CEOs. Whereas before it was solely a question of financial performance, today's leaders must demonstrate a positive impact on society. Reflecting on the great CEOs that came before him – Lou Gerstner at IBM, Jack Welch at General Electric and Chuck Knight at Emerson – Palmisano points to a 'very straightforward measure' of performance. 'It was shareholder-value creation, pure and simple. People looked past how they got there. They really did.'

Lee Scott, the Walmart CEO who lived through the transitional era, agrees. 'Someone like Jack Welch was able just to get up in the morning and drive through the things he felt were best for GE. In those days you acted in the best interests of your investors and your customers and you really did not need to worry too much about the outside world looking in.' Welch worked relentlessly on commercial improvements, whether it was introducing Six Sigma processes or selling any business unit that could not be number one or two in its market. It was enough to develop a well-deserved reputation as the iconic businessman of his age.

During their tenures, it became clear to Scott and Palmisano – as it did to me at BP – that the goalposts were shifting; financial performance alone was insufficient. In all three cases the result was a landmark speech and a change of direction. I followed my 1997 Stanford speech on climate change with the 'Beyond Petroleum' programme. Scott launched Walmart's transformational sustainability strategy in 2005 with an address to his firm's 1.6 million employees on 'Twenty-First Century Leadership'.[5] And Palmisano introduced Smarter Planet in a presentation at the Council on Foreign Relations in 2008.

Google's Eric Schmidt is the one leader we interviewed who believes things have not changed all that much. 'The chief executive's job is still to maximise shareholder value,' he argues, 'and if you're not doing that you will eventually be fired.' That is undoubtedly true, but first, financial performance is now necessary rather than sufficient and second, societal issues are crucial drivers of profitability. To maximise shareholder value, CEOs need to look beyond just the numbers. According to Warren Buffet, Sam Palmisano delivered 'big time' for investors at IBM, driving the stock up 93 per cent and missing only one earnings guidance in almost fifty quarters.[6] According to Palmisano, though, hitting financial targets is 'not going to get you much more than a B-minus when people are grading you as a CEO. You have to define your mission as a CEO and as a company in much broader terms. That's what drove me and it's only going to become more important for the next generation.' Research by Edelman supports Palmisano's argument, at least when it comes to the population at large. As late as 2008, operational excellence (including investor returns) remained the primary driver of corporate reputation among the general public. Just seven years later, it is the least important of the five 'trust performance clusters' that Edelman identifies (the others being engagement, purpose, integrity, and products and services).[7]

The Jack Welch generation was able to choose its stage.[8] Thanks in part to the arrival of twenty-four-hour news and social media, today's CEOs are on every stage, all of the time. The audience, Lee Scott points out, 'is not just your customers and your employees, it's the entire world'. Almost all of the CEOs we spoke to agreed that the job of CEO is harder now than it has ever been. Even in the narrow sphere of financial performance, the judgements are harsher.

Moya Greene, the chief executive of Royal Mail, adds: 'A decade ago, I'd have said that it was harder to be a public official than an executive in the private sector. But the tables have turned. It's tough these days to be the CEO of any business – even a very successful one with a balanced view of the corporation's position in society.'[9]

It is a new world for chief executives and I believe it requires a new way of thinking about the job. In our view, business leaders should focus only on issues that define and enact the company's core purpose. There are two things to say about this. The first is that for most companies societal concerns tend to be at the centre of that purpose, alongside long-term financial growth. The second is that CEOs can only maintain the focus by delegating management more effectively to their teams.

The best founder-CEOs in Silicon Valley instinctively do this better than their counterparts in traditional industries. As protective owners and founders they care deeply about long-term vision. As technologists they understand the importance of anticipating disruptive external trends and discontinuities. As young, often politically engaged, people they grasp the need to get on with society at large. And as recent college graduates in their first jobs, the most self-aware realise they lack the experience to manage a large and growing organisation.

The model seen in these companies was a founder-CEO who focuses on the future of the product and industry, and on the company's relationship with the outside world, leaving a large proportion of management responsibilities to an experienced president or chief operating officer. The most striking example was at Box, the cloud-storage company started by Aaron Levie as a nineteen-year-old from his dorm room, now after its IPO

Aaron Levie, CEO of Box (third from right) celebrates with Dan Levin, COO (second from right) at the IPO of the company Levie started aged nineteen. January 2015.

in 2015 worth more than $2 billion. Having reached the age of twenty-nine, Levie has handed over the day-to-day management of his company to industry veteran Dan Levin. 'I run the company,' says Levin. 'The entire executive staff reports to me, and I report to Aaron. He's the head and I'm the neck. He's got the eyes and the ears, he decides what direction we should go, he decides what the next mountain to climb is, and then I try to figure out how to get the body to do it.'

Trusting a number two with his baby sets Levie free. No more than 30 per cent of his time is taken up with operations. He spends the rest of his day (and night: Levie asked to be interviewed at midnight on a Sunday) reading about the history and future of technology, talking to customers, and meeting people from outside the industry to gain fresh perspectives. 'The CEO should be in perennial start-up mode, thinking deeply about the core product, about new business and about rapidly changing external forces in the world.' Levie believes Silicon Valley CEOs are 'ahead of the curve' but fully expects other sectors to catch up because 'no one is exempt from the increased pace of change that will require leaders to focus more on the big picture'. The challenge for companies outside Silicon Valley is the same as for mature technology firms such as Microsoft: how do you replicate the emphasis on long-term vision and purpose without a founder-CEO in charge? John Hennessy, President of Stanford and a Google director, thinks about this problem a lot. 'What happens when the founder is no longer the CEO is one of the most important questions we have to deal with.'

Time is the one asset that senior executives never have enough of. Yet in order to address the challenges and opportunities associated with the business–society relationship, CEOs need to free up space in their schedules. In a recent McKinsey survey, 40 per cent of respondents said that managing external affairs is one of the three top priorities for CEOs.[10] All of the leaders we asked agreed that this is a CEO-level issue. Many told us that they spend on average about 30 per cent of their calendar on it. When Daniel Vasella ran pharmaceutical giant Novartis, it could be anything up to one third of his week. Hank Paulson said that he 'spent more time on this than anything else. It gave me the most satisfaction. But it is the thing I miss the least.'

The common theme in our interviews, though, was a recognition that societal issues take up far more time than people anticipate. The danger is that they get relegated because they are not defined as a principal part of the job. During Paul Otellini's tenure at Intel, the chip-maker started to attract questions about anti-trust issues from regulators and politicians due to its market dominance. 'I ended up going to Washington twelve times a year,' he remembers. 'I didn't go anywhere twelve times a year, let alone somewhere which wasn't a customer! But I had to get used to it because this went to the core of our ability to grow.' Helge Lund, who used to lead Norway's Statoil, admits to 'giving much more time to stakeholder engagement than I originally thought I would'.

It is critical that time is set aside specifically for this function. Of course, that time needs to be used wisely. Sam Palmisano recalls the flood of requests that began as soon as he announced his intention to define IBM's purpose as something broader than purely financial. 'They'll parade you off on every taskforce known to man if you're not careful. With many of these things you are just a show pony. I had to fight to stay disciplined: I tried to spend my time only on projects that generated serious returns for society and for IBM.'

The question that arises, then, is what should CEOs do with the precious time they give to societal connection? The answer depends on the company and on the industry, but the CEO has a uniquely broad perspective with which to assess the societal and environmental issues that are going to affect business. As Lloyd Blankfein told us, it is his job to 'figure out what is secular versus what is cyclical'. The CEO also has to lead on this topic, both internally and externally. We will come later to the technical management approaches that companies can redirect towards stake-holder issues, but for the CEO the priority should be the emotional rather than the instrumental.

In my experience, leadership is best defined not by personal qualities but by what a leader provides. You need to offer clear direction, values and priorities, with the right tone from the top. This means, in amongst other things, making it clear to your staff that you care deeply about how the company connects with society, and dedicating time to speak to people as individuals about it. It means telling stories of success and failure. And it means identifying role models, people who have performed well in this field, to serve as champions and mentors.

Setting the right tone from the top often comes from small but symbolic gestures. In 2000, a media storm blew up about the denial of health–care benefits to same-sex couples in the oil industry. The episode served as a trigger for BP to cut a distinct path as a leader on diversity. Rodney Chase, my deputy CEO, realised that this would require a challenging change in culture, and he pushed me to appoint a well-respected outsider who could drive the initiative forward. And so it was that Patti Bellinger arrived to become vice president of Global Diversity and Inclusion.

'As an African-American woman, with a title like that, I stood out like a sore thumb,' Bellinger chuckles. 'The suits in BP's St James's Square offices could not believe what they were seeing. They thought it was some sort of nonsensical PR exercise dreamt up in America.' By the end of her first week in the job it was clear to BP's entire management team that they had better give Bellinger exactly what she wanted. On day one, Rodney Chase cleared his calendar and met with her for four hours straight. On day two and day three he did the same. Through his floor-to-ceiling glass walls, the message went out to anyone walking the corridor of power that the woman in charge of diversity and inclusion had the boss's ears. 'Rodney wanted to send a signal that this mattered,' says Bellinger. Chase followed the meetings with calls to each of the senior decision-makers in BP – from Bob Dudley to Tony Hayward – asking them to prioritise the diversity agenda. Over the next few years, BP more than doubled the number of women in leadership positions and empowered local employees to rise to the top in places like Colombia and Egypt. It also became a leader in LGBT inclusion.

Redefining the way a company thinks about itself requires leaders to promote their vision again and again with unremitting energy. Unilever's Paul Polman sees it as his role 'to give people outside and inside the company the confidence that the Unilever Sustainable Living Plan is a winning strategy'. That involves a significant personal risk because you have to take on incumbents who benefit from the status quo. All of the leaders we spoke to had met with resistance from other executives, shareholders, and competitors. Daniel Vasella puts it well: 'When people believe change will only cost them, you can be sure they will do everything to make change fail or not even start.' Leadership requires you to put your reputation on the line and to bring people with you.

For leaders to take on this challenge, they need to know they will be around to see the consequences of good or bad corporate behaviour. As Ngaire Woods, dean of Oxford's Blavatnik School of Government, points out, the average tenure of a CEO is currently far too short. If we expect CEOs to adopt long-term thinking, then we must make sure they have longer tenures.

The Pink Parasol

As with anything else in business, your relationship with society is ultimately defined by the quality and skill of your people. 'It is all about the people,' says Hank Paulson. 'Every time we had a screw-up it was the people, not the systems. It can be a dangerous lone ranger or just someone who doesn't know what they're doing.' Even at the CEO level, many of our interviewees were candid about their lack of preparation to engage stakeholders beyond customers, investors or employees. Intel's Paul Otellini was not the only one who admitted that he felt 'entirely unprepared' for his interactions with government.

Companies need the right people with the right skills and experience to include external considerations in their decision-making. That starts at the top, as Helge Lund explains. 'We have to have three-hundred-and-sixty-degree leaders. They have to be good business people who can develop talent and build business relationships, but they also have to genuinely understand the requirements and the expectations of society.' CEOs are responsible for ensuring that their senior teams are as capable at societal connection as at internal management and that the necessary skills are valued, promoted, and developed throughout the company. At the moment, fewer than 30 per cent of executives believe their companies have the talent necessary to succeed in this area. Just 21 per cent say that people are taught the skills to connect with society.[11]

McKinsey managing director Dominic Barton argues that restoring trust in business will require executives to become what Harvard professor Joseph Nye calls 'tri-sector athletes' – competent in navigating the private, public, and social sectors.[12] Moya Greene comments on how valuable this 'tri-sector' grounding can be in practice: 'My public-sector experience has helped me to understand how easily sound policies can be derailed by small, symbolic things. It may not matter that the policy change you are advocating is the product of fantastic analytics or years of brilliant stakeholder management; the tiniest little spark can become a flash fire, something that takes hold and transforms perceptions in ways that don't seem rational. If you work in the public sector, you learn the value of developing antennae for popular perceptions and keeping them finely tuned.'[13]

Another part of the solution is formal training. A company would never allow a new recruit from finance to go in front of an auditor without basic accounting experience; the same should be true of someone meeting a regulator or NGO worker for the first time. For specialist functions such as government affairs, companies will only build world-class capabilities by hiring experts and providing intensive, regular training. Employees in more traditional areas of the company also need training if societal issues are ever going to be considered in day-to-day commercial activity. At the lowest levels of the company, this can be fairly mechanical: every worker and contractor must understand the importance of the relationship with the external world and know the company's policy on social issues. For senior staff, however, things can be a little more complicated. Unilever, for example, teaches new brand managers how to market their products' green credentials.

One of the most innovative approaches I have witnessed was at Goldman Sachs, where Hank Paulson invited prosecutors and regulators into the heart of the company to coach senior executives. This is an approach that some of the most successful sports teams have adopted for several years. When Sir Clive Woodward was building England's first World Cup-winning rugby team, he realised that most of his competitors took the rules for granted, despite the huge impact officials could have on results. So he made sure that a professional referee participated in every single training session in the run-up to the 2003 tournament. Whenever the referee awarded a penalty against one of his players, Woodward repeated a simple message: 'You've just cost us the World Cup.' In the final against Australia, an unpredictable South African referee appeared to be blowing England out of contention by penalising their scrum. On came the veteran, Jason Leonard, to steady the ship. 'He went straight across to Andre Watson [the referee], put his arm around him and told him there would be no more penalties because he was the most experienced scrummager in world rugby.'[14]

For Goldman Sachs, the equivalent to the South African referee was Eliot Spitzer, New York attorney general, scourge of Wall Street and later a governor who was forced to resign. Spitzer had made a career out of his attacks on bankers, but Paulson made a concerted effort to work with him. He arranged for Spitzer and a selection of other senior prosecutors and regulators from around the world to speak at a regulatory and accountability training programme for 1,200 managing directors, which Paulson led. 'These guys really scared our people, but in a good way,' says Paulson. When I was on the board of Goldman Sachs, I saw Hank dedicate thirty-five days of his time to the initiative. That was a powerful signal to the executives. 'We talked through tough cases which had no black-and-white answers. We discussed what a legal conflict was and what a moral conflict was. They helped us flag all the areas we could get into trouble; and the regulators loved it because they saw us trying to do the right thing.' While the idea was right in principle, it was not enough to prevent some difficult times for Goldman in the wake of the financial crisis.

Training is important but it is helpful to remember that the rigours of business provide most people, at least at the senior levels, with the skills they need to deal with societal connection. Experience in marketing equips executives to analyse and communicate with stakeholders just as experience in operations teaches them how to deliver change on the ground. The real challenge is how to get people to adapt and then use these skills in a different context. Dealing with a politician or an environmentalist is different from traditional commercial activity. They do not work for you. They are not contractors. And they are different from customers; this is not about an 'offer'. There is an ambiguity and equality in negotiations that executives do not always experience in their day-to-day jobs.

Much of the connected leadership training I initiated at BP was designed to help people develop their ability to negotiate. There were master classes with leaders like Madeleine Albright and Henry Kissinger, politicians who really knew how to align diverse interests effectively and get a deal done. These 'Diplomacy and Statecraft' courses were wildly popular; they empowered attendees to use skills they already possessed in different and meaningful arenas.

The sessions also aimed to encourage people to step back and see the bigger picture within which business operates. One of the best moments was delivered by Max Bazerman, a Harvard Business School professor. He showed a video of an amateur basketball game played by a team in black and a team in white. Before it began, he gave his participants a very simple task: count the number of passes made by the players in white. Halfway through the action, a second film was superimposed on to the screen so that a Southern belle holding a pink parasol appears to stroll right across the court.[15] At the end of the movie, Bazerman asked if anyone had noticed anything strange. Not a single one of BP's assembled senior leadership team saw the lady with the pink umbrella, even when questioned directly about her. It was a superb lesson in the importance of 'noticing'. Focus is often lauded as a prized quality in business, but it can be detrimental too, causing people to miss important changes in their surroundings. You only see what you want to see.

Ready, Fire, Aim

There is something very exciting about the private sector's potential to channel its world-class management acumen towards its interactions with society. One of the most impressive recent examples originates in Bentonville, Arkansas. Walmart decided to do something about their deteriorating reputation, and their approach was to throw their well-tuned management machine at the problem. The company had received heavy criticism for its treatment of workers and its impact on communities. That criticism was beginning to drive customers away.

The turning point came in the aftermath of Hurricane Katrina, when the company's response demonstrated the gulf in operational skills between business and the public sector. 'We were the first onsite,' then-CEO Lee Scott explains. 'We beat the government to it and pretty much everyone else too. Our people did a remarkable job in adversity. The question was: "Why can't we be that company, that Walmart, all the time?"'

In a perfect demonstration of 'win the game versus play the game' thinking, the firm's leadership decided to prioritise the environment as an area in which Walmart could be distinctive, while ensuring they performed adequately on other issues. 'We really tried to step up where we thought we could make a difference,' explains Scott. So the company did their best to set the record straight on pay while pushing Congress to increase the minimum wage. As the largest employer of African Americans, they also called for a reauthorisation of the Voting Rights Act while launching programmes to promote women and minorities. On the environment, however, they truly did begin to lead.

Scott and his team were determined to make the most of Walmart's scale. 'In so many areas of business,' he explains, 'as you get larger it simply makes things more complex. You get more criticism, you have more legal challenges, and so on. But we had focused so much on the negative aspects of size that we had forgotten to ask where the areas are where size is an advantage; how can we use our size to make a significant difference?' As the world's biggest retailer, they have the ability to change the behaviour of millions of people. Between 2005 and 2010, Walmart sold 460 million energy-efficient light bulbs. This had the equivalent impact on greenhouse gas emissions as taking 25 million cars off the road. In keeping with the company's focus on value, it also saved customers $15 billion in electricity bills.[16] Walmart's size also means that when they set higher environmental standards, those standards drive up performance among a huge proportion of the world's suppliers. For example, they were instrumental in pushing Unilever to take their leadership position on environmental impact.

All of this has been achieved by integrating sustainability into every commercial conversation. The company's top executives were given responsibilities and asked to apply their operational and strategic excellence to a new problem. Lee Scott recalls: 'In every meeting with store managers, every meeting with buyers, every meeting with suppliers, I talked about resources and energy efficiency. We had to make it a core part of our business process.'

Walmart is a fairly hierarchical organisation, so once the message went out from Scott and Chairman Rob Walton that sustainability mattered, things started to change very quickly. The company is founded on a 'ready-fire-aim' business model that requires executives to implement decisions at speed. An organisation that was able to open 300 stores in a year now directed its management capabilities at environmental improvements. Rocky Mountain Institute co-founder Amory Lovins tells a story which illustrates this dynamism. In a meeting with a senior buyer, an activist was explaining the dangers of endocrine-disrupting plastics contained in certain Walmart products. The buyer broke in: 'Are you saying this stuff is in what we're selling?' On being told it was, she picked up the phone, called the head of the relevant product lines and told them to take them off the shelves immediately, return any unsold inventory, and tell the suppliers why.

The Walmart story is still evolving and the company, like all others, is far from perfect. It is impossible to deny, however, that their progress has been extraordinary. Billions of dollars of energy and packaging costs have been cut. By the end of 2012, carbon emissions from existing stores had been reduced by 20 per cent one year ahead of schedule, not to mention the impact on the vast chain of consumers and suppliers.[17] Walmart has revitalised its reputation by demonstrating genuine leadership on one of the world's most pressing problems.

Companies that achieve outstanding relationships with society do not view this activity as something woolly or unable to be quantified. They see it as a critical contributor to long-term growth and profitability; and as such they approach it with four core tools of great management: creating capability, organising to win, establishing process, and measuring outcomes. There are literally thousands of management treatises that explain how to wield these tools. Here we focus simply on their application to connected leadership.

Rethinking organisational design goes to the heart of this book's main recommendation: it is only possible to integrate society's needs by changing the roles and responsibilities of teams and individuals. The most important point here is that societal and environmental issues must be taken on by core commercial functions. This starts with the redefinition of the CEO's role, but it must cascade down throughout the company so that people 'in the line' consider the wider context as part of their day-to-day activity. That is the only way to ensure that vital external forces are addressed by high-performing, powerful executives rather than people in CSR who may not 'get' business. Only the business line has the resources, the influence, and the knowledge to transform a company's relationship with the world. When Unilever want to change the way they source ingredients to ensure security of supply and an improved life for farmers, they instruct their procurement team, not the CSR department.

However, while CSR units should be abolished altogether, companies will still need staff to analyse stakeholders and examine trends in society's expectations and behaviour. That work should serve as an input into the decisions of commercial managers, who have their own, more senior, engagement responsibilities. There is also a balance to be struck between head-office control and local freedom. The former can ensure a coherent approach to outsiders, but executives on the ground have a much better understanding of the local context, of what realistically can be achieved.

Societal connection must be formally incorporated into business processes from the boardroom to the shop floor. Whether setting corporate strategy, making investment decisions, designing products or planning projects, every process must include consideration of the impact on stakeholders and the consequences of that for the business. At the moment, just 27 per cent of firms achieve this.[18] Reflecting on his time at Statoil, Helge Lund told us that 'stakeholder interests, dialogues, risks and opportunities are deeply integrated in every business decision that we take. Every single project or investment decision comes with reflections, risk maps, and mitigation actions, around the particular topic that we're discussing. You have to make sure that you create processes and operating models that ensure that the issues are dealt with at the right level at the right time.' In setting process, clarity is essential: a build-up of conflicting policies, standards, guidelines and initiatives can be counterproductive, creating overload and confusion. BHP Billiton has worked hard to avoid this, by discarding old guidance and establishing what CEO Andrew Mackenzie describes as 'a series of group-level documents that clearly articulate the minimum standards that must be in place at all company assets, to ensure that all managers and employees fully understand the company's corporate expectations'.

A relentless concentration on outcomes is the final piece in the jigsaw as companies attempt to professionalise their approach to societal connection. It is all too easy to get diverted by process or, even worse, an ill-defined sense of 'doing good'. To retain a focus on outcomes, it is essential to set bounded targets, measure progress against them, and link incentives to their achievement. As with costs, production or safety, if leaders stop checking up on progress, the plan never happens.

Ideally, firms should measure outcomes in terms of quantifiable value added to the business and to stakeholders. Sometimes the commercial impact is very clear. It could be the cost savings from a resource efficiency programme, or the revenues achieved by launching a new, affordable health-care product in a poor community. In other cases, measurement may be more diffuse. Unilever's Sustainable Living Plan, for example, sets targets for fifty metrics, including total water consumption and emissions of greenhouse gas. A traffic-light system summarises the societal and commercial impacts of an innovation as compared to existing products. 'We drive this using hard numbers, not fluffy feelings and hunches,' says CEO Paul Polman. Unilever are also leading the way on so-called 'integrated reporting', the movement to incorporate societal profit-and-loss statements into annual reports.

Measuring connected leadership outcomes is by no means easy. Only 16 per cent of respondents to our survey said their companies quantify the financial impact of their activity.[19] The difficulty arises because the financial benefits of connected leadership are sometimes indirect and far in the future, or can only be quantified against an unobserved counterfactual. In practice, businesses can observe various proxies for the value added, of varying degrees of accuracy. The closest proxy is satisfaction among stakeholders, weighted according to their importance to the business. Clearly, putting polls out is not always appropriate. Sometimes the only option is to track activities instead of outcomes, such as the number of meetings with NGOs. This is a last resort, however, and great care must be taken to ensure that activity is not being undertaken for its own sake.

There is undoubted truth in the old saying, 'What gets measured gets treasured.' Yet on occasion leaders have to act on instinct, comfortable in the knowledge that the results will remain unknowable for the foreseeable future. Of course, that is equally true of many areas of business. Metrics such as Return on Marketing Investment may have added rigour to marketing, for instance, but advertising can still resemble an act of faith. Martin Glenn, CEO of United Biscuits, makes the comparison with connected leadership: 'Over the course of my thirty years in packaged goods, rarely have I seen advertising expenditure pay back in the short term. Yet people still do it because they know it can build long-term value and profit. The same goes for some of the actions you take to improve your relationship with society.' It takes courage for business leaders to make decisions like that. When the US pharmacy chain CVS stopped selling tobacco in 2014, they knowingly took a significant financial hit in the belief that it would pay off in the long term.

World-class management would still be incomplete without the power of leadership. The word 'motivation' has become hackneyed, but when it is absent little can be achieved. This section began with Walmart directing their management machine towards societal concerns. They are leaders when it comes to process and operational excellence; but they also understand the need to motivate. For former CEO Lee Scott, this was every bit as important as the procedural and mechanical changes. 'We used to bring our managers together in these Saturday-morning meetings. After all the numbers, we would have time to tell stories about the people who were really taking a lead on sustainability. You have to celebrate people. You have to make it special.' Walmart's progress also demonstrates how important it is for leaders themselves to genuinely believe in making the world, as well as their business, a better place. It is the combination of the emotional and the technical that brings the best out of business, and both are required if companies are to apply truly world-class management and leadership to their interactions with society.

11

THE FRONT FOOT

'Engage Radically'

Through the Mud

Fixing a relationship that has been intermittently dysfunctional for over 2,000 years will take some doing. In my experience, companies that follow the tenets of connected leadership outlined in the preceding chapters ('map your world', 'define your contribution', and 'apply world-class management') achieve significantly better results in their societal interactions. The fourth and final tenet, though, is perhaps the most important. If business wants a fundamentally different relationship with the external world, it needs to adopt an entirely new attitude. It needs to 'engage radically'. This means being far more open than in the past. It means meeting important stakeholders regularly and making friends before they are needed. And it means communicating to outsiders in clear language, without resorting to propaganda. Openness sounds simple but in fact it contradicts an inherent corporate preference for tight controls on the flow of information. Companies will never make peace with society as long as they treat stakeholders with the suspicion traditionally reserved for enemies.

The most successful and innovative example of radical openness during my time at BP occurred on the island of Papua, in Indonesia. Remembering BP's time in conflict-ravaged Colombia, I was determined that we would not make similar mistakes in an equally difficult but new environment. In 2002, Papua remained a battleground between separatist insurgents and a state-backed security apparatus with a very poor human-rights record. The social breakdown and violence surrounding the only other Western-owned natural-resources facility on the island vividly demonstrated the potential for disaster.

At the local level there was also a real danger that BP could disrupt a fragile, almost untouched community. The proposed site for the liquefaction plant that would enable exports of LNG (Liquefied Natural Gas) from the supergiant Tangguh gas field was in Bintuni Bay. This beautiful and remote part of Papua was home to a tiny population which had very little contact with the outside world. Muslims, Catholics and Protestants lived peacefully together amidst a stunning but delicate natural backdrop. In one meeting, a local elder simply said: 'Whatever the company does in Bintuni Bay, please don't disturb the religious harmony that we have here.' With a vulnerable local community and a broader context of armed conflict, the situation had all the ingredients for a potential corporate blunder.

BP's innovation was to establish an independent advisory panel to hear community concerns, encourage debate, examine BP's activities, and report its findings publicly and fully, all without any influence from BP. Senator George Mitchell, who had been instrumental in the Northern Ireland peace process, chaired a panel that also featured Lord Hannay, formerly Britain's ambassador to the UN, Sabam Siagian, ex-editor of the *Jakarta Post*, and Herman Saud, a local Papuan religious leader. They had their own independent staff resources.

Every year, the Tangguh Independent Advisory Panel held meetings with all of the affected parties, including the Indonesian government, provincial authorities, security services, NGOs, British and American ambassadors, the World Bank, the UN and the British Council. They also sat outside for hour upon hour in the stifling heat and torrential rain, listening to the villagers. At the end of the visits, they published an independent report in multiple languages which contained recommendations and an assessment of BP's progress on such issues as local employment, resettlement, security and environmental impact. Given the high levels of illiteracy in the area, the panel persuaded BP to fund two radio stations so that everyone could receive regular updates.

I have already highlighted the success of the community-policing strategy in contrast to the deployment of the army in Colombia. This was crucial, but there were two even more funda-mental benefits to working with an external committee. First, their independence and pedigree lent credibility to BP and enabled people to believe that the company genuinely wanted to achieve a project that was in everyone's best interests. Second, their outside perspective and varied expertise generated valuable insights and ideas that would have escaped an internal management team. The panel was approachable in a way that BP may not have been, as an episode from the maiden trip demonstrated.

As they inspected the site for the first time, the four members were met on the beach by a group of dishevelled men climbing out of canoes. They were the elders of Taroi, a village thirty miles away on Bintuni Bay's north shore, and they had paddled the entire distance in order to express their concerns. Unlike the villagers on the south shore, who were being resettled, the inhab-itants of Taroi would be remaining in situ. Far from being relieved at not needing to move, they were upset that they were missing out on improved facilities. Senator Mitchell immediately suggested an unscheduled visit. With the tide out, Mitchell and the others had to leave their boat and walk the final few miles through deep, viscous mud. It was a perfect symbol of their desire to listen. After seeing the abject poverty of the north shore, the

panel asked BP to buy new jetties and fishing nets. Compared
to some of the other costs, these investments were tiny; but
without the panel, the company would never have known and
an enemy would have been created.

Senator George Mitchell (front centre) crosses to the northern shore
of Bintuni Bay, West Papua, to hear at first hand the concerns of
villagers living near BP's proposed development. 2002.

There were many other examples of the panel helping BP to
avoid unnecessary conflict. The most sensitive issue was the relocation of two villages, Tanamera and Sayanga, to make way for the
LNG plant. The two Indonesians on the panel immediately realised
that great care was required when it came to moving ancestral
headstones which the villagers worshipped. Any kind of misunderstanding here could have derailed the entire operation. Later,
during the construction phase, the panel made sure that the
contractor did not slip on the commitments to local employment.
'At first it looked like they weren't giving anything like enough
emphasis to Papuan jobs,' says Hannay. 'In our view that risked

losing the support and trust of the community, so we really pushed them hard for three years. By the end, they had Papuans in the control rooms and were training people up to higher education.'

Looking back a decade later, it is clear that success in Indonesia was only made possible by the radical engagement that the independent panel represented. They engaged in a multidimensional challenge that could have gone wrong in any number of directions, from environmental degradation and disputes over ancestral ownership, to human-rights abuses, excessive migration and cultural disrespect. On its own, the company would never have been able to foresee all of the problems or to generate the credibility required to move forward.

Protestors against Freeport-McMoRan's operations in West Papua show how important it was for BP to get engagement right in Tangguh. March 2006.

For BP, the project was another step towards more international gas production. That step was allowed to happen because the

company's local and national hosts felt they could trust the
newcomer. At a meeting in Jakarta, President Susilo Bambang
Yudhoyono took the hand of BP's Dev Sanyal, and said: 'Thank
you for what you have done for my country.' Indonesia has
certainly prospered as a result of the Tangguh development.
It remains one of the world's largest exporters of natural gas.
Western NGOs, which had initially questioned whether the panel
would be truly independent, now lobby BP to continue the
system. At a local level, the residents of sleepy Bintuni Bay remain
committed supporters of BP's presence. There are new jobs,
better facilities and dramatically lower rates of diarrhoea and
malaria.[1] These societal interventions were not the results of CSR;
they were the considered price negotiated with parties who were
treated by BP as equal partners.

Not everyone inside BP welcomed the independent reporting
body. Understandably, people were worried that BP's errors
would be revealed before there was a chance to address them.
They feared that individuals would be blamed and vilified in
the media. Yet trust and learning only come about if organisations are willing to acknowledge mistakes. Being open requires
companies to step boldly out of their comfort zones and to take
calculated risks.

Unilever's Paul Polman is convinced the rewards outweigh the
risks. He recently invited Oxfam to audit its supply chain in
Vietnam, only for the report to reveal that employees were not
earning enough to satisfy basic needs, despite being paid more
than the legal minimum wage. However, because Oxfam respected
the company's transparency and desire to improve, they included
in their press release a summary of Unilever's plan to fix the
problem. Polman explains: 'We published Oxfam's report, which
included criticisms, and we say this is a great thing because it
helps us be better and it helps Vietnam be better. You didn't see
the press jumping on us. You didn't see people saying that Unilever
was irresponsible. In fact, I'd argue perhaps the opposite. So you

create this transparency that builds this trust, which ultimately is the basis for prosperity.'[2]

King Cnut

Openness has always been the most effective way to build trust. Today, thanks to the rise of the Internet and mobile connectivity, transparency is no longer optional. The flow of information is more liquid than ever before and we have only seen the first signs of the flood to come. Companies can either embrace it or fight a doomed battle, ordering back the waves like King Cnut.[3] This does not mean admitting defeat. Digital media act as amplifiers of good behaviour as well as bad. Businesses can turn online transparency to their advantage if they have nothing to hide, if they are willing to have a genuine dialogue, and if they use the proliferation of data without overstepping privacy boundaries.

Our search for a class in digital engagement took us beyond the corporate world to Chicago's start-up scene. Harper Reed is the founder of Modest, a mobile commerce company. He was also the brain behind Barack Obama's unexpectedly convincing re-election victory. As chief technology officer for Obama 2012, Reed pulled off the most successful Web-based campaign in the history of politics. His system allowed the Obama campaign to understand voters in more detail than ever, to solicit more dona-tions, to change more hearts and minds, and eventually to get more votes.

Code-named 'Narwhal' after the Arctic whale, Reed's digital initiative integrated previously disparate databases to build an astonishingly complete picture of potential supporters. Data gath-ered from previous elections was combined with publicly posted material on Facebook and Twitter, responses to campaign emails, census records and donor lists. 'What we wanted to do,' explains Reed, 'was to use existing technology to help us listen very, very closely to people's priorities and preferences.' Having listened, the campaign was able to target tailor-made messages and fundraising requests. Where previously mass emails had to avoid the most divisive issues, now individualised intelligence meant it was possible to raise topics such as abortion without any risk of offence. Once a supporter had agreed to link their BarackObama.com account with their Facebook profile, the campaign was able to figure out which of their friends were likely to be undecided voters. The supporter would then be prompted to persuade these valuable fence-sitters to vote for Obama, a peer-to-peer form of contact that is far more powerful than any other. These conversations could either happen online or over the phone. A digital tool called Dashboard made it simple for volunteers to call 'undecideds' and to feed yet more crucial data into Narwhal's grateful hands. One of the most important considerations was to ensure that individuals did not feel uncomfortable with the amount of information the campaign seemed to know about them. Achieving the right tone was every bit as relevant as sticking to strict privacy laws.

Throughout the process, Reed assumed he was merely applying the status quo in corporate America to politics. His post-election career as an adviser to companies convinced him otherwise. 'I thought we were copying business,' he says. 'Turns out we were copying what business *said* it was doing, but actually wasn't.' Reed had sat through countless conferences listening to chief technology officers reel off all the right buzzwords only to realise that 'business just isn't as savvy as we had thought'. In particular, he argues that many companies lack the quantitative rigour that enables organisa-tions to mine the emotional insights related to stakeholders' beliefs and intentions. 'Even firms that are usually super metrics-driven often only have one or two basic metrics when it comes to social media, and they only measure them once or twice per year. It's impossible to understand what people feel about your business on that basis, or to judge the success of your communications.'

Reed also criticises the 'sterility' that typifies corporate interac-tions in social media. 'Authenticity is everything,' he stresses.

'If people don't feel that they've had a genuine conversation, you have a serious problem.' As an example of unnecessary boundaries, he cites a friend's hedge fund that instructs staff not to post their job titles on LinkedIn: 'How are they supposed to build any kind of rapport?' Often companies clam up out of an understandable fear of employees going 'off message'. With over three thousand paid staffers and hundreds of thousands of volunteers, the balance between openness and discipline was something the Obama campaign had to confront directly. The key was to provide clear guidelines that set out the no-go areas, leaving people comfortable to discuss anything else, armed with the latest campaign facts and figures. On the most difficult issues, junior staff could simply re-tweet designated spokespeople, political surrogates or Obama himself. This set free an army of 'ordinary' supporters to persuade their networks in a way that traditional spokespeople and candidates could not. The strength of peer-to-peer communication is as relevant to business as it is to politics. According to research by Edelman, chief executives are among the least credible media voices, ranking below employees, academics, and NGO representatives.[4]

Our research revealed that just 52 per cent of companies use social media to understand and influence stakeholders other than customers.[5] Only a small proportion excels. There are, however, a handful of companies that are catching up fast, adopting a combination of analytical horsepower and bold commitment to openness. Pepsi, for example, has exploited its innovative digital-marketing capabilities to track societal attitudes. Its Gatorade brand has a 'mission control' in Chicago where analysts monitor online conversations and gently correct inaccurate accusations. More radically, the pharmaceutical giant AstraZeneca decided to publish raw clinical-trial data on its website when the US Food and Drug Administration's director questioned the side effects of its cholesterol drug Crestor. It is always possible to draw different statistical inferences from the same data, but AstraZeneca saw that trust could only be regained if independent researchers were allowed to decide for themselves. It took the risk and was rewarded with renewed trust and restored market share for Crestor.[6]

On the Front Foot

One of the most tangible things companies can do to improve their relationships with society is sit down early and often with the people they affect. It should be a discussion, continuously building understanding, cooperation and connections, in order to keep informed and to establish the reservoir of goodwill that every company needs. It should not just occur when things go wrong. Statoil's former leader Helge Lund is mindful of the practical hard work required: 'Gaining stakeholder trust is not something that you achieve once and for all. You can lose it very quickly. We have to be continuously working on this subject, even when we do not necessarily have big issues to deal with. It has to be developed as part of the DNA of the company.' Our survey found that 65 per cent of CEOs think they should proactively engage the external environment, but only 38 per cent actually do so.[7]

A common mistake is to leave things until it is too late. The temptation for busy and cost-conscious executives is to ignore the outside world until a problem arises. By then the likelihood of a positive interaction is slim. Helge Lund saw Statoil fall victim to this pitfall just before he took over as CEO. In 2003, Statoil started confidential merger talks with Hydro, a Norwegian oil and gas company. It was, Lund explains, an 'obvious decision' from a commercial point of view. 'The logic was outstanding in terms of synergies and financial capabilities.' It was the only way Statoil could compete in a consolidated global industry that values scale above all else. Yet while the business case may have been sound, the companies did not pay sufficient attention to the political ramifications; for years there had been an unspoken rule that Norway would maintain two companies for oil and gas. 'The deal didn't happen because the boards and the management of the companies had not been effective in creating a dialogue with critical stakeholders ahead of the proposal. News of the talks was leaked and it was quickly deemed impossible to do.' Two years later, after a marathon process of meetings, explanation and reassurance, the merger went ahead with almost no serious opposition.

Engaging early offers a clear advantage, but it is also crucial to maintain relationships consistently over the long term. It is easy to watch issues such as the environment slip down the political agenda and then reduce the time spent with green NGOs. The smart companies realise that the cycle is short and they prepare for the future while they can still do so on their own terms. Companies have to make friends before they need them. It sounds obvious, but our research confirmed that when firms increase their interactions with societal actors from a 'rare' basis to 'often', they more than triple their chance of mutually beneficial outcomes.[8] Top companies identify important stakeholders and work with them using a 'key account management' approach that borrows from leading sales techniques. BP tried this method when I was CEO. The government-affairs specialist staff designated 'owners' for specific stakeholders, setting out exactly who should see whom, and when. It helped to avoid outsiders being confused by multiple visits from executives with conflicting messages, and the lack of duplication also made it harder for BP's emissaries to be played off against each other. Unilever have taken this account-management system to a new level of sophistication and complexity. In each country they have a vast web of contacts that the company cultivates with pinpoint accuracy and professionalism. The environmentalist Jonathon Porritt, who advises Unilever, describes the pattern of engagement as 'mind-bogglingly sophisticated'. Anji Hunter, now a senior adviser at PR firm Edelman, has seen an 'explosion' in the number of NGOs, journalists and activists which companies must engage. 'Before now it was a handful of NGOs and a handful of newspapers. Now everyone has a voice, thanks to social media.'

External contacts need to be developed from the lowest levels of an organisation right to the very top. At BP, I was responsible for relationships with statesmen ranging from Tony Blair and the president of Azerbaijan to Arnold Schwarzenegger. CEOs have an important role to play in developing effective working relationships with senior leaders from government, NGOs, and civil society, although they may not always be the best messengers for a wider audience. If the company has decided to operate in new countries, its management team has to find a way to work with the local leadership that both gets the job done and ensures independence.

Lingua Franca

Sitting down early and regularly with the people most affected by the company is a great start, but executives still have to know what to say. One area where many companies fall down in their relationship with the external world is their inability to speak the right language. Sometimes this is literally about adopting local languages, as Facebook's Mark Zuckerberg did in 2014 when he astonished a Chinese audience by speaking Mandarin. It is also about using the phrases which demonstrate that the business has understood stakeholders' concerns. More broadly, it is the ability to put oneself in the shoes of the relevant society.

Sir John Vickers, formerly chairman of the UK Office of Fair Trading, also chaired Britain's Independent Commission on Banking in the aftermath of the financial crisis. He was surprised in both roles by the 'frequency with which companies made bad points unattractively', but it was during his work on bank reforms that some of the most striking examples occurred. While some banks engaged constructively with the ICB, some others, despite the ICB having published a paper of issues in advance of hearings, 'seemed not to have grasped what we were trying to do'. Even

Facebook's Mark Zuckerberg takes questions in Mandarin at Tsinghua University's school of economics and management in Beijing. October 2014.

after British Chancellor George Osborne used a 2011 Mansion House speech to support the commission's intention to recommend the ring-fencing of retail banks, senior executives of some institutions continued to lobby Vickers for unrealistic alternatives. 'Some were pushing for options that would hardly affect them. The idea that I would be persuaded by it, never mind [fellow commissioner] Bill Winters sitting next to me, was preposterous.' At the start of the ICB's work some bankers objected even to the fact that the government had established it. 'A surprising example of how not to engage,' Vickers told us, 'came from a senior figure in one of Britain's principal banks. He didn't speak to us at all until we were more than a year into the process.' Others engaged directly and constructively with the commission's work.

It is not only defensive stances that tend to result in clumsy interactions with stakeholders. Often it is simply a failure to think about issues from their point of view. Consider the proposals made by US businesses for government funding under the American Recovery and Reinvestment Act of 2009. A surprising number did not mention job creation at all.[9] On a more practical level, many companies fail to use the 'budget math' of the organisations such as the US Congressional Budget Office when debating the impacts of proposed legislative or regulatory changes.

The best companies get these basics right and then manage to express with great clarity how they intend to provide a service to society. This goes back to purpose and the need to define a contribution. Simple but powerful facts can achieve the 'cut-through' that advertising executives search for in a world characterised by information overload. Mining company Rio Tinto regularly points out that it is the largest private-sector employer of Indigenous Australians. Similarly, the American car industry highlights its role as one of the country's most important employers in its conversations with government.

Of course, it is not just what you say and how you say it that matters: the messenger is important too. A misconception in the corporate world is that traditional authority figures still command respect. In our survey of executives, a 'trustworthy CEO' was the second-most cited reputational strength, yet on average less than half of the world's 'informed public' perceive CEOs to be credible spokespeople.[10] There is a massive trust deficit between institutions and their leaders. Edelman's 2013 trust barometer focused on this crisis of leadership, showing that while 50 per cent of Americans trust business, just 15 per cent trust corporate leaders to tell the truth.[11] As IBM's former boss Sam Palmisano puts it: 'All celebrity CEOs will be gone, just like all the tsars are gone.'

Soviets and Missionaries

In 2003 I travelled to Moscow to address the new employees of TNK-BP, a historic joint venture between BP and AAR. Just before I stepped on to the podium, one of my Russian business partners pulled me to one side and said: 'I suggest you remember that after seventy years of Soviet rule, these people can smell propaganda a mile off. Talk only about human failures, not glorious successes.' It was sound advice. Business has a propensity to allow its conversations with the outside world to descend either into propaganda or aggression. Instead, societal connection should be understood as a negotiation with intelligent and powerful equals who deserve respect. Repeatedly saying how brilliantly a company behaves inevitably invites scepticism and scorn. Clearly, this is particularly true if the firm's actions do not justify its words. Hypocrisy, as former UK foreign secretary David Miliband reminded us, is the greatest sin in a media environment that thrives on catching people out. Consumer-facing companies have to be especially careful not to allow their strong marketing departments to spin a good story that misrepresents the reality of their everyday activities.

Even companies with genuine substance to their claims need to be careful how they express themselves. It is obviously crucial that they are able to make a case for their positive impact, and at the moment too few do so. For example, 62 per cent of companies do not communicate their sustainability activities to investors.[12] However, people have a limited capacity for propaganda which focuses only on unalloyed success. Sometimes it is better to leave outsiders to report good work. That was Daniel Vasella's approach at Novartis. The former CEO worked closely with governments and private-sector partners on issues of global health, and often allowed others to deal with the media. 'I have an aversion against missionaries,' he says. 'I don't like to go out as a missionary and preach, and then be accused of preaching for my own parish, even if I'm right.'

Stories of success inspire people, shining the spotlight on excellence that can be emulated. It ceases to be credible, though, when there is never any mention of challenges and mistakes. Stories of failure are vital for any organisation that wants to learn and to gain trust. They keep everyone realistic about the scale of challenges, and prevent insiders from losing touch with reality. An obsession with successes is not actually the fault of individuals; it is the result of an organisation's induced behaviour. To tell stories of failure, you need to record them. Yet in most companies and governments, failure is still frowned upon, rather than accepted as the inevitable and desirable consequence of informed risk-taking.

Being open about failure tends to generate trust and understanding. As an example, Unilever's annual reports on their Sustainable Living Plan is free of most sugar-coating. Certainly, there is an account of the year's most impressive accomplishments but also a bluntly phrased list of areas requiring serious improvement. Compare this with the gushing nonsense produced in Enron's Corporate Responsibility Annual Report only a few months before it imploded in a flurry of criminal self-destruction.

If propaganda is one common extreme, the other is naked aggression. Too many businesses view regulators and NGOs as the enemy, unsophisticated combatants to be swatted away as swiftly as possible. They forget that these interactions tend to last far into the future. It might be possible to fool an activist group once, but eventually this type of behaviour backfires. In repeated games, reputation and trust matter.

Senator George Mitchell, who chaired BP's independent panel in Papua, is possibly the world's most successful negotiator. In addition to his well-known role in the Northern Ireland mediation, Mitchell has also facilitated Arab–Israeli talks and is an experienced commercial mediator. In his view, business people often make poor negotiators because 'they cannot stomach giving up any ground whatsoever, which is a prerequisite for any chance of consensus'.[13] In most cases, if companies are willing to cede some ground, mutually advantageous outcomes are possible. When one side holds out, however, negotiations are unlikely to reach what the experts call the 'Zone of Possible Agreement'.

Knowing when to lose purposefully in order to win later does not come naturally to business people. They are trained to win every time. Perhaps surprisingly, the competitive world of finance has been rather enlightened about this in recent times. Some investment banks have realised that it would be futile to fight against the inescapable surge of post-crisis regulation. Even if they disagree with the logic of some legislation, the more astute players realise that their collective responsibility for the crash of 2008 leaves them in no place to argue. Sir Howard Davies, chairman of Royal Bank of Scotland and a former non-executive director of Morgan Stanley, explains the thinking: 'There are some respectable intellectual arguments to say that the amount of capital and liquidity regulators are now demanding is probably counterproductive in the long run for the development of the market economy. But it isn't worth making this point,' he says, 'because the recent past experience is so bad that you know you're not going to win that argument. You just have to swallow your pride and actually do what the regulators are telling you, even if you think it's probably counterproductive and is rather damaging. You must simply focus on meeting these requirements, whatever they are. However high the regulators say you must jump, you must jump, because appearing to contest it at the moment would be foolish. You just have to get on with it.'

It is a sentiment shared by Goldman Sachs CEO Lloyd Blankfein, who has an open relationship with the Obama administration despite the travails of the banking crisis. 'It is still easy to see us as the dark beast, but actually the government welcomes our view.' Goldman Sachs tries to emphasise the mutual goal it shares with government for a transparent, robust and liquid market. When it comes to unpopular government intervention it does not 'pound the table' because, as Blankfein puts it, 'you need to accept that over-regulation in response to public anger at industry and at regulators is inevitable. Our approach is just to engage supportively and try to help them do it effectively and, in the long term, productively.'

I am not suggesting for a moment that business should meekly accept unfair and harmful regulation as a matter of course, but sometimes the hole has already been dug and the intelligent move is to accept your fate. Even when companies are defending their point of view more robustly, it is worth heeding Senator George Mitchell's first rule of negotiation: 'Never fail to act with patience and humility.'

There will, of course, be moments when business needs to stand up resolutely for itself. The aim is not to please everyone. Sometimes mutual advantage is impossible, collaboration will not yield an acceptable outcome, and an entirely legitimate negotiating strategy is to attack. For example, in a legal dispute with a regulator in which the law is on your side, there may be no point in seeking compromise. If an activist group is making ridiculous demands that will win no sympathy with broader society, it may be best to show them the door. That is what Martin Glenn, then CEO of BirdsEye, did when an NGO criticised his approach to the sustainability of fish stocks on his first day in office. Instead, he pressed ahead with his own agenda. Glenn unilaterally announced an end to trawling, a controversial fishing technique, and shifted half of his fish-finger business from scarce cod to abundant pollock within three years. 'You don't have to manage all of your stakeholders equally,' reflects Glenn. 'Some people who think they are stakeholders might not be. You have to decide whether they are truly critical to the long-term health of your business or not.'

More often than not, companies do need to take the call or hold the meeting. They need to do so early and regularly, with a commitment to openness and a resolve to avoid both propaganda and aggression. Sometimes they should act alone, while sometimes they must join forces with competitors and other organisations to broaden their impact. Above all, they should approach their interactions with the external world with an overwhelmingly positive and inclusive attitude. That is the meaning of radical engagement. It is the only mindset that can repair a relationship damaged by centuries of mistrust.

EPILOGUE

PEOPLE RISING

The Future

Vague but Exciting

'It is entirely possible,' a quiet, serious voice announces, 'that stream of consciousness is just a small piece of code.' Tim Berners-Lee is used to people ignoring his big ideas. Down an incongruously choppy telephone line from Boston, the inventor of the World Wide Web digresses from his précis of artificial intelligence to describe how his greatest contribution to humanity almost never happened.

After years experimenting in his spare time, Berners-Lee was approached in 1989 by a colleague at CERN, who casually suggested that he should write up his big idea. So in March of that year the young scientist released a paper entitled 'Information Management: A Proposal'. Over a few short pages, he had summarised what would one day become the World Wide Web. A year later, someone asked him what had happened to his idea. Had he done anything about it? 'Nothing actually,' Berners-Lee explained. 'It never really caught on.' Adopting an admonishing tone, his friend shook his head. 'You really should write a memo, Tim.' Exasperated, Berners-Lee went back to his room and reprinted the same article, 'with March 1989, May 1990 on it, just to make my point'. This time, it was read by a supervisor, Mike Sendall, who allowed his young charge to develop the project in between pushes to advance the CERN accelerator. Within a decade the World Wide Web had transformed the world.

At around this time Mike Sendall died of bone cancer. Among his papers was the original copy of the Web proposal. His only comment, written in faint pencil at the top of the page, was: 'Vague but exciting . . .' Berners-Lee laughs warmly at the memory. 'Imagine if he had said "Exciting but vague." There would be no Web! He would not have let me do it!'

Tim Berners-Lee's early-draft proposal for the World Wide Web, marked with a crucial comment of support from his supervisor, Mike Sendall. March 1989.

When he tells you that artificial intelligence (AI) is about to explode and that it has in many ways already taken over the corporation, the wise reaction is to listen carefully. The rise of disruptive technologies in general and of AI in particular is one of three major trends that I believe will profoundly alter the relationship between business and society. AI promises radical solutions to some of the worst problems for which people blame business. Yet the extraordinary power it may place in corporate hands could trigger new levels of distrust if companies do not tread carefully. Even worse, the potential automation of whole swathes of manual and knowledge work threatens to undermine the best reason people have to accept business.

The second trend is the shift in the economic centre of gravity towards emerging economies. This shift means that the main theatre of action in the old drama of business–society relations will be a new world, with attitudes and cultures which are altogether different from those of the West. The differences are crucial, but the core principles of connected leadership can and should be applied all over the world; the real hurdle is implementing those principles in more challenging arenas.

The third trend is the emergence of a new global generation that will demand more than ever from business because of increasing wealth, education and access to information, as well as shrinking government budgets. The growth of emerging markets will play a central role in this trend, exacerbating many social and environmental problems and simultaneously enabling previously voiceless populations to push companies to solve them. Technology has a big part to play here too, exposing the worst business practices and providing the tools for the best responses.

These three trends will change the nature of the business–society relationship, creating a moving target that even the most enlightened companies will have to chase with a commitment to renewal and learning. Above all, the trends will amplify the relevance of this relationship to the successful future of both sides.

ARTIFICIAL INTELLIGENCE

The Valley

In the autumn of 2013, looking for a view of AI, we set off in search of a secretive Silicon Valley start-up, Vicarious. There is no name on the building, no sign on the lift, and no address on the website. Having made it through layers of anonymity, we are greeted by a piece of reassuringly Californian eccentricity. Co-founder Scott Phoenix steps away from, or rather off, his 'desk', a treadmill that stands below a raised monitor and keyboard. He walks eight miles a day while he works.

He and his partner Dr Dileep George have been given $65 million and fifteen years by investors including Mark Zuckerberg and Jeff Bezos to 'build software that thinks and learns like a human'. The holy grail for Vicarious is a computer that possesses the common sense and reasoning ability of a person. We are here to witness the results of the first stage in their journey: visual perception. Tomorrow, Vicarious will announce the invention of software that can solve the most widely used test to distinguish between humans and computers. A CAPTCHA (Completely Automated Public Turing Test to Tell Computers and Humans Apart) is the ubiquitous anti-spam program that asks Internet users to prove they are human by typing words disguised in garbled and unique graphics. As of this moment, it can no longer reliably tell the difference.[1]

Using reasoning rather than big-data search, the software attempts to explain what it perceives, just as a human brain would. Astonishingly, it also possesses imagination. Confronted with an 'A' that is missing half of the character, it imagines the missing part. Given an optical illusion, it switches back and forth between the various interpretations exactly like a person. Using the same capability, it can stare at a sky and imagine a dog in the clouds. Unlike other entrepreneurs and academics, Vicarious's founders can press ahead without short-term pressure to deliver a product. The range of possible applications is endless, though, as Dileep George explains: 'If I give you a black box and say: "This can do anything humans do with our eyes," it's not hard to come up with uses for a vision system.'

These are exciting times for the field of AI. Since the 1950s, academics have predicted the advent of 'the singularity', the moment when machine intelligence surpasses that of the human brain. Ray Kurzweil's book, *The Singularity is Near*, points to confidence that major breakthroughs are imminent. While few experts other than Kurzweil are willing to forecast an exact date for the singularity, most that we spoke to believe it has a good chance of happening in their lifetimes. 'I find it hard to imagine that it won't,' says Tim Berners-Lee. For John Hennessy, president of Stanford University, 'the last decade has shown that human beings are not that complicated after all. Our deductive reasoning is not that good compared to a computer. We are just very good learning machines.'

This confidence is based on a string of tangible successes. The most public belonged to IBM's supercomputer, Watson. In 2011, it took on and beat two chess grandmasters on the television quiz show *Jeopardy*. 'We were just trying to compete and not screw up,' recalls former CEO Sam Palmisano. 'We were just hoping it wouldn't crash on TV or something. And then it goes and beats the best people to have played the game!' The victory was a small indication of the vast potential of AI that does not even come close to singularity-level capability. Compared to the Vicarious software, Watson uses a sledgehammer approach. It digests and analyses huge amounts of information very, very quickly, but does not 'think' in the way that a human does.

The question of the singularity itself is in some ways a distraction. However long it takes for machines to attain 'general' intelligence, the 'narrow' tasks in which they surpass mankind are becoming so numerous and so complex that AI is unquestionably going to change the world in a big way. If 'software eats the world', as Web-browser pioneer Marc Andreessen claims it does, AI will sit at the head of the table throughout the next century. Our aim is to understand how it will impact the way society perceives business.

Moonshots

The potential for AI to help business solve humanity's biggest problems is perhaps most evident inside the world of Google. We met Sebastian Thrun, the German inventor of Google's driverless car, in Mountain View. Thrun is an evangelist for the positive change artificial intelligence will bring. His own, very personal, story is a symbol of technology surmounting human suffering.

As an eighteen-year-old in Germany, Thrun lost his best friend to a split-second bad decision to speed on ice. Years later, Thrun's Stanford colleague went to pick up breakfast before a meeting about self-driving cars. At an intersection, someone crashed into her at 55 miles per hour, sending her into a coma from which she would never wake up. 'This senseless, brutal loss of life is something almost every human being on the planet has been exposed to,' says Thrun. 'More than a million people die as a result of car accidents every year. Eventually I just thought: "I need to do something about this."'

In 2004, Thrun was a spectator at the inaugural DARPA Grand Challenge, a competition for autonomous cars funded by the Pentagon's Defence Advanced Research Projects Agency. Anyone whose car made it across 150 miles of desert in one piece would receive the $1 million prize. The most successful vehicle travelled a miserable 7 miles before it crashed in a ball of flames. Almost all of the other entrants went up in smoke or got stuck behind rocks. Thrun was convinced he could do better and spent much of the next year in the Mojave Desert with his Stanford students, building a self-driving car that could compete.

The technology was based on machine learning. 'We would take the car, which we named Stanley, into the desert and make it learn by watching me drive. Then it was Stanley's turn to copy what it saw. Whenever it made an error, we explained what had gone wrong and helped it to adjust.' The car would need to continue to learn during the race in real time: there was no opportunity to rehearse the specific journey because the co-ordinates were only released one hour before the race. The car had to make decisions not only on steering and where to go, but also on how fast to move. The desert terrain was so uneven that any misjudgement in speed would cause a crash.

In 2005 Stanley was one of five cars to complete the course. As the first across the line, Thrun and his team took home the prize money, which had now doubled to $2 million. More importantly, he was introduced to Google's co-founder Larry Page, who had turned up under the cover of sunglasses to see what all the fuss was about. Two years later, Page managed to persuade Thrun that the best place to realise his vision for a worldwide network of driverless cars was Google. He was right. Google's fleet of autonomous cars have not caused an accident in the more than 1 million miles they have covered in self-drive mode.[2] They can run for the equivalent of four years of human driving (50,000 miles) without requiring the attention of a real person at all.

Clearly, there is still room for improvement. However, Thrun expects an improved consumer version to be launched within five years. Google's director of research, Peter Norvig, confirmed to us that the company is in regular contact with car manufacturers. Politically, the barriers may be less difficult to overcome than many observers had anticipated. California, Nevada and Florida have all passed legislation to allow some form of self-driving vehicles to operate on public roads. However, there are both legal and psychological barriers to overcome. The issue of liability in the case of a crash remains unresolved. And surrendering driving control to a computer will take some people a little while to accept.

Sebastian Thrun celebrates victory in DARPA's driverless car challenge
of 2005. Thrun went on to pioneer Google's work on autonomous
vehicles. October 2005.

The impact on society could be enormous. Millions of deaths
and injuries could be avoided. Carbon emissions could be slashed
as journeys become vastly more efficient. Blind and elderly people
could regain their mobility. Much of the fifty-two minutes that
the average American worker wastes inside a car each day could
be put to better use. Finally, the vast areas of land that are taken
up with roads and parking spaces could be reclaimed. It is easy
to see why 60 per cent of LA's land is reserved for cars when
you consider that traffic-filled highways are only 6 per cent occu-
pied even at their highest capacity and that there are three parking
spaces for every American car.[3] But with self-driving cars there
would be less redundant space as cars return home when not
needed or are free to be used for other purposes than simply the
daily commute.

The self-driving car is just one example of how AI and robotics
could give companies an unprecedented toolkit to address the

societal issues for which business is often held responsible. Google alone has a startling number of projects under way at its clandestine Google X lab, including one effort to reproduce the human brain. Astro Teller, whose title is Captain of Moonshots, oversees the development of 'science-fiction-sounding products that can solve the world's biggest problems'. There are encouraging efforts taking root outside Silicon Valley, too. Organic crops could be harvested so efficiently that monoculture farms would no longer be necessary. Robots could take the place of humans in the aftermath of nuclear meltdowns. Live audio translation could break down the misunderstandings that so often trigger conflicts.

Perhaps the most exciting and tangible application of AI is likely to be in health care. Every expert we interviewed cited the potential for automated diagnosis to improve accuracy and to save billions of dollars if experts were no longer required to infer the meaning of X-rays, cardiograms and other visual data. IBM chose to direct Watson to health care before other industries because, as Sam Palmisano puts it, 'society needed to be able to relate to the technology and not be threatened by it. Early on, that was more important than the ridiculous money hedge funds would have paid for this capability.'[4]

So that is the upside, and it is undoubtedly significant. The possibilities for spectacular breakthroughs are almost endless. Unfortunately, there are also important downsides.

Paper Robot

The risks associated with AI are many and varied. There are those, for instance, who fear a world overtaken by super-machines which can continuously improve themselves to the point that humans lose control. I want to set that scenario aside, not because it is entirely fantastical but because the implications lie beyond our scope. The only point to make is that business had better take great care if it ever has the responsibility to program a computer with potential volition. Dr Stuart Armstrong of Oxford University's Future of Humanity Institute told us that the precautions adopted by cutting-edge technology firms are currently often 'ludicrously inadequate'.

A more immediate security concern is that even today's AI technology could wreak havoc in the hands of hackers, cyber-criminals or terrorists. There is a reason why Vicarious is so hard to find and why the founder of CIA-backed data-analytics firm, Palantir Technologies, is reportedly accompanied by a bodyguard wherever he goes.

The first risk to explore in detail is not about the *abuse* of AI, whether by malign machines or criminals. Rather, it is about the *misuse* and the misunderstanding of the technology by business: in essence, the delegation of corporate decision-making to intelligent machines by companies that do not truly understand their electronic companions. For Peter Norvig, director of research at Google, this is a very real issue: 'I don't think the threat is that computers are going to have a revolt and try to kill us all. But there could be societal damage anyway because they act in ways that we don't understand. In fact, we already have software acting in ways that we don't understand, and as we make it smarter and give it more responsibilities that very well could get worse.'

Tim Berners-Lee believes we are much further down this road than many people appreciate. Speaking so fast that you feel his words cannot keep up with the sheer speed of his brain, he paints a picture of the automated corporation, a paper robot with all of the rights that human beings enjoy and much more power: 'People wonder when robots will be sufficiently intelligent to be given access to the rights of a human being: the right to a trial in front of their peers; the right to open a bank account; the right to fund political campaigns. Well,' he says, 'I think that that particular transition has already taken place. The corporation has all of those rights and it is increasingly operated by artificially intelligent computers. Look at the companies where the trading is done by

computers, or the hiring is done by computers. The fastest path
to a dystopian reality is not from robots on two legs running
around dominating the world; it is robots running corporations.
Some people might say that we have got there already.'

Berners-Lee undoubtedly has a more extreme view of this risk
than our other interviewees, but in his reference to trading he
finds the one current piece of evidence that is impossible to
ignore. High-frequency trading, the use of complex algorithms
and supercomputers to exploit tiny changes in stock prices by
the millisecond, now accounts for over half of the volume on
many stock exchanges. It has helped to increase liquidity, improve
efficiency and cut transaction costs for traditional traders. Indeed,
rebates worth fractions of a dollar per trade are provided by
exchanges to reward this public good.

The problem, as the Bank of England's Andy Haldane explains,
is that high-frequency traders provide 'fair weather' liquidity. 'They
are the new market makers, because they're always there. They're
always doing business. Well, they are, except when they're not.
And they're not there when, of course, you most need them,
which is when prices are tumbling and you're looking for someone
to make a market for you.' This is exactly what happened during
the Flash Crash of 6 May 2010, when the Dow Jones stock index
lost and regained almost 10 per cent in a matter of minutes. After
a large automated 'sell' trade by a mutual fund triggered an initial
drop in the market, the high-frequency traders' algorithms took
fright and abruptly stopped trading. The conventional market
makers having been driven out, there was no one left to take up
their slack.

The most worrying aspect of the US regulators' report was not
that it apportioned significant blame to the high-frequency traders,
but that it took six months for them to unpick what had occurred.
In a staggeringly candid interview for someone who has been
responsible for financial stability at the Bank of England, Andy
Haldane conceded that government and business alike have no

proper understanding of how high-frequency trading (HFT) affects market dynamics. 'What's very interesting is, even now, we don't understand flash crashes. And you can't, because it's in the nature of HFT business that it's almost unknowable. Not just because of the speed of execution, but also because of the speed of evolution, because the algorithms they use themselves evolve at incredible speed. No one can have any sense of the collective consequences of these evolving, superfast algorithms colliding,' he said, 'which is why no one could make any sense of any of the mini flash crashes. It's almost unknowable. Which means, could a much, much worse flash crash happen tomorrow? Of course it could. What guarantee have we got that it won't happen? We haven't got any. In fact, all the signs are that it could.'

According to Haldane, the only way regulators can intervene is to switch the whole system off when it starts to spiral out of control. 'Most people now accept that if you can't understand it, at least you should have a mechanism for flipping the switch.' In terms of preventative safeguards, he argues, all that governments can do from a position of ignorance is slow the trades down with pauses, transaction fees or minimum resting periods. None of those solutions involve anyone actually understanding how the algorithms work. Sebastian Thrun, the automated-car inventor and AI specialist, shares Haldane's concern that companies have unleashed computers which they do not comprehend. 'With the decision cycles on machines outpacing humans by so many orders of magnitude,' he explains, 'and the decisions being so much more global in their scope, chain reactions could come to creation within milliseconds that could wipe out financial markets. This is being realistic. This is not because machines are malicious. It's because we just don't understand complex systems.'

If companies are seen to cede control to computers which they do not understand well enough to correct, any positive developments associated with artificial intelligence will be utterly eclipsed by the mistakes. As Google's Peter Norvig puts it: 'If your self-driving car cuts the number of accident deaths in half you wouldn't expect to get fifty per cent thank-you letters – you might expect to get up to fifty per cent lawsuits from the families of the bereaved.' Whether it is an individual car crash caused by a robotic malfunction or a global financial crisis triggered by corrupt algorithms, society will make the companies responsible feel its wrath.

The Jobs Compact

The second risk associated with AI is by far the most profound in its potential damage to the relationship between business and society. It is the automation of knowledge work and the consequent possibility that unemployment could rise significantly in specific, politically sensitive parts of the economy. If that were to happen, the most important bond between companies and the population would be sorely tested. Whether explicitly or implicitly, workers accept corporate profit primarily because of the jobs they provide. It is highly probable that this compact will be challenged severely in the next few decades; the question is to what extent and where?

In the most extreme scenario, large-scale copying of machines that are more intelligent than humans could cause mass unemployment. Three of our interviewees, Google's director of research, a senior Silicon Valley venture capitalist, and a leading educator, all believe this is a possibility, albeit an unlikely one. But none of them dismissed the idea. However, even without superhuman machines, if AI technology continues to unearth specific tasks where the computer outperforms the human, sections of society will suffer badly. It will be no consolation to those groups if the jobs are made up in other demographics or countries.

Of course, dramatic technological progress is nothing new. Yale economist William Nordhaus estimates that computer performance improved by a factor of at least 1.7 trillion over the twentieth century. Most of the increase has taken place since 1945, with an average improvement rate of 45 per cent per annum.[5] This has automated routine tasks, for example in manufacturing and transactional work. In the past 40 years, more than half of American transaction jobs have been eliminated. Bank cashiers lost out to ATMs; travel agents gave way to self-service systems; typists and telephone operators disappeared almost entirely. Now, computers can increasingly analyse giant sets of information, make subtle judgements, learn, and respond to complex requests via natural user interfaces such as Apple's Siri. Those capabilities are about to sweep through the service sector, which employs more than 80 per cent of the developed world. Of the activities individuals are paid to perform, 45 per cent can be automated by adapting currently demonstrated technologies. The automation of activities will redefine occupations.[6]

However, commentators have tended to overstate the extent of machine substitution for human labour and ignore the strong complementarities.[7] Tasks that demand skills which are only understood tacitly have proved vexing to automate. Examples are developing a hypothesis or organising a cupboard. This is a manifestation of Michael Polanyi's paradox which he set out in 1966: 'We know more than we can tell.' Technology has also increased the demand for highly skilled workers such as managers, doctors, lawyers and scientists. The result has been a polarisation of demand, with middle-skill cohorts losing out to both high- and low-skilled employees.[8]

Paul Graham, the programmer, essayist and founder of Y Combinator, has tweeted: 'Technology has been eliminating jobs for centuries. But not net jobs'.[9] The 2000s, for example, was a decade of falling world inequality thanks to China and India. Nonetheless the polarisation of skill demand, combined with the rapid growth of low-cost manufacturing in China, has driven a large growth in inequality in Western countries.[10] This places tension on the social compact between workers and business, and

contributes to the rise of nationalism in Western countries, especially spurred by low-skill employees seeing their jobs disappear
to robots, to foreign nations and to their more productive immigrant counterparts. As LSE's John Van Reenen has noted, resolving
these tensions is fundamentally about dealing with inequality in
the acquisition of human capital.[11] There is a major need in the
US and UK, for example, to improve education and skills for
those in the lower half of the distribution, a major theme of the
LSE Growth Commission of which I was a member. This conclusion should not distract from the value of rapid technological
progress, which is the engine of growth which itself creates better
possibilities of redistribution.

In this context, what of AI? As Sebastian Thrun observes: 'We
haven't got to the point where AI replaces all jobs and we might
never replace all jobs. But we will certainly replace massive numbers
of jobs. We're not that far off software being developed by AI and
not by human programmers. A company like Google might actually lose most of its software engineers and replace them with
AI.' Thrun himself now plays a central role in the automation of
education, another profession that is ripe for productivity gains.
As the founder of Udacity, he is one of the earliest proponents
of MOOCs (Massive Open Online Courses). Collaborating with
Peter Norvig, Thrun started by making his Stanford artificial-
intelligence class available to hundreds of thousands of students
from countries as diverse as New Zealand and Iran. To date,
Udacity has opened up first-class university content to almost
6 million people, using artificial intelligence to grade papers.
Thrun somewhat boldly predicts that only ten mainstream univer-
sities will survive the digitisation of learning.

Common business functions such as administrative support,
customer service and what remains of human call centres all seem
particularly vulnerable to automation, but more skilled professional
jobs are clearly also at risk. Stanford president John Hennessy
anticipates a 'hollowing-out of employment, starting with the

semi-skilled jobs but rapidly moving on to at least the moderately skilled jobs'. Tim Berners-Lee agrees: 'You will find information jobs being taken by computers bit by bit.'

The days of enormous legal teams sifting through columns of files so high they reach the ceiling are almost over already. At the press of a button, a computer can review thousands of briefs and the entirety of case history. This is work that traditionally has provided hundreds of thousands of billable paralegal hours. Today, it only takes a couple of lawyers to check the computer's output. Symantec's Clearwell software was able to analyse more than 570,000 documents in two days for one recent case.[12]

The implications of this phenomenon for business are severe. What role do companies have if they are no longer the drivers of employment in their industry or their local community? The most extreme scenario of structurally higher unemployment has not been thought through.[13] There are merely vague murmurings in Silicon Valley of states providing guaranteed basic incomes and of the populations' 'cognitive surplus' being applied to public good projects such as Wikipedia.

Of course, the probability based on history is that AI will instigate a whole new class of jobs to replace the ones it automates. An apocryphal story about the economist Milton Friedman pokes fun at the natural human instinct to fear technology. On a visit to Asia, Friedman saw thousands of workers building a dam with shovels. 'Why aren't you using mechanised diggers?' he asked the foreman. 'That would put people out of work,' came the reply. 'Oh,' said Friedman. 'If you're looking for jobs, why don't you take away their shovels and give them spoons.'

There are those who see AI augmenting rather than replacing people, helping us to achieve more in a fewer number of hours and to accelerate the pace at which we achieve extraordinary things. This is certainly the view of Dileep George of Vicarious. 'People say that we are going to be slaves to machines once machines become intelligent. Actually, I think we are slaves to machines now because machines are *not* intelligent.' He quotes the inventor Arthur C. Clarke, who 'said that the goal of the future is full unemployment, so we can play. What Clarke meant was that technology gradually takes over the drudgework and liberates us to spend our time doing more creative, more human things. AI can be a great amplifier of that trend.' Others point out that the most recent disruptive technological force, personal computing and the Internet, has driven the number of hours we work up, not down.

The optimists may be right about AI; but the truth is that no one knows. Just because new technological dawns have replaced the jobs they destroyed in the past, does not mean the same will happen in the future. If we cannot imagine the new industries that will be required to keep the world's population busy and maintain the employment-based compact between business and society, we cannot be sure that they will ever arrive. The onus is on business to create those industries and, together with education systems, to train the world to work alongside intelligent machines. Stanford president John Hennessy does not mince his words on the topic: 'Anybody who doesn't want to be flipping burgers somewhere should think very hard about their education and their continuing professional learning.'

Even if AI leaves the overall employment rate unchanged, particular demographics and industries will lose out. The adjustment process will probably be 'slow, costly, and disruptive'[14] with business taking the brunt of the blame. It also seems inevitable that information technology will accelerate changes in the *nature* of work, which will make people rely less on big business.

It has never been easier to leave a job with a large company and create a small business. A combination of reduced capital costs and the Internet means anyone can become an entrepreneur. Twenty years ago the serious start-up was a fifty-person company competing with IBM. Now the fifty-person company is a big company and the start-up comprises two students working from a coffee shop. Apps such as Uber allow drivers to leave their taxi firm, drive for themselves, and get more work. Google's Peter Norvig summarises the impact of these changes to working life: 'We will need big business much less than we used to.' More negatively, however, technology is continuing to erode job security. People now expect to stay with a company for a few years; eventually that could decrease to a few months. In an Internet-connected world full of intelligent machines, the fluidity and availability of labour is rising rapidly. Companies no longer need to pay people's salaries in the periods when they do not really need them in the hope that they have someone in place when they do.

Artificial intelligence can provide business with unprecedented ammunition to solve society's problems and generate economic growth. But it could cause unintended, unknowable mistakes and its threat to employment in traditional sectors may deeply shake society's faith in business. These are challenges which the corporate world must tackle with urgency and subtlety. Companies should be fostering an open debate about the ethical and practical risks associated with super-intelligent machines. They should also be working closely with government to prepare the workforce for a very different future.

EMERGING MARKETS

Gravity Shift

In the first year of the Common Era, the world's centre of economic gravity was somewhere in the hills between Afghanistan and Pakistan.[15] Global economic power was distributed largely according to population sizes and so, with limited migration, the centre of gravity remained firmly in Asia for almost 2,000 years. Then, from the nineteenth century onwards, the economic map started to change considerably, as industrial revolutions in the West shifted the balance first to Europe and, by the 1950s, to the US. That transition was important but the current shift in power is even more dramatic. In the first decade of the new millennium, the fastest economic shift in the history of the world took place. The centre of economic gravity travelled east and south at a speed of 140 kilometres per year, 30 per cent faster than the previous top speed. It is now hovering in the middle of Russia, well clear of the West, and will continue to draw ever closer to China over the next ten years. We are living through arguably the world's biggest ever economic event.

China's growth is occurring at ten times the speed of the first country to urbanise, the UK, and is one hundred times the scale. It took the UK 154 years to double GDP per capita during the Industrial Revolution. That same achievement has taken just twelve years in China and sixteen in India.[16] Between 2007 and 2010 alone, three more Chinese cities reached the 'megacity' threshold of 10 million people. By 2025, a further seven Chinese cities will achieve this status, while only one developed-world metropolis (Chicago) will reach that stage.[17] There will be volatility along the way but, in the words of Goldman Sachs's Lloyd Blankfein, 'it is very clear that China will advance to its rightful place in the world'.

Much has been written on the growth of emerging markets; but what is relevant for us? Why is this our second of three trends for the future? The most obvious, but nonetheless meaningful, point to make is that the main arena of connection for business and society will change for the first time in hundreds of years. The key players will increasingly be Asian and Latin American, whether it is companies, people, governments or NGOs. The emerging nations' share of the leading five hundred companies is forecast to increase from 5 per cent in 2000 to nearly half by 2025, while an extra billion city-dwellers are expected to join the world's 'consuming class', swelling the commercial importance of developing-world populations.[18] In a new arena, with new

EVOLUTION OF THE EARTH'S ECONOMIC CENTER OF GRAVITY

1 CE to 2015

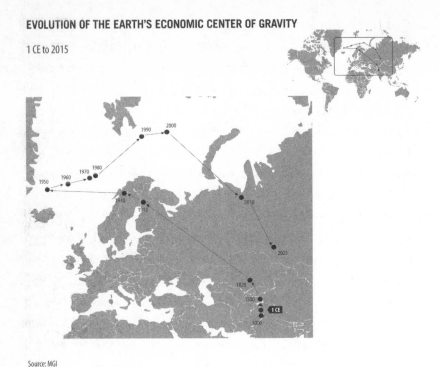

Source: MGI

players and diverse cultures, the great business–society game will inevitably look different.

The developing world is hardly a unified 'place', but it is worth teasing out some common differences from the West. First, and on a positive note, attitudes towards large companies are on average more sympathetic. According to Edelman's Trust Barometer, trust in big business is consistently higher across the developing world. Moreover, the tendency in the West to lionise small business over big business is reversed in countries such as China, where 80 per cent of respondents said they trust big companies compared to 61 per cent for small firms.[19]

So there is an opportunity for big business in emerging markets to work from a position of strength and make the most of populations that, for the moment, are more forgiving than their Western counterparts. It is not clear, though, that this breathing space is the hard-earned outcome of outstanding connected leadership. Barring some notable exceptions, in our experience companies in emerging markets lag behind their developed-world competitors in their desire and ability to connect effectively with the full range of societal stakeholders. Hank Paulson highlighted this message in a recent talk to the top one hundred Chinese CEOs. 'I told them that they are screwing up their reputation around the world. I told them that they have outstanding firms in China but no world leaders yet. The world's leading businesses do not have governance issues. They do not report to the government. They lead on technology, on the environment, and on training.'

Paulson also told his audience that he understands they face a far more challenging external environment than US, Japanese or European firms. Connected leadership is simply harder in developing countries, whether you are a local company or a Western multinational one. Foreigners and locals alike face a quagmire of barriers and potential problems.

First, bureaucracy remains chronically unwieldy and fragmented accountability means decisions do not get made. India ranks 184th out of 189 countries for the difficulty of dealing with construction permits.[20] Land-use reform moves at a snail's pace because the buck is passed between local, state and national governments. Second, some regulatory institutions are still developing their capabilities and resources. In China, for example, decentralisation makes it difficult to implement government policy and enforce regulations, contrary to the popular belief that a one-party state can drive through whatever change it wishes. China's Ministry of Environmental Protection has fewer staff than Mao's mausoleum.[21] As journalist and academic Sam Geall points out, the reliance of the ministry's regional bureaus on local corporate-tax dollars means there is often a lack of independence. Third, patchy rule of law creates massive uncertainty and distrust in all directions. Laws are often enforced inconsistently, as I discovered in Russia, home of some of the most stringent and most tactically applied environmental regulations in the world. And fourth, the cancer of corruption lives on.[22]

Given that business environment, it is no surprise that the default engagement position in developing markets is defensive. However, a proactive approach is not only possible in these circumstances, but the context rewards radical engagement even more than in developed markets: firms that excel can open up large gaps between them and their competitors. The best example we came across was the rise of the Indian software industry, as described by Narayana Murthy, the founder of India's second-largest IT outsourcing firm, Infosys.

Votes not Notes

Setting up Infosys in India in the 1980s, Murthy experienced all of the difficulties just outlined and more. In his case, the typical bureaucratic minefield of developing countries was laced with the uniquely Indian distrust of big business that defined the era. He faced a state apparatus that was 'convinced large corporations would become omnipotent and hijack the nation's agenda', a condition Murthy dubs 'East India Company Syndrome'. He also faced a political elite who wooed the rural majority instead of the urban, business-employed minority. The upshot was that 'if the government's incompetence didn't discourage private enterprise enough, its rules certainly did'.

Murthy had to secure more than forty approvals from various officials just to start the company. 'It then took almost three years and fifty visits to Delhi to get a licence to import a computer that was worth fifty thousand dollars in those days. Every trip cost me one thousand dollars, so by the time I got the paperwork I had already given the government the price of the computer.' The official import duties were even worse at about 150 per cent, 'because computers were seen as instruments of capitalism in some sense'.

Despite the best efforts of the Indian state, Murthy persevered and built up a promising young company. Nonetheless, his first decade in business had taught him two valuable lessons about the government. The first was that Infosys would never fulfil its potential if it continued to be restricted by hostile regulation. The second was that Murthy and his small team were powerless to change anything in isolation. In 1988, Infosys joined forces with its peers in the outsourcing and IT industry to form the National Association of Software and Services Companies (NASSCOM). Murthy was its third president.

NASSCOM became arguably the most successful trade association in history, from the government's as well as the industry's point of view. At a time when India was embarking on economic reform, NASSCOM was able to change the government's perception of the software sector entirely. Belying the varied interests of its members, the group managed to align everyone around a few key points and speak with one common voice. It was then able to translate its narrative into a compelling message focused on quality jobs and the generation of precious foreign exchange. Its informal mantra was 'votes not notes'; 500-page reports were important but insufficient. Finally, having grasped that it was not necessarily the best advocate of its own message, it let others do the talking. Representatives from Microsoft and Cisco met with officials to communicate how difficult Indian's regulatory environment made it to do business in the country.

The government listened, and in doing so supported the growth of an industry for India. 'They have indeed become a catalyst rather than an obstructionist,' says Murthy. 'Today there is no negative vibration from the government. My children think I am exaggerating or lying when I talk about the old days, because, you know, in the last twenty-two years, I have not gone to Delhi for a single approval.' Formerly hostile politicians and regulators slashed taxes, eased foreign-exchange controls and established dozens of software technology parks with state-of-the-art facilities and duty-free import arrangements.

While other Indian sectors continue to struggle through the paralysis of bureaucracy and over-regulation, the software industry has demonstrated how powerful a proactive approach to societal connection can be when the intuitive response might be to batten down the hatches. The interface between business and society might have different local conditions in the emerging world, but the fundamental rules of engagement remain constant. Narayana Murthy grasped that truth and used it to build a powerhouse. 'Unless a corporation has the goodwill of society, unless a corporation lives in full harmony with all of its constituents, it is unlikely that it will be a long-term proposition. This is true whether it is a developed market or a developing market.'

The Campus

At their core, underneath the local differences, the connection issues that companies face as they deal with society are similar all over the world. The best emerging-economy companies are starting to tackle these issues on the front foot.

I am the UK chairman of Huawei, one of China's most exciting technology companies. Its biggest business activity is carrier networks that underpin telecommunications, serving forty-five of the world's fifty largest communications providers. It also sells IT services to corporate customers and smartphones to consumers. Across all three divisions, the twenty-six-year-old company is designing leading-edge technology at a fraction of the prices charged by its US and Korean competitors. Its flagship product in that regard is in development: a $49 smartphone that could win the billions of low-income consumers poised to come online in the next decade.

The future is bright, but Huawei faces two critical societal-connection challenges, each with a distinctly Chinese flavour and a universal underpinning. The first is to build a culture that will attract and retain the brightest minds. Like most of the developing world, China lags far behind the West when it comes to working conditions. For Huawei to continue its exponential growth, however, it must maintain a steady stream of world-class local and international talent flowing through its doors. That means raising its level of employee engagement to the standard of the most innovative companies on the planet.

When I flew from Silicon Valley to Huawei's Shenzhen head-quarters in the autumn of 2013, Huawei's role model became apparent. With the low-rise steel-and-glass buildings set among landscaped gardens and idyllic water-features, this could easily have been Google's campus; it was only the specially imported Yunnan trees that gave it away. Google's Eric Schmidt has a well-known philosophy that 'in our case as a modern technology company, every employee contributes to the intellectual property of the firm and so we have to really treat them very well. We are not dealing with fungible assets.' Huawei clearly shares that approach. Its global team of seventy thousand engineers with an average age of twenty-nine is run from a research-and-development centre clad with columns that echo the White House. Nearby Huawei University has one hundred classrooms and space for three thousand trainees. Lunch is a ninety-minute affair consisting of healthy, fresh food. On sunny evenings, young computer scientists take advantage of an outdoor swimming pool that might belong in a luxury resort but is actually the centrepiece of a community of employee apartments called Bai Cao Garden. Their health care is provided for and they have the potential to share serious financial rewards as Huawei grows: the company is owned by its employees, and the dividend payments to top performers have been enough to see some retire in their forties.[23]

If Milton Hershey or George Cadbury were alive, the Huawei campus is exactly the type of project they would have admired. Through their transformation of working conditions, the chocolate barons addressed the Industrial Revolution's squalid underbelly just as they mastered its technological breakthroughs. Huawei's founder Ren Zhengfei is attempting to do something similar to China's double-edged development revolution. There is a long way to go, of course. Huawei has outsourced manufacturing to Foxconn and the suicide-prevention netting on the windows of its Shenzhen neighbour serves as a reminder that all twenty-first-century companies are answerable to workers at every level of their supply chain. Yet the efforts that Huawei has made on employee engagement are undoubtedly impressive, a far-sighted investment that is already paying off.

Huawei's testing centre at its campus in Shenzhen, China. April 2015.

Progress on its second societal challenge, trust, has been harder to achieve. Again, there are elements of this issue that are manifestly new-world in nature. Huawei's largest barrier to growth is a widespread suspicion that its networks are riddled with back doors that lead directly to the Chinese security services. For a company that provides the backbone of telecommunication systems around the globe, it is a damaging allegation. So far it has crippled Huawei in the US; the five major communications providers that do not use its equipment are all American.

In October 2012, the US House intelligence committee accused Huawei of being a threat to national security, claiming that networks in America could be switched on remotely to relay data to China. It also claimed that it 'provides special services to a body that is believed to be an elite group within the People's Liberation Army dealing with cyber-warfare'.[24] Huawei protests that Ren Zhengfei's previous career as a member of the People's Liberation Army has been used to smear the company.[25]

The animosity in the US is palpable. We spoke to a technology-industry heavyweight who was in line to take on a political role had the 2012 presidential election gone differently. Their face contorted into anger at the very mention of Huawei: 'I would have allowed those guys in over my dead body.' That attitude has been largely shared across the aisle. In 2010, the US government scuppered a multibillion-dollar deal for Huawei to supply network infrastructure to Sprint Nextel, one of the country's largest network operators.[26] Following the 2012 House intelligence committee briefing, one congressman insisted that 'this is not trade protectionism masquerading as national security'. Given the speed with which Huawei is threatening the dominance of America's telecommunications industry, that statement does not seem wholly credible, however genuine the security concerns might be.

Huawei's response to its international trust deficit has had mixed results. Beyond taking the obvious step of denying the allegations, it has become better at defining its contribution to host societies by focusing on the creation of high-quality jobs. That has worked well in the UK. Responding to Huawei's intention to build a new research base, UK chancellor George Osborne said in 2013: 'I know that there are some countries which are a little bit nervous of Huawei. That is not the United Kingdom.'[27] In the US, where a Huawei research-and-development centre in California employs 1,000 scientists and engineers, the strategy is yet to change opinions.

Huawei is not alone as a developing-world company struggling with trust overseas. According to Edelman, firms with headquarters in emerging nations suffer far lower trust ratings than their developed-world counterparts, largely driven by suspicion in the West. Indian and Chinese-headquartered firms are trusted on average by 34 and 36 per cent of people around the world, compared to 75 per cent for German-headquartered companies.[28] It is important to remember, however, that the nationalist impulses that Huawei face in their dealings with the US are experienced by companies from every country. So-called 'non-tariff' trade barriers, restrictions on imports that are not traditional custom tariffs, are a fact of life for companies of all nationalities operating in countless jurisdictions. Regardless of the country you are in, the only sensible option is to connect as effectively as you can under your own steam and then seek the help of your own government to negotiate with hostile hosts.

Huawei may not have achieved the uniform success with foreign governments that it has managed with employees but, like Infosys, it has proved that proactive, connected leadership is even more crucial in the emerging-market context, despite the temptation to become insulated and defensive in the face of such complexity. As the developing world experiences the most extreme economic transformation in history, the business–society relationship will take on new twists and unexpected guises; it will, however, only become more relevant.

DEMANDING GLOBAL POPULATION

People Rising

Our third and final trend is the advent of a global population that will demand more from business than any previous generation in history. Armed with unprecedented access to education, information and technology, people will hold companies to a higher standard at a time when economic growth in emerging markets will exacerbate many of the societal and environmental problems that business has to solve. The East's rise will simultaneously generate raised expectations and higher hurdles. The companies which meet this challenge positively will share the spoils of the greatest period of growth the world has ever seen. The laggards will not see the journey through.

The lion's share of the growth will be driven by urbanisation, which is important because city dwellers are more likely to participate in the dialogue with business. Between 2010 and 2025 47 per cent of global economic growth will come from four hundred and forty developing world cities. Twenty are well-known 'megacities', but the rest are middleweight cities, such as Surat in India or Porto Allegre in Brazil. Physical co-location makes it easier to form communities and engage with business, yielding 'agglomeration benefits'. It also has a significant impact on education.[29] In rural India, schoolteacher absentee rates are nearly 25 per cent.[30] McKinsey predicts that higher educational attainment in India will increase five times as fast in urban households as in rural households. The upside is vast. There are hundreds of millions of people still waiting to be pulled out of ignorance – 26 per cent of Indians above the age of seven are illiterate[31] – and when that happens, business will have a whole new swathe of knowledgeable stakeholders to connect with on more equal terms.

Technology will help. Thanks to people like Sebastian Thrun, anyone with an Internet connection now has access to the same course materials and lectures enjoyed by Stanford computer-science undergraduates. Technology is also collapsing the information asymmetry between traditional institutions of power such as business and previously uninformed populations. Narayana Murthy of Infosys reflects on how, in 'nations with poor communities which have been suppressed for a long time, access to technology has brought people closer to mainstream society. Even television, which is now available in every Indian village, gives them an opportunity to see what is happening in state capitals, in Delhi and in the boardroom. They are part of the debate and they feel so much closer. They feel empowered.'

Those televisions are only the beginning, since Internet connectivity and social media are democratising the flow of information and improving transparency. By the end of the decade there are expected to be 50 billion connected devices. Business practices will be exposed to ever brightening sunlight and the most educated and informed generation to have lived will not tolerate the excesses of the past.

Technology will continue to act as a great leveller, providing innovative companies with the means to overtake those who do not treat stakeholders with respect. Narayana Murthy remembers the week that Infosys installed its first ATM money dispenser at its Bangalore campus. He asked a janitor who was standing in the queue ahead of him how he liked the new machine. '"Sir, I like this ATM very much. When I used to go to the bank branch, the clerk would not treat me well, because I was not dressed nicely, I was not educated, and therefore he just would not treat me with respect and dignity. On the other hand, when I go to this machine, I put in the card and it treats me exactly like it treats you."'

Consumers, those most fundamental of stakeholders, have simply not been treated well enough in developing markets. One leading Chinese entrepreneur we spoke to is planning to use technology to do something about it. He plans to harness mobile commerce to put the nail in the coffin of China's shops. 'The stores are terrible, the service is terrible. Why should people put up with it?' he says. Physical stores, this mogul told us in Beijing on condition of anonymity, are dead except in their most sophisticated and convenient incarnations.[32] It is not only customers that technology will empower. Intelligent companies will use innovation to fix problems that upset all sorts of stakeholders and in doing so they will render obsolete the companies that benefit from a dearth of choice.

As wealth pours into emerging economies, expectations for better business behaviour will soar. Rising incomes are associated with increased demand for health and well-being, environmental protection, corporate ethics, and the rule of law. In China the natural environment has started to appear in polls as the second-most mentioned concern after the economy. Yet the same growth that drives higher standards also generates more issues for whichever business is responsible. Consumer growth is currently outpacing infrastructure development, and business will need to move fast to partner with governments and build the necessary roads, airports and utilities. As China used up resources to fuel its development, increases in the prices of energy, land, food and water in the first decade of the millennium wiped out a century's worth of falling prices, now being corrected to some extent by the sharp decline, in the second half of 2014, in the price of oil.[33] The world's 'consuming class' is set to double by 2025 and as a result the planet could face increased levels of stress and shortage of resources.[34] This was an issue highlighted repeatedly in conversation with former prime minister Tony Blair. 'As these huge numbers of Chinese, Indian, Far Eastern and then African consumers come on to the market, you can't tell them not to consume,' he emphasised. 'You've got to provide the means of them consuming sustainably.'

Indeed, providing the means to solve all of these new challenges will play an increasingly important role in determining commercial success in the years ahead. Companies will have to respond, both out of immediate self-interest and in order to remain socially acceptable. Four of the world's six most expensive social costs are facilitated largely by companies: smoking, obesity, alcoholism and climate change.[35] People will expect more from business and so will governments, whose budgets are likely to face continued cuts as welfare costs rise.

SELECTED GLOBAL SOCIAL BURDENS

Estimated annual global direct economic impact and investment to mitigate selected global burdens, 2012 GDP, $ trillion

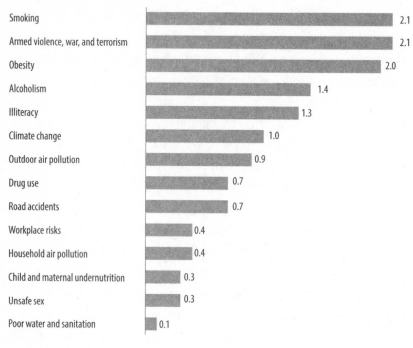

Smoking	2.1
Armed violence, war, and terrorism	2.1
Obesity	2.0
Alcoholism	1.4
Illiteracy	1.3
Climate change	1.0
Outdoor air pollution	0.9
Drug use	0.7
Road accidents	0.7
Workplace risks	0.4
Household air pollution	0.4
Child and maternal undernutrition	0.3
Unsafe sex	0.3
Poor water and sanitation	0.1

Source: MGI

We are already starting to see business respond to the challenge. Local emerging-market firms have begun to address their growing responsibilities. Taking their lead from the Chinese government minister who told *Der Spiegel* that 'the Chinese miracle will end soon because the environment can no longer keep pace', a new group of business leaders is taking action against the phenomenon that threatens China's commercial hubs.[36] During Beijing's 2011 'airpocalpyse', a property developer named Pan Shiyi launched a campaign on social media to push authorities to bring forward clean-air legislation and publish detailed pollution data. As someone who owns large chunks of Beijing, he depends for his business on the city being an attractive place to live. He is one of a growing number of influential businessmen known as 'Big Vs' in reference to the letter that signals to followers that their Sina Weibo accounts have been verified. He has more than 17 million followers on the micro-blogging platform and his voice carries weight. The Chinese government bowed to his pressure and agreed to release air-quality data in real time. Using a range of mobile apps, Beijing's citizens now know exactly when the atmosphere is 'unhealthy' or even 'hazardous'. So far that remains the case too often, but the transparency is spurring change.

Just outside the city, I visited the company which is at the heart of the pollution problem and which now hopes to be part of the solution. Shenhua is the world's second-largest coal company. It knows that the societal harm its product causes has placed its long-term future in serious doubt. John Hennessy, who as presi-dent of Stanford oversaw the university's divestment from coal stocks, explains why: 'In my opinion, a person wisely investing an endowment should probably avoid coal because it faces exis-tential regulatory threats. Investing in companies which have a significant amount of assets held in coal reserves which may or may not be usable in the future does not make sense.' Shenhua has seen the writing on the wall. In some of the most advanced wet labs I have seen, a team of 'a thousand talents' from around the globe is working on alternative uses for coal.

Across China, new industries are springing up as companies strive to meet society's evolving needs. Some of the most successful are smaller local businesses, masters of the country's *shanzhai* (tink-ering) culture. Solar hot-water heaters were developed by a local company and have now spread across China to such an extent that it is now the largest producer and consumer of the technology. The same thing is happening with electric bikes. In contrast to some of the less successful state-backed firms, companies like these are genuinely market-led innovators.[37]

Of course, the responsibility does not lie entirely with devel-oping-world companies. There are extraordinary opportunities for

Western multinationals willing to serve a more demanding global population. They will need to avoid the mistakes of the past. As a former Motorola manager, Indra Nooyi witnessed emerging markets leapfrog cable and fibre straight to wireless. Now, as the Pepsi CEO, she wants to achieve something similar with food and drinks. 'There's no reason to believe that we need to go in and do traditional carbonated soft drinks and traditional salty snacks, then migrate to "good-for-you products" and "better-for-you products",' she told reporters. 'If we go back to the US, up until about 1990 the market was largely carbonated soft drinks and slowly started expanding into non-carbonated beverages. Over time, beverages got better and better for you. It was slow progress, but it doesn't have to be that way elsewhere.'[38]

The under-served needs for healthy food, medicine, water and education that can be met profitably are almost endless. Companies can create new revenue streams from thin air by aiding the development process in a sustainable way. The drug company Novartis has reached an extra 42 million people by funding clinics and health-care professionals in rural India.[39] They think that a decade from now they will be selling more medicine through this model than their traditional one. If that happens, they will need to match their commercial vigour with the highest ethical standards. The days of pharmaceutical companies using poor countries to rush through trials they would not get away with in the West are numbered. People will not stand for it. A generation is about to emerge that is at once the most lucrative ever for business and the most challenging.

Breaking the Cycle

Sir Martin Sorrell, CEO of WPP, the world's largest advertising and PR company, believes that only two things have truly changed in business over the last twenty years. 'Technology and geography. That's it.' We think that these two changes, which underpin our first two trends for the future, have the potential to shake the very core of the bond between business and society. Of all the technological developments, artificial intelligence offers the greatest hope for solutions to many of society's great challenges; but it could also fuel distrust of companies whose inability to understand super-intelligent machines may cause chaos in financial markets and beyond. In many industries, it also threatens the central compact between large companies and workers: jobs. Meanwhile, the geographic swing to the East is rewriting the global economic map faster than ever before, shifting the main arena for business–society interaction. The combination of changing geography and technology causes our third trend, the emergence of the most demanding set of people to have inhabited the planet.

All three of these trends will alter the nature of the dialogue between business and society, its talking points, its participants, its cultural connotations and its locations. Most importantly these trends will amplify the intensity and importance of that dialogue. Companies that excel today in their dealings with the external world will need to adapt to new circumstances. Stragglers are running out of time to evolve.

There has never been a better time to challenge the cycles of anti-business sentiment that have spanned the length of history, from ancient China's great debates to Beijing's social-media campaigns. From Andrew Carnegie and his hellish steel plants to the Wall Street bankers who lost their sense of purpose, people at the top of business have ignored the same simple lesson again and again: mistreating any constituent of society eventually leads to collapse, while successful connection is rewarded with lasting commercial success. In perhaps our most striking example of recidivism, the failure of China's merchants to learn from the past created a wave of anger against private enterprise that eventually contributed to the great empire falling behind the West. Future global development will be constrained just as badly if business is hamstrung by the hate it generates so self-destructively.

I firmly believe that the cycle can be broken. This must happen because in an age of transparency the public can alter the fortunes of companies in a matter of minutes. Change is possible if leaders are able to break the shackles of conservatism which grip big companies. History is full of pioneers who showed just how powerful a strong relationship with society can be. Milton Hershey built an iconic brand out of his reputation as a good employer. Henry Heinz helped his small enterprise sell ketchup to the world by embracing legislation on pure food. Today, connection with society is the new frontier of competitive advantage.

I am optimistic that companies will be an enormous force for good in the future. Companies have never been more accountable for the positive contribution they make to people's lives. The connected firms of the future will push the boundaries of human possibilities in their quest to contribute. They will not fracture their bonds with society.

Acknowledgements

My interest in the subject of this book started thirty-five years ago when I was at the Graduate School of Business at Stanford University, California. There I learned that business could not be conducted in isolation from the context of society, public policy and human feelings. Business was a wonderful weave of humans and numbers.

My thanks go to all the people who contributed to this learning and to all the people with whom I have done business over these last forty-nine years. For good or bad they have shaped my thinking.

This project was a partnership with my collaborators Dr Robin Nuttall and Tommy Stadlen who contributed enormously to the intellectual and practical backbone of the book. I am deeply grateful to them both. Without them it would never have seen the light of day.

I want to thank McKinsey & Co., their employer, and Dominic Barton, the firm's global managing director, for their support and encouragement. We also thank other members of the firm who made significant contributions, notably Scott Beardsley, Richard Dobbs, David Dyer, Luis Enriquez, Massimo Giordano, Ian Gleeson, Martin Hirt, Rik Kirkland, Alberto Marchi, Ellora-Julie Parekh and Kurt Strovink.

I am very grateful to Professor Arnaud De Meyer, president of Singapore Management University; Professor Rana Mitter of the University of Oxford; Professor John Van Reenen of the LSE; Professor David Yoffie of Harvard Business School; Spencer Dale; Ian Davis; Mark Hutchinson; Emran Mian; John Seifert; the Rt Revd David Urquhart; and David Yelland who read various versions of the book and gave invaluable feedback.

Over seventy people agreed to be interviewed. I want to thank them for spending time with us and giving us great insights. Quotations from many are in this book. Some are not quoted but they gave us equally interesting views and opinions.

I would also like to thank Gail Rebuck and Ed Faulkner of Random House, my agent Ed Victor and my present and former executive assistants – Matthew Powell, Brook Hewett and David Rawcliffe – who worked on different vintages of the book.

As always my thanks go to my partner, Nghi Nguyen, for his support and encouragement on this project.

John Browne
London, April 2015

Picture Credits

PART ONE

Chapter 1. The Nothing New

page 5   Excerpt from Joseph Needham's copy of the *Yan tie lun*. Text first published 81 BCE. East Asian History of Science Library, Needham Research Institute.

page 8   Wall Street bankers face to face with protestors against financial services companies. September 2013. Photo by Andrew Burton/Getty Images.

page 14   Graphic showing the four tenets of connected leadership.

Chapter 2. Chocolate Villages

page 18   A depiction in *Harper's Weekly* of the battle between workers and private security agents at Andrew Carnegie's Homestead steel plant, Pennsylvania, USA. July 1892. Public domain.

page 22   Milton Hershey with children on the steps of the Hershey Industrial School. *C.*1910. Hershey Community Archives.

page 78 Rachel Carson testifies before a Senate subcommittee on pesticide regulation. June 1963. Associated Press.

page 81 The Greenpeace ship, *Rainbow Warrior*, after being sabotaged by French intelligence officers. July 1985. AFP/Getty Images.

Chapter 6. Queen and Servant

page 94 Turkish protestors in Istanbul's Taksim Gezi Park. June 2013. Associated Press.

page 95 A protestor uses her phone to report news on unrest around Taksim Square. June 2013. Ozan Kose/AFP/Getty Images.

page 97 Martin Cooper makes the first public cell-phone call in New York City. April 1973. Courtesy of Martin Cooper.

page 108 A Keralan fisherman makes a call on a mobile phone to coordinate with nearby boats. April 2004. Deshakalyan Chowdhury/AFP/Getty Images.

Chapter 7. The Reservoir

page 117 Akio Toyoda, president and CEO of Toyota, makes a formal apology at a press conference. March 2010. Feng Li/Getty Images.

page 122 BP's Deepwater Horizon rig on fire in the Gulf of Mexico. April 2010. US Coast Guard via Getty Images.

page 127 A Greenpeace boat approaches Shell's disused Brent Spar oil platform in the UK's North Sea. May 1995. Photofusion/UIG via Getty Images.

PART TWO

Chapter 8. History Rhymes

page 138 Enron's former CEO Ken Lay is led into Federal Court in handcuffs. July 2004. Associated Press.

page 138 A framed copy of Enron's code of ethics on a former employee's desk. June 2015. Author's collection.

page 142 Graphic showing the four tenets of connected leadership.

Chapter 10. Professional Era

page 180 The team at Box Inc. celebrate a successful IPO of the company that founder Aaron Levie started aged nineteen. January 2015. Associated Press.

Chapter 11. The Front Foot

page 198 Members of the Tangguh Independent Advisory Panel cross to the north shore of Bintuni Bay, West Papua, to hear the concerns of villagers living near BP's development. 2002. Courtesy of BP plc.

page 199 Protestors against Freeport-McMoRan's operations in West Papua. March 2006. Associated Press.

page 207 Facebook's Mark Zuckerberg speaks in Mandarin at Tsinghua University, Beijing. October 2014. Courtesy of Tsinghua University's school of economics and management.

Epilogue: People Rising

page 214 Tim Berners-Lee's proposal for the World Wide Web with a comment of support from his supervisor, Mike Sendall. March 1989. Courtesy of CERN.

page 220   Sebastian Thrun celebrates victory in DARPA's driver-less car challenge. October 2005. Gene Blevins/Reuters/Corbis.

page 232   Map showing the evolution of the earth's economic centre of gravity. McKinsey Global Institute.

page 238   Huawei's testing centre at its campus in Shenzhen, China. 13 April 2015. Photo by Ouyang Yang, courtesy of Huawei Technologies Co. Ltd.

page 244   Chart showing the cost of global social burdens. McKinsey Global Institute.

Notes

PART ONE

Prologue

1   Robin Nuttall and Sergio Sandoval, 'The New Value at Stake in Regulation', *McKinsey Quarterly*, January 2010.

2   Alex Edmans, 'The Link Between Job Satisfaction and Firm Value, With Implications for Corporate Social Responsibility', *Academy of Management Perspectives* 26(4), 1–19, November 2012. The variable tested here was employee engagement – just one aspect of connected leadership. The financial outperformance is likely to be even higher for firms able to excel across multiple aspects. Edmans found that 'a value-weighted portfolio' of the '100 Best Companies to Work for in America' earned an annual four-factor alpha of 3.5 per cent from 1984 to 2009, and 2.1 per cent above industry benchmarks. His results 'are robust to controls for firm characteristics, different weighting methodologies, and the removal of outliers'.

3   McKinsey & Company Insights and Publications, 'McKinsey Global Survey results: External affairs at a crossroads', May 2013. This research shows that although most firms understand the power of societal stakeholders, only 21 per cent report 'frequent successes' in shaping their decisions.

Chapter 1. The Nothing New

1   Esson Gale (trans.), *Discourses on Salt and Iron* (Leyden: Brill, 1931), p. xxvi.

2   Terms such as 'industrialist' and 'government intervention' post-date the period in question, but the basic concepts are timeless and I use them freely here.

3   Esson Gale, trans., *Discourses on Salt and Iron*, op. cit.

4   The great historian of the age, Sima Qian, criticises the 'lawlessness, excesses and usurpation' of the Zhuo, Cheng and Kong iron families in his *Biographies of the Moneymakers*. Other observers note with distaste their 'notorious' displays of extreme wealth. New brides were accompanied by a hundred carriages into wedding parties that rivalled imperial feasts for the quality of cuisine. Joseph Needham and Donald Wagner, *Science and Civilisation* in China, Volume 5, Part 11 (Cambridge: Cambridge University Press, 2007), pp. 142–3.

5   John Vickers charts the development of the concepts of competition from Adam Smith to John Stuart Mill, Friedrich Hayek and Joseph Schumpeter. John Vickers, 'Concepts of Competition', *Oxford Economic Papers* 47 (1995), pp. 1–23.

6   Esson Gale, trans., *Discourses on Salt and Iron*, op. cit.

7   Kenneth Pomeranz, *The Great Divergence: China, Europe, and the Making of the Modern World Economy* (Princeton: Princeton University Press, 2000), p. 65.

8   Rana Mitter describes how this official distrust of commercial culture persisted long into the second millennium. Rana Mitter, *A Bitter Revolution: China's Struggle with the Modern World* (Oxford: Oxford University Press, 2004), pp. 90–101.

9   Edelman Trust Barometer 2015.

10 Gennady Estraikh, of the Skirball Centre of Hebrew and Judaic Studies at New York University, notes that moneylending has also been derided among Jews (and Muslims). This is rooted in the Bible's (and Koran's) proscription against such practices. Jews began

to play the role of a compromise: they did not lend money to other Jews, but did so to non-Jews. Hence the despised (albeit extremely important) 'mission' allocated in European economies to the Rothschilds and their ilk.

11 Earlier, in the twelfth and thirteenth centuries, assets seized from Jewish moneylenders regularly accounted for a seventh of the Crown's total revenue. An Exchequer of the Jews administrated the proceeds from a trade the state publicly denounced. As Simon Schama puts it: 'The Jews were obliged to do the dirty work and get the odium while the Crown got the profit.' Simon Schama, *The Story of the Jews: Finding the Words 1000 BCE–1492 CE* (London: The Bodley Head, 2013), pp. 315–16.

12 Francis Bacon, 'Of Usury'.

13 Edelman Trust Barometer 2014. 18 per cent of global respondents said they trust business leaders to tell the truth.

14 McKinsey & Company Insights and Publications, 'McKinsey Global Survey results: External affairs at a crossroads', May 2013.

15 Dominic Barton, 2011, 'Capitalism for the Long Term', *Harvard Business Review*, March 2011. See also Dominic Barton and Mark Wiseman, 2015, 'Where Boards Fall Short', *Harvard Business Review*.

16 Ian Davis, 'Business and Society', *The Economist*, 28 May 2005.

17 Michael Porter, 'Strategy and Society: The Link Between Competitive Advantage and Corporate Social Responsibility', *Harvard Business Review*, December 2006.

18 See Philipp Kruger, 'Corporate Goodness and Shareholder Wealth', *Journal of Financial Economics*, forthcoming. Kruger finds that CSR announcements are often value destructive, as measured by event-study stock-market returns. He does find that CSR announcements can be shareholder value-enhancing under certain circumstances, in particular in firms where agency problems are less likely to be present (as measured by firms having high leverage) and when the positive CSR news is the result of managerial efforts aimed at offsetting prior corporate social irresponsibility.

19 A.G. Lafley was CEO from 2000 to 2009. P&G rehired him as CEO, president and chairman in May 2013. Karen Dillon, 'I Think of My Failures as a Gift: An interview with A.G. Lafley', *Harvard Business Review*, April 2011.

Chapter 2. Chocolate Villages

1   For detailed accounts of the Homestead incident, see Kevin and Laurie Hillstrom, *The Industrial Revolution in America: Iron and Steel* (California: ABC-Clio, 2005); Peter Krass, *Carnegie* (Hoboken: John Wiley & Sons, 2002); Paul Krause, *The Battle For Homestead, 1880–1892* (Pittsburgh: University of Pittsburgh Press, 1992);

2   David Nasaw, *Andrew Carnegie* (New York: Penguin, 2006).

3   Carnegie admitted the negative impact on President Harrison, who had previously promised to protect workers' rights. He wrote to Frick: 'I fear that Homestead did much to elect Cleveland.'

4   Peter Krass attributes this quote to the *London Financial Observer* in his book *Carnegie* (Hoboken: John Wiley & Sons, 2002).

5   In her biography, Frick's great-granddaughter describes him as 'ice cold, with a mysterious underlying passion that was visible in his art collection and in his occasional bouts of rage.'

6   The two donated a combined total of over $505 million. Measured in terms of relative economic power, that figure was worth $111 billion in 2015. Calculations were made via measuringworth.com, which measures the amount of wealth relative to a country's GDP.

7   The account of Hershey draws on Joel Brenner, *The Emperors of Chocolate* (New York: Random House, 1999); Michael D'Antonio, *Hershey* (New York: Simon & Schuster, 2007); Carol Off, *Bitter Chocolate* (Toronto: Random House, 2006); and Tim Richardson, *Sweets* (London: Bantam Press, 2002).

8   Kevin and Laurie Hillstrom, *The Industrial Revolution in America: Iron and Steel* (California: ABC-Clio, 2005), p. 218.

9   The description of Cadbury draws on John Bradley, *Cadbury's Purple Reign* (Chichester: John Wiley, 2008); Joel Brenner, *The Emperors of Chocolate* (New York: Random House, 1999); Carol Off, *Bitter*

Chocolate, op. cit.; Tim Richardson, *Sweets*, op. cit.; and Anne Vernon, *A Quaker Businessman* (London: Allen and Unwin, 1958).

10 Fry's, the company that pioneered eating chocolate in Britain, started out as an apothecary. Chocolate was first advertised in Britain in 1657 as an 'excellent West Indian drink that cures and preserves the body of many diseases'.

11 Edward Cadbury, *Experiments in Industrial Organization* (London: Longmans, Green and Co., 1912), p. 274.

12 Ibid., p. 282.

13 After Richard's death in 1899, the company's paternalism transformed into welfarism. George's son, Edward, was aware that the factory-town model risked accusations of interference. He attempted to ensure that 'no coercive attitude is assumed by the employer'. Unlike Lord Lever's Port Sunlight, the town of Bournville had a degree of independence as it was administered at arm's length from the company. Of the residents, 60 per cent did not work for Cadbury.

14 Alex Edmans, 'The Link Between Job Satisfaction and Firm Value, With Implications for Corporate Social Responsibility', *Academy of Management Perspectives* 26(4), 1–19, November 2012.

15 Edward Cadbury, *Experiments in Industrial Organization*, op. cit., pp. xii–xiii.

16 Ibid., pp. 263–4.

17 Childless, Hershey 'decided to make the orphan boys of the United States my heirs'. The school's endowment is now worth over $9 billion, eclipsing all but a handful of the world's richest universities, including Columbia, the University of Pennsylvania and Duke. Notable alumni include William Dearsden, CEO of Hershey in the 1970s.

18 Richard Cadbury, *Cocoa: All About It* (London: Sampson Low, Marston and Company, 1896), p. 58.

19 The 2015 Edelman Trust Barometer found that 'regular employees' are significantly more credible spokespeople than CEOs.

20 Richard Cadbury, *Cocoa: All About It*, op. cit., pp. 67–8.

21 Cadbury, 'Cadbury World: A case study', 2009. A report produced by Cadbury World Market Team exploring the history, product development, operations and marketing functions of Cadbury World.

22 Fair Labor Association, 'Independent Investigation of Apple Supplier, Foxconn', March 2012. http://www.fairlabor.org/report/foxconn-investigation-report.

23 'Audit Faults Apple Supplier', *Wall Street Journal*, 30 March 2012.

24 'Light and Death', *The Economist*, 27 May 2010. According to Foxconn, the suicide rate is less than one tenth of the national rate.

25 External stakeholders in China are also beginning to demand improved labour practices. Pressure from local governments and mass riots in Foxconn's factories in 2012 drove the company to allow collective bargaining for the first time. With China's working-age population starting to decline earlier than expected, one of Foxconn's main barriers to growth will be the supply of new workers.

26 At BP, I appointed Patti Bellinger as head of diversity to drive through an agenda on diversity and equality. As I said in 2002 at the Women in Business Conference, diversity was smart business as well as the right thing to do: 'The people we have form our human capital. To me that is a more important corporate asset than all the plant and equipment, all the oilfields and pipelines. If we can get a disproportionate share of the most talented people in the world, we have a chance of holding a competitive edge.'

Chapter 3. Meatpackers and Muckrakers

1 Former BP chairman Eric Drake faced a similar experience during the OPEC oil embargo that followed the Yom Kippur War. British prime minister Edward Heath summoned Drake to Chequers and demanded that BP maintain regular deliveries to the United Kingdom at the expense of other European nations. Drake did not scare easily. He had been one of the last men out of Abadan, Iran, having been threatened with the death penalty when Mohammad Mossadegh nationalised the oil industry. On his return

he was rebuked by Winston Churchill, then leader of the opposition, for failing to deploy his pistol. 'Drake,' Churchill growled, 'you can finish a man with a pistol. I know because I have.' Heath, by comparison, was nothing to be scared of and Drake reminded the prime minister that the government had agreed not to interfere in company management when it took a 51 per cent stake in 1914. However, secret papers uncovered by James Bamberg later showed that Drake eventually bowed under persistent pressure to provide 'under-the-counter supplies to Britain'. James Bamberg, *British Petroleum and Global Oil, 1950–1975: The challenge of nationalism* (Cambridge: Cambridge University Press, 2000), pp. 483–4; Daniel Yergin, *The Prize: The Epic Quest for Oil Money and Power* (New York: Free Press, 2009, originally published in 1991), p. 445.

2   'Novartis Seeking Vaccine Payments', *Wall Street Journal*, 6 May 2010, and 'Novartis Chief Warns State Over Cancelled Vaccine Orders', *Independent*, 27 January 2010.

3   Joseph Stiglitz et al., *The Economic Role of the State* (Oxford: Basil Blackwell, 1989).

4   EBITDA is earnings before interest, tax, depreciation and amortisation.

5   Robin Nuttall and Sergio Sandoval, 'The New Value at Stake in Regulation', *McKinsey Quarterly*, January 2010.

6   Reinier Musters, Ellora-Julie Parekh and Surya Ramkumar, 2013, 'Organizing the Government Affairs Function for Impact', *McKinsey Quarterly*, November 2013.

7   McKinsey & Company Insights and Publications, 'McKinsey Global Survey results: External affairs at a crossroads', May 2013.

8   Microsoft CEO: Governments need to catch up to Big Data. https://www.youtube.com/watch?v=F7aM0XsaToI&feature=y outu.be. Published on 18 March 2015. Microsoft CEO Satya Nadella shares his thoughts on data and privacy with CNN's Maggie Lake.

9   Andre Dua, Robin Nuttall and Jon Wilkins, 'Why Good Companies Create Bad Regulatory Strategies', *McKinsey Quarterly*, June 2011.

10 Ian Phimister, 'Zimbabwe: The Path of Capitalist Development', in D. Birmingham & P.M. Martin, *History of Central Africa*, Vol. ii (London: Longman, 1983), p. 261.

11 Ibid., p. 252.

12 Ilyse Barkan, 'Industry Invites Regulation: The Passage of the Pure Food and Drug Act of 1906', *American Journal of Public Health* 75 (1), January 1985, p. 22.

13 James Young, *Pure Food* (Princeton: Princeton University Press, 1989), p. 231.

14 Ilyse Barkan, 'Industry Invites Regulation', op. cit., p. 25.

15 James Young, *Pure Food*, op. cit., p. 177.

16 Heinz inaugural CSR report, 2005.

17 Andrew Smith, *Pure Ketchup: A History of America's National Condiment With Recipes* (Columbia, SC: University of South Carolina Press, 1996), p. 105.

18 Ibid., pp. 86, 97.

19 Heinz engaged as successfully with its employees as it did with regulators and customers. It won numerous awards for its treatment of workers. Harry Sherman, grand secretary of the National Brotherhood of Electrical Workers of America, described the Heinz factory as 'a utopia for working men'. Quentin Skrabec, *H.J. Heinz, A Biography* (Jefferson, NC: McFarland, 2009), p. 233.

20 Quentin Skrabec, *H.J. Heinz, A Biography* (Jefferson, NC: McFarland, 2009), p. 154; Andrew Smith, *Pure Ketchup*, op. cit., p. 110.

It will be no surprise to learn that a similarly enlightened strategy had been implemented some years earlier in Britain by George Cadbury. At a time when confectionary companies regularly used brick dust, red lead and even arsenic in their products, consumers increasingly placed their trust in the reliable Quaker family firms. Cadbury saw an opportunity to emphasise its reputation for purity by lobbying government to impose regulation. He particularly targeted the drinking-cocoa market which was divided into 'pure' and 'mixed' products. The issue here was quality rather than safety: mixed cocoa was adulterated with flour and starch. The Adulteration of Food Acts of 1872 and 1875 forced the industry to label any adulterants. Cadbury seized upon the publicity his policy intervention had generated to redefine his cocoa brands. He discontinued his profitable mixed cocoas even though it meant compensating his independent sales force, and launched a thirty-year advertising campaign using the slogan 'Absolutely Pure, Therefore Best'. John Bradley, *Cadbury's Purple Reign* (Chichester: John Wiley, 2008), pp. 12–13.

21 'A Leader for the Uber Campaign', *Uber.com*, 19 August 2014.

22 McKinsey interview with Airbnb co-founder and CEO Brian Chesky, 'The Future of Airbnb in Cities', November 2014.

23 The National Diet of Japan, 'The Official Report of the Fukushima Nuclear Accident Independent Investigation Committee: Executive Summary', 2012, p. 17.

24 Ibid., p. 20.

25 Following the Gulf of Mexico accident in 2010, many pointed to regulatory capture of the Minerals Management Service.

26 'System Bred Tepco's Cosy Links to Watchdogs', *Financial Times*, 19 April 2011.

27 Ibid.

28 'Culture of Complicity Tied to Stricken Nuclear Plant', *New York Times*, 26 April 2011.

29 'Japan Nuclear Energy Drive Compromised by Conflicts of Interest', *Bloomberg*, 12 December 2007.

30 The National Diet of Japan, op. cit.

31 Yoichi Funabashi, 'The End of Japanese Illusions', *New York Times*, 11 March 2012.

32 'Fukushima Disaster Was Man-Made, Investigation Finds', *Bloomberg*, 5 July 2012.

33 'Executive Dealing with a Corporate Meltdown', *Financial Times*, 21 October 2012.

Chapter 4. The Last Nabob

1 Yuval Atsmon, Peter Child, Richard Dobbs and Laxman Narasimhan, 'Winning the $30 Trillion Decathlon: Going for Gold in Emerging Markets', *McKinsey Quarterly*, August 2012.

2   McKinsey Global Institute, 'Urban World: The Shifting Global Business Landscape', 2013. Report.

3   Nicholas B. Dirks, *The Scandal of Empire: India and the creation of imperial Britain* (Cambridge: Harvard University Press, 2006), pp. 42–43.

4   This was the sum uncovered by the Select Committee Inquiry of 1772. It is safe to assume that the actual total was far higher. Nicholas B. Dirks, *The Scandal of Empire*, op. cit., p. 43; £12 billion figure measured in terms of relative economic power in 2015. Calculations were made via measuringworth.com, which measures the amount of wealth relative to a country's GDP.

5   Nicholas B. Dirks, op. cit.

6   George K. McGilvary, *Guardian of the East India Company: The Life of Laurence Sullivan* (London, Tauris Academic Studies, 2006), p. 91.

7   Rajat Datta, *Society, Economy and the Market: Commercialization in rural Bengal c. 1760–1800* (New Delhi: Manohar, 2000), pp. 287–88; Nicholas B. Dirks, *The Scandal of Empire*, op. cit., p. 54.

8   Contemporary accounts disagreed on the method employed. Some suggested a penknife to the throat, others a massive opium overdose. Modern historians have explored the possibility that Clive never meant to kill himself and merely overdid the opium by mistake.

9   Nick Robins, 'Loot: In Search of the East India Company, the World's First Transnational Corporation', *Environment & Urbanisation*, Vol. 14, No. 1 (2002), p. 79.

10 Ibid., p. 83.

11 C.A. Bayly, *The New Cambridge History of India*, Vol. ii: *Indian Society and the Making of the British Empire* (Cambridge: Cambridge University Press, 1988), p. 90.

12 It is estimated that by the 1780s roughly one out of every ten seats in the House of Commons was owned by a nabob. Nick Robins, 'Loot', op. cit., p. 83.

13 Nicholas B. Dirks, *The Scandal of Empire*, op. cit., p. 63.

14 Ibid., p. 67.

15 Jonathan Duncan, as governor of Bombay during the 1790s, allowed the overseer of the company's factory in Malabar to acquire

low-caste Pullars to work as slaves. Nancy Gardner Cassels, *Social Legislation of the East India Company: Public Justice versus Public Instruction* (New Delhi: Sage, 2010), pp. 7, 165, 178.

16 Christopher Hibbert, *The Great Mutiny: India 1857* (London: Allen Lane, 1978), pp. 50–53.

17 Ibid., pp. 53–4.

18 Denis Judd, *The Lion and the Tiger: The Rise and Fall of the British Raj, 1600–1947* (Oxford: Oxford University Press, 2004), pp. 71–72.

19 Ibid, p. 71.

20 John Flint, *Cecil Rhodes* (London: Hutchinson & Co., 1976), pp. 204–5.

21 A long line of Rhodes Scholars have gone on to lead their countries, starting with Norman Manley of Jamaica (Jesus College, 1914), and culminating with Bill Clinton (University College, 1968) via the connoisseur of Oxford pubs, Bob Hawke of Australia (University College, 1953).

22 P. Slinn, 'Commercial Concessions and Politics during the Colonial Period: The Role of the British South Africa Company in Northern Rhodesia 1890–1964' in *African Affairs*, Vol. 70, No. 3 (Oxford: Oxford University Press, 1971), p. 381–2.

23 Ibid., p. 382.

24 The story of OPEC's rise to power is based on two superb histories: Dan Yergin's definitive history of the oil industry, *The Prize: The Epic Quest for Oil, Money & Power* (New York: Free Press, 2009); and Jim Bamberg's history of BP, *British Petroleum and Global Oil 1950–1975: The challenge of nationalism*, Volume 3 (Cambridge: Cambridge University Press, 2000).

25 Saudi Arabia compensated the companies but many others, including Libya and Venezuela, did not. In Kuwait, BP and Gulf Oil assumed their long-standing relationship with the rulers would ensure preferential access and adequate compensation to the tune of $2 billion. They were offered just $5 million. On being asked what would happen if the terms were rejected, the Kuwaiti oil minister replied: 'We will just say thank you very much and goodbye.' D. Yergin, *The Prize*, op. cit., p. 629.

26 Ibid., p. 616.

27 The UK Bribery Act forbids UK companies from paying bribes anywhere in the world. It goes further than the US Foreign Corrupt Practices Act, which makes it illegal to make improper payments to foreign officials, by noting that some business expenditure on hospitality can be employed as bribes. In the UK, companies have a duty to do their best to prevent bribery, but there is a grey area when it comes to contractors and subcontractors.

28 For more information, see John Browne, *Beyond Business* (London: Weidenfeld & Nicolson, 2010), p. 101.

29 F.A. Hayek, *The Road to Serfdom*, (Chicago: University of Chicago Press, 1944).

30 'Locals Tap Oil Majors' Niger Delta Retreat', *Financial Times*, 27 August 2014.

31 There were also concerns about the integrity of the pipeline in the event of an earthquake creating the possibility of an oil spill in the Gulf of Alaska. Of course such a spill subsequently occurred, though mainly due to human error, in the *Exxon Valdez* disaster.

32 He was joined by a stringer from the *Manchester Guardian* and a Scot named 'Scotty'.

Chapter 5. Silent Spring

1 This is what economists term an 'externality' following A.C. Pigou, or 'missing market' following Kenneth Arrow. See A.C. Pigou, 1920, *The Economics of Welfare*, and Kenneth J. Arrow, 1969, 'The Organization of Economic Activity: Issues Pertinent to the Choice of Market Versus Non-market Allocations', in 'The Analysis and Evaluation of Public Expenditures: The PPB System', a compendium of papers submitted to the Subcommittee on Economy in Government of the Joint Economic Committee, Congress of the United States 1 (Washington DC: Government Printing Office), pp. 47–64, OCLC 26897.

2 Europe's flagship scheme, the EU Emissions Trading System, has been affected by mismanagement. The overall number of credits

distributed was too high and when emissions fell in the recession the price of carbon dropped dramatically. It is critical that the overall cap continues to be lowered so that a reasonable carbon price is achieved, providing an incentive for companies to cut emissions.

3   To understand why, see the explanation of public goods in the section 'The tragedy of the commons' further on in this chapter.

4   Garrett Hardin, 'The Tragedy of the Commons', *Science*, Vol. 162, No. 3859, December 1968, pp. 1243–48.

5   Eliza Griswold, 'How *Silent Spring* Ignited the Environmental Movement, *New York Times*, 21 September 2012.

6   Frank White, *The Overview Effect* (Boston: Houghton-Mifflin, 1987).

7   Buckminster Fuller was a man of many talents and even more ideas. Most famous for championing geodesic domes, Fuller was also a serial experimenter. He developed (and for two years implemented) what he called the Dymaxion sleep pattern, consisting of four naps of thirty minutes per day. This, he suggested, could be the key to victory in the Second World War. As a frequent flyer, he used to wear three watches: one for the time zone of departure, one for the current zone, and one for the destination zone. 'Science: Dymaxion Sleep', *Time*, 11 October 1943.

8   Former secretary of agriculture Ezra Taft Benson wrote to former president Dwight Eisenhower that Carson was 'probably a communist'. Linda Lear, *Rachel Carson: Witness for nature* (New York: Henry Holt & Company, 1997), p. 429.

9   Rachel Carson, Speech to the Garden Club of America, New York, 8 January 1963.

10 DDT use had declined 70 per cent from its peak by the time of the ban. It had been abandoned in agriculture except on cotton farms. Steve Maguire, 'Contested Icons: Rachel Carson and DDT' in Sideris, Dean and Moore, eds., *Rachel Carson: Legacy and challenge* (Albany: State University of New York Press, 2008), p. 200.

11 Union Oil's response displayed the callousness that BP would be accused of following the Macondo spill. 'I don't like to call it a disaster,' Union Oil's president Fred Hartley said, 'because there has

been no loss of human life. I am amazed at the publicity for the loss of a few birds.'

12 Marc Eisner, *Governing the Environment: The transformation of environmental protection* (Boulder: Lynne Rienner, 2007), p. 63.

13 In 1791, Britain's Society for the Abolition of the Slave Trade led a boycott of sugar produced by slaves. The boycott hit sugar plantations and retailers hard, reducing demand by between a third and a half, and helped build momentum towards the Abolition of the Slave Trade Act in 1807.

14 Carolyn Merchant, *The Columbia Guide to American Environmental History* (New York: Columbia University Press, 2002), p. 182.

15 Ernest Saunders quoted in M. Brady, 'Food for Infants: How the Baby Food Industry Competes with Breastfeeding' in J. Madeley, ed., *Hungry for Power: The impact of transnational corporations on food security* (London: UK Food Group, 1999), pp. 11–12.

16 Richard Pagan Jr, the PR executive and inaugural NCCN president, quoted in M. Brady, 'Food for Infants', op. cit., p. 12.

17 On a global average basis among 'informed publics', NGOs have been more trusted than business, media and government since 2008. Edelman Trust Barometer, 2015.

18 Aon Benfield, 'Annual Global Climate and Catastrophe Report', 2012.

19 Yuval Atsmon, Peter Child, Richard Dobbs and Laxman Narasimhan op. cit.

20 'China Smog Cuts 5.5 Years from Average Life Expectancy', *Financial Times*, 8 July 2013.

21 Sam Geall, 'Would You Swim in China's Rivers?', *New Statesman*, 24 June 2013.

22 'Apple Agrees to China Pollution Audit', *Financial Times*, 15 April 2012.

23 Edelman Trust Barometer, 2015. Edelman define 'informed publics' as follows: '25–64, college-educated, in the top quartile of household income per age group in each market and report significant media consumption and engagement in business news and public policy.'

24 WWF and CDP, 'The 3% Solution', 2013.

25 Data from Walmart 2014 Global Responsibility Report, available at www.walmart.com.

26 Ibid.

27 Ibid.

28 Edward Humes, *Force of Nature: The unlikely story of Wal-Mart's green revolution* (New York: Harper Collins, 2011) p. 20.

29 Walmart's sustainability programme has won tributes from a wide range of environmental NGOs as well as the Environmental Protection Agency which cited the company as the leading corporate user of onsite renewables. When President Obama made his landmark climate-change speech in June 2013 he singled out Walmart for praise.

30 IEA, 'World Energy Outlook', 2012.

31 Unilever, 'Sustainable Living Plan', launched in 2010 with targets for 2020.

32 'Walmart Announces New Commitments to Dramatically Increase Energy Efficiency and Renewables', Walmart press release, 15 April 2013. Continuity at Walmart is boosted by the ongoing presence of Chairman Rob Walton, a member of the founding family.

33 IPPR, 'Consumer Power: How the Public Thinks Lower-carbon Behaviour Could be Made Mainstream', September 2009.

34 Tommy Stadlen, 'Climate Skeptics', *International Herald Tribune*, 28 May 2010.

Chapter 6. Queen and Servant

1 McKinsey Global Institute, 'Disruptive Technologies: Advances that Will Transform Life, Business, and the Global Economy', May 2013.

2 'Internet of things' and 'Mobile Internet' represent two of the twelve 'disruptive technologies' identified by MGI as having significant potential to drive economic impact and disruption by 2025. The full list of disruptive technologies is as follows: Mobile Internet; Automation of knowledge work; The Internet of things; Cloud technology; Advanced robotics; Autonomous and near-autonomous

vehicles; Next-generation genomics; Energy storage; 3D printing; Advanced materials; Advanced oil & gas recovery; Renewable energy. See McKinsey Global Institute, 'Disruptive Technologies', op. cit.

3   China Internet Network Information Center, 'Statistical Report on Internet Development in China', January 2013.

4   '2 Billion Consumers Worldwide to Get Smart(phones) by 2016', eMarketer, 11 December 2014.

5   McKinsey Global Institute, 'The Social Economy: Unlocking Value and Productivity through Social Technologies', July 2012.

6   Microsoft, 'Data Privacy Day Privacy Survey', 2013.

7   See discussion on regulation and nuclear safety in Chapter 7.

8   Mark Aldrich, *Safety First: Technology, labor and business in the building of work safety, 1870–1939* (Baltimore: Johns Hopkins University Press, 1997). Data for 2013 from the United States Department of Labor, available at www.msha.gov.

9   Dan Gardner, *Risk: The science and politics of fear* (London: Virgin Books, 2008).

10 Although the shale revolution is a story about market forces, it is important to recognise the role of government support. The US government contributed almost $100 million to critical research into the application of hydraulic fracturing. See US Department of Energy press release, 'DOE's Early Investment in Shale Gas Technology Producing Results Today', 2 February 2011.

11 'The Father of Fracking', *The Economist*, 3 August 2013.

12 Ibid.

13 US Energy Information Administration, www.eia.gov.

14 US Census Bureau, 'Petroleum as a Percent of the Total Trade Deficit', www.census.gov.

15 The substitution of gas for coal has helped the US reduce carbon emissions from domestic energy by 8.6 per cent between 2005 and 2012 without ever really intending to do so. John Broderick and Kevin Anderson, 'Has US Shale Gas Reduced CO2 Emissions?', Tyndall Centre for Climate Change Research, Manchester University, October 2012.

16 'The Industry Can No Longer Simply Focus on the Benefits of Shale Gas', *The Economist*, 1 August 2013.

17 Cass Sunstein, 'Of Montreal and Kyoto: A Tale of Two Protocols', *Harvard Environmental Law Review* 31 (1), 2007, p. 4.

18 Council of Economic Advisers, *Economic Report of the President* (1990: Washington DC: U.S. Government Printing Office, 1990), pp. 210, 223.

19 'Indra Nooyi's Pepsi Challenge', *Fortune*, 11 June 2012.

20 Robert Jensen, 'The Digital Provide: Information (Technology), Market Performance, and Welfare in the South Indian Fisheries Sector', *Quarterly Journal Of Economics*, Vol. CXXII, Issue 3, August 2007.

Chapter 7. The Reservoir

1 The Conference Board CEO Challenge, 2015. http://www. conference-board.org.

2 Game theory has formalised the concepts of 'trust' and 'reputation', which can both apply in situations of asymmetric information.

In game theory, trust is a situation 'when agents expect a particular agent to do something'. For example, as Luis Cabral explains, oligopoly competitors might trust each other regarding an implicit or explicit price-fixing agreement; a developing country would like to be considered a trustworthy borrower; more generally, implicit contracts (employment, partnership, lending, etc.) involve some amount of trust between contracting parties. The essence of the mechanism is repetition and the possibility of 'punishing' off-equilibrium actions.

By contrast, reputation is a situation 'when agents believe a particular agent to be something'. For example, governments would like to be perceived as rigorous on inflation; some incumbent monopolist would like to have the reputation for being tough with respect to entrants; a seller would like to have the reputation for selling good-quality products. The essence of the reputation mechanism is Bayesian updating and possibly signalling as well. As Fudenberg and Tirole comment on p. 367 of *Game Theory*: 'Intuitively, since reputations are like assets, a player is more willing to incur the short-run costs to build up his reputation when he is patient and his planning horizon is long. A player with a short horizon will be less willing to make investments, so we should expect that investments in reputation will be more likely in long relationships than in short ones, and more likely at the beginning of a game than at its end.'

See 'The Economics of Trust and Reputation: A Primer', Luis M.B. Cabral, New York University and CEPR, 2005; and Fudenberg and Tirole, *Game Theory* (Cambridge: MIT Press, 1991).

3 Richard Tedlow and Wendy Smith, 'James Burke: A Career in American Business (B)', Harvard Business School Case Study 9-390-030, 2005, p. 2.

4 Stephen Greyser, 'Johnson & Johnson: The Tylenol Tragedy', Harvard Business School Case Study 9-583-043 (revised), 1992, p. 1.

5 Richard Tedlow and Wendy Smith, 'James Burke', op. cit., pp. 3, 8.

6 Ibid., p. 3.

7 Ibid, pp. 6–7.

8 Grahame Dowling, *Creating Corporate Reputations* (Oxford: Oxford University Press, 2001), p. 253.

9 Johnson & Johnson Credo, www.jnj.com.

10 Jim Collins, 'The 10 Greatest CEOs of All Time', *Fortune*, 21 July 2003.

11 Richard Tedlow and Wendy Smith, 'James Burke', op. cit., p. 7.

12 Ibid, p. 4.

13 Ibid, pp. 2–3, 11. J&J dealt with the second crisis as brilliantly as the first.

14 Ibid, pp. 1–2.

15 Ibid, p. 6.

16 'Toyota Memo Shows $100m Savings Over Floor Mat Recall', *Guardian*, 22 February 2010.

17 David Austen-Smith, Daniel Diermeier and Eitan Zemel, 'Unintended Acceleration: Toyota's Recall Crisis', Kellogg School of Management Case Study 5-311-504, 2011, p. 10.

18 'Fire Hazard', *The Economist*, 11 October 2012.

19 Rory Knight and Deborah Pretty, 'The Impact of Catastrophes on Shareholder Value', Oxford Executive Research Briefing, 1997.

20 'BP settles Deepwater Horizon spill for $18.7bn,' *Financial Times*, 2 July 2015.

21 'Spills and Bills', *The Economist*, 9 February 2013.

22 This speech is available to watch at gsb.stanford.edu.

23 BBC Two television broadcast, 'BP: $30 Billion Blowout', released 9 November 2010.

24 'Tony Hayward, Genel Energy CEO: Now He Has His Life Back', *Financial Times*, 14 September 2014.

25 'How Bad was Andersen?', *The Economist*, 4 December 2003.

26 'Andersen Auditor Pleads Guilty', BBC News, 10 April 2002.

27 'Back in Court', *The Economist*, 28 April 2005.

28 The conviction was later overturned by the U.S. Supreme Court on the grounds that the trial judge's instructions to the jury were incorrect. Essentially a technicality, this was in no way an exoneration of Andersen's guilt. A retrial was deemed unnecessary by prosecutors given the demise of the firm.

29 Amos Tversky and Daniel Kahneman, 'Availability: a Heuristic for Judging Frequency and Probability', *Cognitive Psychology* 5, No. 2 (1973), pp. 207–232.

30 David Anderson QC, *The Terrorism Acts in 2011: Report of the Independent Reviewer on the operation of the Terrorism Act 2000 and Part 1 of the Terrorism Act 2006* (London: The Stationery Office, 2012).

31 'Ash Halts Flights over Northern UK and Ireland', *Financial Times*, 4 May 2010.

32 'Brent Spar's Long Saga', *BBC News online*, 25 November 1998; 'Brent Spar: Battle that Launched Modern Activism', *Ethical Corporation online*, 5 May 2010.

33 'Interview with Former Shell Chief Sir Mark Moody-Stuart', *Financial Times*, 29 May 2014.

34 'Environmentalists Apologise to Shell for Using Faulty Data: Greenpeace Admits Slip on Oil Rig Risk', *New York Times*, 6 September 1995.

35 Nuclear Energy Agency, *Comparing Nuclear Accident Risks with Those from Other Energy Sources* (OECD, 2010).

PART TWO

Chapter 8. History Rhymes

1 Daniel Kahneman, *Thinking, Fast and Slow* (London: Penguin, 2010; UK edition), p. 258.

2 Heather Mahar, 'Why Are There So Few Prenuptial Agreements?', Harvard Law School John M. Olin Center for Law, Economics and Business Discussion Paper Series. Paper 436, September 2003.

3 Richard Thaler and Cass Sunstein, *Nudge* (London: Penguin, 2009; revised UK edition), p. 36.

4 Daniel Kahneman, *Thinking, Fast and Slow* (London: Penguin, 2010; UK edition), p. 251.

5 Kim Gittleson, 'Can a Company Live Forever?', *BBC News*, 19 January 2012.

6 Ibid.

7 CECP, 'Giving in Numbers', 2012. Carried out in early 2012, the survey of 2011 corporate giving data received 214 responses, including 62 of the top 100 companies in the Fortune 500.

8 When Lee Scott decided to turn Walmart into a world leader in energy efficiency, the reaction from his younger staff was: 'It's about time.' As Scott explains: 'They wanted us to be doing things they could be proud of besides hitting our quarterly numbers.'

9 Enron, Corporate Responsibility Annual Report, 2000.

10 It was this type of distraction from the core business that Milton Friedman reacted against in his articles about shareholder value.

11 Michael Porter and Mark Kramer called for a more integrated approach to societal and environmental issues with their 'Creating

Shared Value' concept, as did Ian Davis, our colleague at McKinsey, when he called for a new 'social contract' between business and society. Michael Porter and Mark Kramer, 'Creating Shared Value', *Harvard Business Review*, January 2011; Ian Davis, 'The Biggest Contract', *The Economist*, 26 May 2005.

12 Robert Bradley, *Capitalism at Work: Business, Government, and Energy* (Salem: Scrivener Press, 2009), p. 309.

13 Peter F. Drucker, *Managing in Turbulent Times* (New York: Harper & Row, 1980).

14 Arthur Page, speech presented at the Bell Telephone System's Publicity Conference, 28 April 1927. www.thepagecenter.comm. psu.edu.

15 Michael Porter and Mark Kramer, 'Creating Shared Value', op. cit.

16 Robin Nuttall and Sergio Sandoval, 'The New Value at Stake in Regulation', *McKinsey Quarterly*, January 2010.

17 By shrinking packaging by 5 per cent, Walmart saves $3.4 billion per year, the equivalent of its third-quarter profit in 2010. Edward Humes, *Force of Nature: The unlikely story of Wal-Mart's green revolution* (New York: HarperCollins, 2011), p. 145. See www.walmart.com for 2010 third-quarter earnings report.

18 Sheila Bonini and Lenny Mendonca, 'Doing Good by Doing Well: Shaping a Sustainable Future', McKinsey article, March 2011.

19 Ibid.

20 'Starbucks to Pay £20m UK Corporate Tax', *Financial Times*, 6 December 2012.

21 John Vickers quoted at a Competition Commission Roundtable held at Victoria House, London, on 30 March 2009. www.competition-commission.org.uk.

Chapter 9. On Purpose

1 US Geological Survey online: http://earthquake.usgs.gov/research/parkfield/eq_predict.php.

2 Andre Dua, Robin Nuttall and Jon Wilkins, 'Why Good Companies Create Bad Regulatory Strategies', *McKinsey Quarterly*, June 2011.

3 Intel's former CEO Paul Otellini summarised the impact of the two iconic CEOs: 'Gerstner saved the company; Palmisano transformed it.'

4 The 'unstructured' data produced by sensors, video footage, tweets, audio files, medical images and geolocation information is harder to manipulate than the structured data common to spreadsheets and other traditional relational databases.

5 IBM Smarter Planet Leadership Series, 'Memphis PD: Keeping Ahead of Criminals by Finding the "Hot Spots"', 2011.

6 These figures were supplied directly by IBM.

7 According to IBM, Brand Health Monitor research indicates that 'Consideration' and 'Preference' for IBM are substantially higher, up 15 percentage points and 24 points respectively, when decision-makers are aware of Smarter Planet.

8 Data by Interbrand, www.bestglobalbrands.com: Best Global Brands 2008 valued IBM at $59 billion, Best Global Brands 2013 valued IBM at $78.9 billion.

9 'Paul Polman: "The Power is in the Hands of the Consumers"', *Guardian*, 21 November 2011.

10 Unilever's Sustainable Living Plan (USLP) was launched in 2010 the year after Polman took over as CEO. USLP aims 'to double the size of the business whilst reducing [its] environmental footprint and increasing [its] positive social impact'. Unilever reported that by the end of 2013 USLP programmes aimed at improving health and hygiene had reached 303 million people: Lifebuoy hand-washing products had been used by 183 million, Pureit had provided 55 million with clean drinking water and 52 million new consumers were using Unilever toothpaste brands. According to Unilever, the company's use of renewable energy has almost doubled since 2008, and since 2010, waste impact has been reduced by 11 per cent. Unilever have now provided help and training in sustainable methods to 570,000 smallholder farmers.

11 Paul Polman, Bata Lecture on Responsible Capitalism, 11 February 2013.

12 Kim Gittleson, 'Can a Company Live Forever?', *BBC News*, 19 January 2012.

13 While we share Will Hutton's view on the importance of purpose in business, we believe it would be counterproductive to require companies to define their contribution to society from the moment of creation. Will Hutton, *How Good Can We Be: Ending the mercenary society and building a great country* (London: Little, Brown, 2015).

14 'Doing Good by Doing Well: Shaping a Sustainable Future', *McKinsey on Society*, Winter 2011.

15 Gillian Tett, 'Silos and Silences: Why so few people spotted the problems in complex credit and what that implies for the future', *Banque De France Financial Stability Review*, Number 14, July 2010.

16 Ibid.

17 High-frequency trading has all the hallmarks of a creed waiting to turn bad. Those inside the industry, which makes small margins on trades conducted in milliseconds, argue that they are helping to improve market efficiency and liquidity. In reality, they pose a significant risk of flash crashes, such as the one that occurred on Wall Street in May 2010.

18 Krishna Guha and Gillian Tett, 'Last Year's Model: Stricken US Homeowners Confound Predictions', *Financial Times*, 31 January 2008.

19 'Sweden's Back-to-the-Future Banker', *Financial Times*, 13 January 2013.

20 SNL Financial, cited in 'Handelsbanken is Championing an Old Way of Doing New UK Business', *Daily Telegraph*, 24 August 2013.

21 Alan Blinder, *After the Music Stopped: The financial crisis, the response, and the work ahead* (New York: Penguin, 2013), p. 6.

22 Accenture, 'Consumers' Trust in Utilities Lowest in Four Years, New Accenture Research Shows', 28 June 2013.

23 'Utility Firms Least Trusted by UK Consumers', *PR Week*, 19 April 2012.

24 Novo Nordisk, Company's Annual Report for 2012.

25 Ibid.

26 McKinsey Global Institute discussion paper, 'Overcoming Obesity: An initial economic analysis', November 2014.

Chapter 10. Professional Era

1   John Wanamaker was an American businessman and political figure who lived 1838–1922.

2   See 'We're All Marketers Now', *McKinsey Quarterly*, July 2011.

3   The professionalisation of marketing is a good case study to follow for connected leadership in all but one sense. As David Reibstein, professor of marketing at Wharton Business School, puts it: 'The rigour with which marketing is now undertaken has played a role in shaping society's negative view of business. People have a sense that corporations' omniscient marketing departments convince us to buy products we don't want.'

4   McKinsey & Company Insights and Publications, 'McKinsey Global Survey results: External affairs at a crossroads', May 2013. Reinier Musters, Ellora-Julie Parekh, and Surya Ramkumar, 2013, 'Organizing the Government Affairs Function for Impact, *McKinsey Quarterly*.

5   Walmart Annual Report 2005.

6   Transcript of CNBC interview with Warren Buffett, 14 November 2011.

7   Edelman Trust Barometer 2015. The five 'trust performance clusters' identified by Edelman are: Engagement; Integrity; Products and Services; Purpose; and Operations. Operations include financial returns, ranking as a top global company, and widely admired top leadership.

8   Palmisano and Scott both pointed out that they had every reason to believe Welch would have adapted and thrived in today's more multi-dimensional era.

9   Interview in 'Leading in the 21st Century', *McKinsey Quarterly*, June 2014. Dominic Barton, Andrew Grant and Michelle Horn.

10 McKinsey & Company Insights and Publications, 'McKinsey Global Survey results: External affairs at a crossroads', May 2013.

11 Ibid.

12 Dominic Barton, 2011, 'Capitalism for the Long Term', *Harvard Business Review*, March 2011. This is an idea that Nick Lovegrove and Matthew Thomas have built on in their article 'Triple-Strength Leadership', *Harvard Business Review*, September 2013.

13 Interview in 'Leading in the 21st Century', *McKinsey Quarterly*, June 2014. Dominic Barton, Andrew Grant, and Michelle Horn.

14 'Sir Clive Woodward Relives England's World Cup Final Victory' BBC, 21 November 2013.

15 Search 'Visual illusion – Attention Experiment' on YouTube to see the video.

16 'Exclusive Interview: Walmart's Andrea Thomas, SVP Sustainability', *Triple Pundit*, 19 April 2012.

17 Walmart, 2014 Global Responsibility Report.

18 McKinsey & Company Insights and Publications, 'McKinsey Global Survey results: External affairs at a crossroads', May 2013.

19 Ibid.

Chapter 11. The Front Foot

1 Tangguh Independent Advisory Panel, Seventh Report on Tangguh LNG Project, March 2009.

2 'Interview: Unilever's Paul Polman on Diversity, Purpose and Profits', *Guardian*, 2 October 2013.

3 Of course, King Cnut's actions should not be misread, as they commonly are, as simply a foolish man's attempt to defy the inevitable. Ordering back the waves was a deliberate effort to prove that he was not in fact all-powerful. Cnut knew he was fighting a doomed battle, but his actions are a helpful reminder of the futility of certain efforts.

4 Edelman's Trust Barometer 2015 showed global trust in CEOs as spokespersons fell from 46 per cent in 2014 to 43 per cent in 2015.

5 McKinsey & Company Insights and Publications, 'McKinsey Global Survey results: External affairs at a crossroads', May 2013.

6   Sheila Bonini, David Court and Alberto Marchi. 'Rebuilding Corporate Reputations', *McKinsey Quarterly*, June 2009.

7   McKinsey & Company, 'McKinsey Global Survey results: Engaging and understanding governments', 2012.

8   McKinsey & Company Insights and Publications, 'McKinsey Global Survey results: External affairs at a crossroads', May 2013.

9   'Why Good Companies Create Bad Regulatory Strategies', Andre Dua, Robin Nuttall and Jon Wilkins, *McKinsey Quarterly*, 2011.

10 McKinsey & Company, 'McKinsey Global Survey results: External affairs at a crossroads', 2013; Edelman Trust Barometer 2015.

11 Edelman Trust Barometer 2013.

12 McKinsey & Company, 'How Companies Manage Sustainability: McKinsey Global Survey results', 2010.

13 Mitchell also believes executives lack experience with the added complexity associated with non-financial disputes.

Epilogue: People Rising

1   'AI Startup Says it Has Defeated Captchas', technologyreview.com, 28 October 2013, says Vicarious technology can defeat Captcha 90 per cent of the time.

2   In May 2015, the monthly report for Google's self-driving-car project said its cars had been involved in twelve minor accidents, but there had been no injuries. This occurred in the course of 1.8 million miles of tests, including 1 million miles in self-driving mode since the project began in 2009. It said that not once was the self-driving car the cause of the accident.

3   Data from expert interviews.

4   'Oncologists at Memorial Sloan-Kettering Cancer Center in New York are using IBM's Watson supercomputer to provide chronic-care and cancer-treatment diagnostics by accessing knowledge from 600,000 medical evidence reports, 2 million pages of text from 42 medical journals, and 1.5 million patient records and clinical trials in the field of oncology. It can then compare each patient's individual symptoms, vital signs, family history, medications, genetic

make-up, diet, and exercise routine to diagnose and recommend a treatment.' McKinsey Global Institute, 'Disruptive Technologies: Advances that Will Transform Life, Business, and the Global Economy', May 2013.

5   William Nordhaus, 2007, 'Two Centuries of Productivity Growth in Computing', *Journal of Economic History,* Vol. 67, No. 1.

6   Michael Chui, James Manyika, and Mehdi Miremadi, 'Four Fundamentals of Workplace Automation', *McKinsey Quarterly*, November 2015.

7   David Autor, 'Polanyi's Paradox and the Shape of Employment Growth'. Paper prepared for Federal Reserve Bank of Kansas, Jackson Hole Conference, 22 August 2014.

8   Guy Michaels, Ashwini Natraj and John Van Reenen, 2014, 'Has ICT Polarized Skill Demand? Evidence from Eleven Countries over 25 Years', *Review of Economics and Statistics*, 96(1) 60–77.

9   Https://twitter.com/paulg/status/577239973650399232.

10 Daron Acemoglu, David Autor, David Dorn, Gordon H. Hanson and Brendan Price, 2014, 'Import Competition and the Great U.S. Employment Sag of the 2000s'. NBER Working Paper No. 20395.

11 João Paulo Pessoa and John Van Reenen, 2013, 'Decoupling of Wage Growth and Productivity Growth? Myth and Reality'. CEP Discussion Paper No. 1246.

12 McKinsey Global Institute, 'Disruptive Technologies: Advances that Will Transform Life, Business, and the Global Economy', May 2013.

13 Keynes predicted in 'Economic Problems of our Grandchildren' that too much leisure would be a problem. It hasn't happened yet.

14 David Autor, 'Polanyi's Paradox and the Shape of Employment Growth', op. cit.

15 McKinsey Global Institute, 'Urban World: Cities and the Rise of the Consuming Class', June 2012; data from Angus Madison, University of Groningen. The centre of economic gravity is calculated by weighting national GDP by each nation's geographic centre of gravity; a line drawn from the centre of the earth through the economic centre of gravity locates it on the earth's surface.

16 Richard Dobbs, James Manyika and Jonathan Woetzel, *No Ordinary Disruption: The Four Global Forces Breaking All the Trends*, Public Affairs, 2015.

17 McKinsey Global Institute, 'Urban World: The Shifting Global Business Landscape', October 2013.

18 Ibid.

19 Edelman Trust Barometer, 2015.

20 The World Bank and International Finance Corporation, 'Doing Business', 2015.

21 Interview with Sam Geall, executive editor of *China Dialogue* in July 2014. The Ministry for Environmental Protection in Beijing employs around 320 people. While the regional environmental protection bureaus report to this central ministry, they are financed by local governments and their corporate funders.

22 Bribery is one of the hardest challenges for local firms in developing countries. For Western companies the answer is straightforward: you simply do not pay. An 'engage radically' approach protects them in countries where bribery is a possibility and pushes them out of states where it is a way of life. That may be painful but it is at least possible. Leaving is not an option for local operators, and it is worth remembering that not everyone volunteers in the mafia. Regardless of nationality, it is challenging for any company to stamp out graft thoroughly if it is standard practice in the host country. Larsen & Toubro's executive chairman A.M. Naik has taken one of the boldest anti-bribery stances of any Indian business leader, but even his efforts were unable to cleanse the Indian construction conglomerate at every level. 'World Bank Suspends Larsen & Toubro', *Wall Street Journal*, 8 March 2013.

23 Phil Muncaster, 'Huawei: Inside the Lair of the Not-so-hidden Dragon', *Register*, 30 September 2012.

24 'US brands Chinese Groups Security Threat', *Financial Times*, 8 October 2012.

25 'Huawei "Not Interested in the US Any More"', *Financial Times*, 23 April 2013.

26 Ibid.

27 'Huawei to Build £125m Research Base in Britain', *Sky News*, 16 October 2013.

28 Edelman Trust Barometer, 2015.

29 Anthony Venables, 2008, 'New Economic Geography', *The New Palgrave Dictionary of Economics*, 2nd edition.

30 M. Kremer et al., 'Teacher Absence in India: A Snapshot', *Journal of the European Economic Association*, Vol. 3, No. 2–3, April–May 2005.

31 Office of the Registrar General & Census Commissioner, India, 'Census of India', 2011.

32 The use of mobile devices in-store is already gathering pace in China. QR code scanning increased almost fourfold from March 2012 to March 2013. Imageco, QR Market Study, 2013.

33 McKinsey, 'Resource Revolution: Meeting the World's Energy, Materials, Food, and Water Needs', 2011.

34 McKinsey, 'Winning the $30 Trillion Decathlon: Going for Gold in Emerging Markets', 2012.

35 McKinsey Global Institute, 'Overcoming Obesity: An Initial Economic Analysis', November 2014.

36 Pan Yue, then China's deputy minister of the environment, told the German newspaper: 'Acid rain is falling on one third of the Chinese territory, half of the water in our seven largest rivers is completely useless, while one fourth of our citizens does not have access to clean drinking water. One third of the urban population is breathing polluted air, and less than 20 per cent of the trash in cities is treated and processed in an environmentally sustainable manner. Finally, five of the ten most polluted cities worldwide are in China. Of course I am pleased with the success of China's economy. But at the same time I am worried. We are using too many raw materials to sustain this growth. To produce goods worth $10,000, for example, we need seven times more resources than Japan, nearly six times more than the United States and, perhaps most embarrassing, nearly three times more than India. Things can't, nor should they be allowed to, go on like that.'

'Interview with China's Deputy Minister of the Environment: "The Chinese Miracle Will End Soon"', *Der Spiegel*, 7 March 2005.

37 Sam Geall, *China and the Environment: The green revolution* (London: Zed Books, 2013).

38 'PepsiCo CEO: 'If All Consumers Exercised . . . Obesity Wouldn't Exist", *CNN Money*, 27 April 2010.

39 Novartis, 'Arogya Parivar Fact Sheet', 2013.

Index

Entries in *italics* indicate *photographs* or *illustrations*.

John Browne, chief executive of BP from 1995 to 2007, is now executive chairman of L1 Energy. He is the author of the memoir *Beyond Business*, the popular science book *Seven Elements that Changed the World*, and *The Glass Closet*, a commentary on LGBT acceptance and inclusion in business.

Robin Nuttall is a principal with McKinsey & Company.

Tommy Stadlen is a technology entrepreneur and former McKinsey & Company consultant.

PublicAffairs is a publishing house founded in 1997. It is a tribute to the standards, values, and flair of three persons who have served as mentors to countless reporters, writers, editors, and book people of all kinds, including me.

I. F. STONE, proprietor of *I. F. Stone's Weekly*, combined a commitment to the First Amendment with entrepreneurial zeal and reporting skill and became one of the great independent journalists in American history. At the age of eighty, Izzy published *The Trial of Socrates*, which was a national bestseller. He wrote the book after he taught himself ancient Greek.

BENJAMIN C. BRADLEE was for nearly thirty years the charismatic editorial leader of *The Washington Post*. It was Ben who gave the *Post* the range and courage to pursue such historic issues as Watergate. He supported his reporters with a tenacity that made them fearless and it is no accident that so many became authors of influential, best-selling books.

ROBERT L. BERNSTEIN, the chief executive of Random House for more than a quarter century, guided one of the nation's premier publishing houses. Bob was personally responsible for many books of political dissent and argument that challenged tyranny around the globe. He is also the founder and longtime chair of Human Rights Watch, one of the most respected human rights organizations in the world.

·　　·　　·

For fifty years, the banner of Public Affairs Press was carried by its owner Morris B. Schnapper, who published Gandhi, Nasser, Toynbee, Truman, and about 1,500 other authors. In 1983, Schnapper was described by *The Washington Post* as "a redoubtable gadfly." His legacy will endure in the books to come.

Peter Osnos, *Founder and Editor-at-Large*